The Secret Lives of
FISHES

THE SECRET LIVES OF FISHES

By the same author

THE MARINE FISHES OF RHODE ISLAND (1960) Paperback
edition (1974)
HANDBOOK FOR ADVISERS AMERICAN LITTORAL SOCIETY (1964)
GUIDEBOOK TO HISTORICAL SOUTHERN NEW ENGLAND (1967)
MAN AND THE SEA (1970) Paperback edition (1972)
MARINE CAREERS (1970)
MARINE RESOURCE PERSPECTIVES (1974)
THERE REALLY WAS A DODO, with Esther Gordon (1974)
HURRICANE IN SOUTHERN NEW ENGLAND (1976)
ONCE THERE WAS A PASSENGER PIGEON, with Esther Gordon (1976)

The Secret Lives of FISHES

Bernard Ludwig Gordon

Grosset & Dunlap
A FILMWAYS COMPANY
Publishers   New York

There we'll drop our lines and gather
Old Ocean's treasures in,
Where'er the mottled mackerel
Turns up a steel-dark fin.
The sea's our field of harvest,
Its scaly tribes our grain;
We'll reap the teeming waters
As at home they reap the plain!

From "THE FISHERMEN"

By John Greenleaf Whittier

Acknowledgments

Some of the material in this book has previously appeared as articles in other publications. The author wishes to thank the following publications for permission to use this material: NATIONAL FISHERMAN; NATURAL HISTORY; NATURE MAGAZINE; FRONTIERS, the Magazine of the Academy of Natural Sciences of Philadelphia; THE FISHERMAN; CONNECTICUT CIRCLE; FISHING WORLD; SEA FRONTIERS; The Magazine of the International Oceanographic Foundation; OUTDOOR LIFE; SALT WATER SPORTSMAN; and AQUASPHERE, Journal of the New England Aquarium.

Contents

Author's Note

During the preparation of this book the author received specimens of fish along with personal observations about the various species from many of the commercial fishermen of the American coastal zone. Especially helpful were Captain Willis Clark, Captain Theo Silva and Captain Ellery Thompson.

He would like to express his thanks for past assistance to Donald J. Zinn, and Robert A. DeWolf, retired members of the Department of Zoology at the University of Rhode Island; Mrs. Myvanwy M. Dick of the Division of Fishes, Museum of Comparative Zoology, Harvard University; Richard Wolfe, Rare Book Librarian, Countway Library, Harvard University; John Mason of the Woods Hole Oceanographic Institution; Sal Testaverde, Curator at the New England Aquarium; Charles Wheeler, Director, National Marine Fisheries Service Aquarium, Woods Hole, Mass.; Henry Wise; and Roland Moody, Dean of Libraries, Northeastern University, Boston, Massachusetts.

The author also gratefully acknowledges the advice and encouragement of literary agent and former editor, Toni Strassman; editors Lee Schryver, Margaret P. Zug, and Patricia Fisher; my secretary, Carole Magnuson; Joseph Gordon, who critically reviewed most of the manuscript; and my wife, Esther Saranga Gordon.

Lastly, with humble gratitude the author acknowledges the benefits derived from studying the classic ichthyological works of David S. Jordan, Barton W. Evermann, George B. Goode, Samuel F. Hildebrand, Henry B. Bigelow, William C. Schroeder, and the other chroniclers of piscine lore.

B.L.G.

Introduction

Few people realize that within the seventy-three percent of the earth's surface which is covered with water, there reside over thirty thousand different species of fish. The minute Philippine goby *(Pandaka pygmaea)* with an adult size of one-third inch makes it the smallest vertebrate; the whale shark *(Rhincodon typus)* of tropical waters reaches fifty feet or more.

The purpose of this book is to acquaint the reader with some of the most interesting and curious fishes of the oceans, rivers and lakes which I have observed, whether they seem common or not. Some we think of as ordinary actually have unique habits.

In recent years, more and more persons have taken up the enjoyable pastimes of fishing and skin diving. Sport fishermen, commercial fishermen, and naturalists will find unfamiliar facts here, and the general reader will be amazed at the many watery communities around the world sustaining strange tribes of the sea.

As highly nutritive food, fish in the diet is unsurpassed and increasing. However, serious inroads have been made in the supply of many species. Just when we need them most, thousands of edible fish, together with their eggs and food supply, are destroyed each year by raw sewage, chlorinated hydrocarbons, polychlorinated biphenyls (PCB), and industrial wastes. These substances deplete the waters of essential levels of oxygen or prevent the growth of aquatic organisms on which fish feed. Shad, striped bass, and salmon have been gradually dwindling during the past two centuries on our east coast. In many places action is being taken to return bays and rivers to their pristine conditions. Small numbers of sturgeon and salmon are once again found in the great waters of the Hudson, but a great deal remains to be done. As food prices rise, we must safeguard our fish, not just eat increasing quantities of them.

This book is written not only for the fisherman but for any reader with an interest in knowing more about the importance of the finny denizens of our waters.

B. L. Gordon
Northeastern University
Boston, Massachusetts

Foreword

"Master, I marvel how fishes live in the sea." *Pericles*, Shakespeare

From prehistoric times to the present day fish have constituted an important and apparently inexhaustible source of food. Ancient kitchen middens, especially cave sites, have produced bones from many species of fish representing catches from fresh water ponds and streams and from the sea. The artifacts of the earliest civilizations reflect the extent to which the sea and its inhabitants were incorporated into the living habits of the people. From simple pottery bowls to elaborate wall paintings, the motif of fishes is omnipresent, beautifully portrayed with an accuracy that makes identification readily possible, for man was an observant harvester of the sea's abundance. In Egypt mummified fish have been found in the burial tombs, intended perhaps to be a part of the essential requirements in the next world. From the highly civilized cultures of the Orient and the East to the primitive cultures of other races, fish have been—and are still—vividly portrayed in many forms, depicting their integral part in the life of the community.

Life under the waters has always had the great fascination of the unknown and the mysterious. Strange creatures were glimpsed and became the basis for even stranger beliefs and superstitions. After storms, the sea would sometimes cast upon the beaches monsters, or smaller fantastic creatures that fired the imagination. Even the nets of the fishermen would have their quota of weird life forms. Familiar though the waters of the littoral may have been, the deeper waters were an enigma, even though fishermen braved great expanses in small boats in order to fill their nets and hand lines from these hidden depths. That this world beneath them was filled with countless wondrous creatures was an accepted fact. Professor Gordon has clearly and knowledgeably shown that the gamut of shape, color, and size of fishes is seemingly unlimited, and that they dwell in every conceivable part of the waters of the earth.

Even though the field of ichthyology has been extensively explored, particularly in the last century, there is still an enormous lack of information about the majority of species. Much remains to be clarified taxonomically even within the most familiar groups. Little is known of the life history of all but a few species and the realm of behavior is but slightly understood. The quest for knowledge is constantly pursued in the laboratory and in natural habitats. By small increments, a world fund of information is being accumulated. With our present population expansion and increased demand for protein food, it is essential that this research be energetically extended in order to understand how to protect and maintain our vital fishery resources.

Modern technology has made possible greatly expanded horizons of study. With the development of scuba, or self-contained underwater breathing apparatus, the colorful inhabitants of coral reefs and shallow waters can now be observed *in situ*. Small two-man submarines make the exploration of reef walls and continental slopes possible, and even the deepest waters have been invaded by submersibles, first by the famous bathysphere of Beebe and Barton and now by free-moving submersibles such as the "Alvin." More sophisticated equipment on research vessels has also contributed significantly to our understanding of many facets of oceanography.

The impact of this technological thrust has been of inestimable value to the scientific observer as well as to the commercial fisheries and associated industries. Unfortunately it has not been an undiluted advantage. More efficient equipment has also made possible massive over-fishing in the most productive fishing grounds, seriously depleting the resources that for so long seemed inexhaustible. Even remote atolls of the South Seas are now facing unprecedented depletion of food fishes since the introduction of modern fishing methods.

In delineating the complexity and biological significance of many species of fishes, Professor Gordon has provided an invaluable guide to this increasingly demanding area of human concern. The detailed background he has so lucidly described is the distilled result of many years devoted to personal observation and intensive research. We are indeed fortunate to be able to profit by Professor Gordon's excellent work.

Myvanwy M. Dick, Ichthyologist
Former Acting Curator of Fishes
Museum of Comparative Zoology
Harvard University
Cambridge, Massachusetts

1

Most Delectable to Man

Always nutritious, sometimes flavorful and succulent, fish has been a significant part of the human diet since prehistoric times. These six species are among the tastiest fishes that inhabit the waters of our planet.

Pompano—King of the Table

Its scales glisten with the sparkle of polished silver. Prized by those who savor its succulence, the pompano is acclaimed by many as the most flavorful food fish.

Belonging to the family Carangidae, which includes jacks, lookdowns, moonfish, and scad, the pompano is a deep-bodied, small-

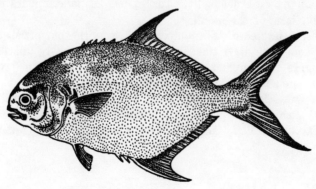

mouthed, rounded, graceful fish. Carangid fish vary somewhat in shape and size, but all have the characteristic of swimming at great speed. When hooked on a fishing line they are wonderful game fish for their size.

The common pompano, or Florida pompano *(Trachinotus carolinus)*, was first described as blue and silvery by Carolus Linnaeus in 1766 from specimens taken by Dr. Garden in South Carolina. It was not observed north of Cape Hatteras until the summer of 1854 when Spencer Baird saw thousands of pompanos in the sandy coves of the outer beach near Beasley's Point, New Jersey. In August 1874, a party of the U.S. Fish Commission hauled a 100-fathom seine on the beach at Watch Hill, Rhode Island, and were much surprised to find quite a few 2-inch pompanos, which they kept alive for some weeks in aquariums. Small pompanos look like silver dollars swimming on their edges. In captivity their graceful movements were carefully studied.

The pompano has been recorded from Brazil to Cape Cod but is uncommon at either of the extreme ends of its range. It becomes abundant from North Carolina south to the Gulf of Mexico and is very common along the sandy beaches of the Keys and islands of the Gulf coast. This fish averages 1 to 2 pounds with one of the largest specimens, reported by Stearns, 19½ inches long and weighing 6¼ pounds.

Along southern beaches the pompano feeds on sand fleas, shrimp, hermit crabs, and small minnows. Because of its excellent flavor and food value, anglers seek out the pompano using small feathered jigs, spoons, and pork-rind lures. The pompano is a very sporty fish to catch with a small spinning or bait casting rod. It puts up a remarkable fight for its size when hooked, rushing out with amazing speed when given the line.

Many epicures consider the pompano to be the supreme food fish of the United States. It is not found in European waters. At Antoine's restaurant in New Orleans, baked or broiled pompano appears as a most expensive item on the menu.

Close relatives of the pompano, such as the butterfish and the runner, sometimes have their fins clipped and are sold by unscrupulous fishmongers as pompano. Although somewhat similar in flavor, the discerning gourmet can easily distinguish the less desirable substitutes.

The true Florida pompano is often confused with several similar species, such as the permit *(Trachinotus falcatus)*, the palometa *(Trachinotus goodei)*, and the gafftopsail pompano *(Trachinotus rhodopus)*. These three species all grow larger than the Florida pompano. But, as James A. Henshall has stated: "No one who has eaten a true pompano can be deceived by these other species."

The name pompano is believed to be derived from the Spanish word *pampana*, which means a "vine leaf." The oval shape of the fish is somewhat leaflike. Mention of a similiar name appears in 1542; M. La Roche, in his *Voyage to Canada*, names bass, carp, and *pimperneaux*.

Experts declare the pompano a game fish of more than ordinary cunning. When hooked, the pompano frequently breaks water in efforts to escape the angler. A number of naturalists have observed pompanos in schools jumping out of the water and sometimes into boats. Henshall states: "I have often had them leap into my boat, both when anchored and moving, but usually when sailing near a school." Charles F. Holder describes the pompano as being able to travel 20 feet or more in its aerial leaps. Holder mentions the following instance of the remarkable leaping powers of the pompano:

> A friend . . . was sailing up a shallow river, and found that he was driving a school of pompano. As the stream grew narrower, they turned and in a body left the water, darting over the yacht, whirling through the air like bullets. Dozens struck the sail and fell aboard, while others cleared the rigging and dropped thirty and forty feet away, making good their escape.

About a million pounds of pompano are caught each year by fishermen, in addition to those taken commercially by haul seines, gill nets, cast nets, and fish traps, and for over a hundred years the pompano has supported a small but significant fishery in Florida and the Gulf of Mexico. During the past decade a number of attempts to farm the pompano have been tried in Florida and along the Gulf coast. The University of Miami used Sea Grant funds to raise pompano in warm-water pools at the Florida Power and Light Company's Turkey Point Plant. Experiments were designed to raise 1- to 2-inch pompano to marketable size. Research in raising pompano was also carried out at Marineland of Florida and by the Minorcan Seafood Company. The captive pompanos were able to adapt to a freshwater environment when the salinity was gradually reduced. However, further research into pompano physiology and reproductive processes is necessary before this fish can become a profitable aquacultural species. The pompano appears to breed in late spring and summer in southern waters, but there are still many unanswered questions about its migratory and reproductive habits.

Broiled or baked pompano can be eaten bones and all, as the skeleton is quite soft. It is one fish that, when properly cooked, will provide a flavorable remembrance for a long time after one has left the dinner table.

The Gregarious Red Snapper

The most sought after member of the tropical snapper family is the red snapper, which is shipped extensively to northern markets. At times called pargo, Mexican snapper, or Colorado, this species of snapper, *Lutjanus campechanus*, was first described by the Cuban ichthyologist Poey. The generic name *Lutjanus* was originally used in 1787 by M. E. Bloch, who derived the name from Ikan Lutjany, an Asiatic name for a member of this group of fish. The tasty red snapper is popular among both sport and commercial fishermen throughout the West Indies, Gulf of Mexico, and Central America. Usually found from Florida to Brazil, it occasionally strays north to New England waters. It reaches lengths of 2 to 3 feet and weights of 10 to 35 pounds.

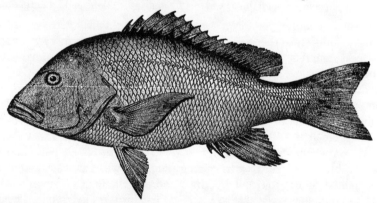

With eyes that are always red, the red snapper can be best described as brilliant and gaudy; a bright red hue on the upper part of its body fades away to pink on its lower sides and white on its stomach. Its fins are also red with the dorsal having an orange margin. Young red snappers have faint black spots on the sides, which disappear with maturity. Somewhat of a deep-sea fish, the red snapper is usually found in water from 60 to 400 feet deep. It is a bottom feeder living in company with groupers.

The growth and development of the red snapper fishery is an interesting story. In the late 1840s and early 1850s, New London, Connecticut, fishermen sailed into the Gulf of Mexico in their 15- to 20-ton sloops, which had been used in cod fishing, seeking new fisheries. On the west coast of Florida they caught many red snappers, which they marketed for good prices in New Orleans. News of their success reached New England, and other northern fishing sloops soon joined them. The catch was sold mostly in New Orleans and Mobile. Gradually the fishery expanded to other southern ports, including Pensacola. Red snappers were also packed in ice and shipped to New York and New England. By 1898 more than forty vessels were engaged in the red snapper fishery in the Gulf of Mexico.

The early fishing sloops had built-in wells where the fish could be kept alive until brought into port. This limited the size of the catch, so instead ice was used to keep the snappers fresh. Pensacola became the center of the red snapper fishery from which boats headed out to the productive Campeche and Tortugas banks. Northern restaurants now fly in fresh snappers, just as they do Dover sole from England.

At the turn of the century the fish were found by continually throwing the lead when the sloop reached the vicinity of the fishing bank. Once the bank was reached, a fisherman standing on the weather rail and supporting himself by a hold on the main shroud, released the line with a baited hook and a 9-pound lead weight. The baited hook went down to a depth of 40 fathoms (240 feet) where the fish, if hungry, took the hook and was brought to the surface. As soon as a fish was taken, a fisherman with gear and bait was launched in a dory to fish the location. The dory either anchored or drifted over the grounds. On productive grounds six men could catch a thousand red snappers in a few hours. When snappers were spawning they often were so abundant around the sloops that they tinted the water red, but they refused to take a baited hook. Then the fishermen's only alternative was to search for other schools.

Today red snappers have an affinity for the more than ten thousand "artificial" reefs, the offshore-oil drilling rigs in the Gulf of Mexico. They gather around the rigs to feed on the marine organisms that attach themselves to the submerged portion of drill rigs. Workmen on the rigs catch quite a few snappers in their spare time, and many boatmen come out to the drill rigs to fish for them, welcomed by the isolated oil crews.

Red snappers are carnivorous fish that feed on shrimp, crabs, and small fish. In the sea their only natural enemies are sharks and the large sea bass. Cut-up bait of skipjack, young shark, or bluefish is used to catch the snapper on an 8/0 hook. When a school of snapper is located, the fish will bite rapidly and furiously.

The Snook—From Bad to Good Reputation

A streamlined, powerful fish of southern waters, the snook resembles the northern freshwater pike. The name snook is derived from the Dutch name *snock*, meaning "pike." It has gained a reputation for flavor even above that of the red snapper.

This silvery green fish was first described in 1792 by M. E. Bloch from a Caribbean specimen taken near Jamaica. Bloch gave it the scientific name *Centropomus undecimalis: Centropomus* because it is a characteristic member of the family Centropomidae, and *undecimalis* to signify "eleven," referring to the eleven fin rays of the soft dorsal fin.

The snook is also called saltwater pike, robalo, ravallin, or sergeantfish, the last referring to the prominent black stripe running on its sides from gill cover to tail. Oddly, it is a close relative of both the 2-inch glass fish and the 200-pound Nile perch.

This long, slender creature has a head about one-third the total

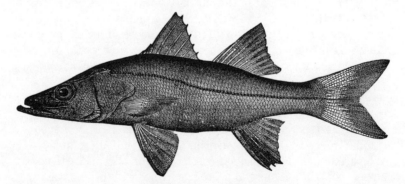

length of its body. Its large mouth is filled with brushlike teeth; a protruding lower jaw juts out slightly.

It is a voracious feeder that preys upon mullet and other small fish, fiddler crabs, and shrimp. As for bait, it will go after eelskin rigs, plugs, spoons, and feather jigs with a furious smashing strike that makes this species an angler's favorite throughout its range. Snook is found in the Caribbean, throughout the West Indies, along the Gulf coast from Florida to Texas and Mexico, then south to Rio de Janeiro. In the Pacific Ocean it ranges from the Gulf of California southward to Callao, Peru.

Usually an inshore fish, occasionally snook will enter deltas and estuaries and swim upstream into fresh water. The fish seems to prefer the quiet waters of mangrove swamp areas, which makes Florida its favorite habitat. Many vacationing fishermen head south to the brackish inlets, where in small boats they find the mangrove roots an intolerable hazard. Floridians, with more experience, know just how to fish for snook.

Fifty years ago snook were very abundant in inshore waters on the east and west coasts of Florida. Without too much effort, anglers could take dozens of them around the bridges and jetties near Naples, West Palm Beach, and Fort Lauderdale. Today snook are not as plentiful as formerly; overfishing, pollution, and destruction of the eastern Florida mangrove coasts have made the snook a prize catch.

Large snook have been known to reach lengths of 3 or 4 feet and weights up to 50 pounds. Today the average snook runs 5 to 8 pounds, rarely more than 25 pounds. The largest snook recorded was taken by Jane Howard on January 9, 1963 at La Paz, Mexico. This record fish was 49½ inches long and weighed 52 pounds 6 ounces.

The snook is a warm-water fish, very sensitive to temperature changes. Studies have shown that the snook has difficulty surviving when water temperature drops below 60 degrees F.

These fish do not tend to migrate any major distance from their home locality, according to Florida tagging studies. When fifty-seven snook were recaptured within a year after being tagged, analysis showed that 73 percent of them were within six miles of their original site of capture.

As an active game fish the snook is a prize catch for anglers, not only for its pugnacity, frantic runs, leaps, and sporting fight, but also for that flavorful delight at the dining table. With firm white and flaky meat the snook is said to taste very similar to striped bass. Some southern restaurants, perhaps under the mistaken notion that it sounds more desirable, have been known to serve snook under the name "sea trout" on their menus. When plentiful, the snook was a poor man's fish; now that it is an increasing rarity, northern sportsmen are all too pleased to catch one, by any name.

Porgy (Scup), the Common Delicacy

Muscuppanog was the name they were called by the Narragansett Indians who went wading into the bays and inlets and speared them with pointed sticks as they swam swiftly by. Early settlers called them *scuppaug* after their Indian name, but today we know these thin silvery fish as porgy or scup. In southern waters they are sometimes called fair maid, maiden, or ironsides, the latter because of their metallic, platelike scales.

Found from Maine to South Carolina, the scup is an abundant and important food fish in the northern part of its range. It is easy to recognize because of its thin, somewhat oval-shaped body, small mouth, and elongated spiny dorsal fin.

Although one of the most abundant shore fish of southern New England, the scup is found here only part of the year. E. W. Whalley of Narragansett Pier made the following statement with regard to the coming of scup in 1871, but it still holds true: "When I see the first dandelion, scup come in. I watch the buds and when the buds are swelled full our traps go in; when the dandelion goes out of bloom and goes to seed, the scup are gone."

Where porgies go in winter was somewhat of a mystery until Bureau of Fisheries biologists attached numbered tags to a large quantity of them in southern New England. Later, some of these tags turned up on fishes found wintering off Virginia and northern North Carolina.

Since 1950 scup have been taken during the winter off New England's coast in depths ranging from 45 to 70 fathoms. This gives reason to believe that only a portion of the scup migrate south in the winter and that others move offshore in the fall and come inshore again in the spring. During their summer visit inshore, porgies tend to hug the shoreline very closely; as a result, very few are found more than six miles offshore.

Usually porgies congregate in schools, and frequently in the late spring, a trap fisherman may find his trap filled to capacity with a large school that has been snared by the netting. Young porgies will come in close to shore and have been found in 2 or 3 feet of water. However, the large jumbo scup prefer water at least 6 feet deep with a rocky bottom, shellfish beds, reefs, or barnacled wrecks.

Porgies are principally bottom feeders, preying upon sea worms

(Nereis), small squid, mollusks, small crustaceans, and fish fry. Like most other fish, adult scup stop feeding during their spawning time, which is principally in June in southern New England but may extend from May to August.

Inshore waters, such as Long Island Sound, Narragansett Bay, and Martha's Vineyard South, are places where the scup deposit their eggs. These eggs are rather small, about the size of a pinhead, transparent and spherical. When the water is as warm as 72 degrees, the egg develops rather quickly, producing a baby fish in 40 hours.

A newly hatched porgy is about 1/16 inch long. It grows rapidly and may reach 2 to 3 inches by September. By November, it may be as big as 4 inches.

Said to reach lengths of 18 inches and weights of 3 or 4 pounds, the largest scup I have encountered was a specimen from Block Island South that was 17 inches long and weighed 2½ pounds. Adult porgies usually run about 12 inches long and weigh from 1 to 2 pounds.

Like many other types of fish, the amount of scup landed fluctuates from year to year. In some years scup of commercial size may be plentiful, in other years very scarce, depending upon favorable spawning conditions and the number of predators. While living on the bottom, porgies are preyed upon by sharks, cod, anglerfish, and other ground fish. Trap fishermen along the Massachusetts and Rhode Island coasts take considerable amounts of scup each year along with the draggers with otter trawls.

The porgy, or scup, is a favorite with anglers all along the Middle Atlantic and New England coasts. It bites a hook baited with squid or clam readily and puts up a spirited fight for its size. It bites best at slack tide and is taken with small hooks.

Anyone handling scup without gloves or a gaff hook has to be very careful of the sharp dorsal spines on its back. It is very easy to get one's hand and fingers punctured by these spines, and it takes a long time for the wound to heal.

The porgy is an excellent panfish. The flesh is tender, flaky, and of appetizing flavor. If rolled in flour, bread crumbs, or cornmeal, the fish fries well and is delicious. It has always been popular with southern black people and now, in northern markets, can be bought inexpensively. Soon perhaps, it may be more popular, and prices will rise. Now, however, it makes a dollar meal possible and more delicious than a number of more costly fishes.

Sea Bass in Lobster Pots

A small fish with a big head and large mouth is the common, or black, sea bass, *Centropristis striata*. Found from Maine to northern Florida, this dark-hued fish is known by a variety of local names including rock bass, black Will, black Harry, blackfish, rockfish, tallywag, and humpback.

Usually found among rocks, wrecks, and reefs, the sea bass is generally located in the company of the tautog and porgy. Sea bass seem to show up in greatest number around rocky ledges and boulders in water 20 to 50 feet deep where they find an almost inexhaustible supply of the many types of invertebrates on which they feed.

Although sometimes called black bass, the sea bass is not a true black but actually dark indigo. There may be a slight range in the coloration of individuals due to sex and age, with females being gray-blue and males a dark blue or indigo. Immature fish take on a greenish or brownish color. Young sea bass are predominantly female, but at five years of age many become functional males.

Male sea bass develop a fleshy hump on the back of the neck in front of the dorsal fin during the spawning season, which is from the middle of May to the beginning of July. During this period, the male takes on a bright blue color. The eggs of the sea bass are about a millimeter in

diameter, the same size as porgy eggs, and hatch in about 4 days with a water temperature of 60 degrees.

Possessing firm, white, flaky flesh, the sea bass when packed in ice does not deteriorate as rapidly as other fish in hot weather and is a favorite at the fish market, even though overfishing has decreased the supply and caused the price to climb in eastern markets. Sea bass is delicious baked, broiled, or in a chowder. It is the great favorite of many Chinese-Americans and should be offered cooked with Oriental seasonings in all Chinese restaurants. Sweet-and-sour sea bass is an unsurpassed dish. Chinese homes serve sea bass for special occasions in much the same way as the French do a huge decorated salmon at New Year's. In Chinatown fish markets, sea bass are usually kept in tanks with nets used to scoop out the fresh fish selected by the customer. Ask your own fish marketer to bring you a sea bass and pick it up as soon as he arrives from the wholesaler's.

In the summer, anglers on party fishing boats who catch numerous sea bass find that these hardy fish live for quite a long time in the wells. (There have been records of sea bass living several months in the same well.) Fishermen who keep sea bass in this manner will find that if they first puncture the fish's air bladder with an awl or sharp-pointed instrument by driving it into the side of the fish, they will equalize the pressure inside the fish with that outside, causing it to adjust itself to the container. If the sea bass is brought up from the depths and is not punctured, it will float on top of the water and soon die.

One must exercise great care in handling a sea bass without a gaff or pick as this fish has very sharp spines on its back and around its gill cover. I find that an easy way to hold a sea bass is to place your thumb in its mouth on its lower jaw and grasp it with the index finger under the jaw with a strong grip. The fish has small teeth so there is very little chance of being bitten.

The sea bass has the unusual distinction of being the first marine fish of U.S. waters on which artificial propagation was tried by fish culturists. In June 1874, Fred Mather of the Noank, Connecticut, station of the U.S. Fish Commission fertilized a number of sea bass eggs. The eggs were carefully observed for several days in shad boxes as they passed through their early stages of development. But a storm interfered with this experiment, and it was not brought to a successful conclusion.

The sea bass is quite plentiful on the Middle Atlantic coast during the summer, and great numbers are taken by anglers and commercial fishermen. Sea bass are hardy fish with a body temperature almost the same as the water in which they swim. They usually appear inshore off southern New England during the first or second week in May and stay until the end of October or November. They spend the winter offshore and at greater depths somewhat to the south.

The average sea bass is about 12 inches long and weighs between 1 and 2 pounds; a few run about 3 pounds. The world's record sea bass taken by rod and reel, according to the International Game Fish Association, was an 8-pounder that was 21 inches long, caught off Nantucket Island on May 13, 1951 by H. R. Rider.

Adult sea bass are chiefly bottom feeders consuming crabs, small lobsters, squid, clams, and small fish. They will readily take a hook baited with squid, clam, or sand worm.

Lobster fishermen quite frequently find sea bass stuck in their lobster pots as the bass often enter the trap to feed on the lobster bait or the lobster itself. The bass, with their large fins, often find themselves snarled in the mesh of the trap. Some fishermen find that sea bass will often enter an empty lobster trap merely out of curiosity.

In 1950, according to the Fish and Wildlife Service, 12,974,000 pounds of sea bass were landed on the Atlantic coast with a value of $1,496,000. By 1975, the U.S. sea bass catch had declined to 5,155,000 pounds valued at $1,597,000. Of this total, the largest amount was captured by otter trawl. Other methods used were pound nets and seines. New Jersey fishermen use a special type of gear in getting sea bass—the fish pot. This device resembles a lobster pot but the height of the funnel is increased to admit the fish. Fish pots are set unbaited on rough bottom with buoys and lines to mark their location. One fisherman set 650 pots.

The Regal Kingfish

"Look here at the fish I caught," said the fellow fishing beside me on the breachway at Weekapaug, Rhode Island. "I think it's some sort of cod."

"You're all wrong," remarked the fisherman on the other side of him. "It's a kind of hake."

I could see the fish clearly and knew at once that it was neither of the two species.

"What you have there is a kingfish," I said. "You can always identify a king by the dark, irregular stripes on its silvery green back and the elongated first dorsal fin on its back."

The angler had caught the fish on a flounder rig with a piece of squid for bait.

"Take your kingfish home, fry it for supper, and you will be in for a taste treat," I told my neighbor as he started back along the rocky breakwater.

For its size, the kingfish is considered by some fishermen to be the gamest saltwater fish. When the kingfish is present, and conditions are favorable, it will bite suddenly and savagely, with vigorous strength that is startling to the unwary angler. Hooked at the end of an angler's line, the kingfish will make a sudden dash, and swerve from side to side with a fury that is unusual for so small a fish. A 1- or 2-pound kingfish will sometimes nibble at a baited hook and then strike suddenly with the force of a 10-pound bluefish.

Jerry Sylvester, the noted saltwater angler, tells of catching kingfish in May near Jones Beach, Long Island. Jerry caught more kingfish than the rest of his fishing party combined. It seems his companions were casting over a long sandbar into shallow water while Jerry's success formula was casting over the sandbar into a deep waterhole where the kingfish were feeding.

Smaller kingfish usually bite during daylight; larger ones take the hook at night. A heavy sinker should be used to keep the bait near the bottom. Kingfish tend to move closer to shore to feed during high tide.

In coastal Atlantic shore areas from spring through fall kingfish can provide a regal thrill for the lucky anglers who hook on to this fighting species.

The northern kingfish, which is known scientifically as *Menticirrhus saxatilis*, may be called by a variety of local names including roundhead, sea mullet, sea mink, king whiting, sea sable, and surf whiting. The name that is most often used for this species, kingfish, was given during colonial times by people in the New York area. They called it kingfish because they considered its excellent taste and colorful beauty far above all other fish. To catch a kingfish was considered the crowning glory by old-time fishermen.

After being relatively scarce in our waters for a few years, kingfish are getting more plentiful. Warmer waters have caused them to increase their numbers north of the elbow of Cape Cod. The general range of this species is from Pensacola and Key West, Florida, to Massachusetts, with stragglers of the species found as far north as Casco Bay, Maine. The greatest number of these fish are found in the area bounded by Chesapeake Bay and Long Island Sound.

There can be little question about the identification of a kingfish once one is familiar with its characteristics. In addition to the metallic green color, it has dark, irregular side bars and a first dorsal fin with a long, filamentous spine. The snout and the tip of the head are somewhat rounded. The upper jaw projects beyond the lower one, and a little barbel, or flesh whisker, is found under its chin. Its jaws are filled with numerous small teeth, and its lips are fleshy. Kingfish grow to a maximum length of 17 inches and a maximum weight of around 3 pounds.

The kingfish is a member of the drum family and should not be confused with the large king mackerel of the mackerel family, which is called cero but is sometimes referred to as kingfish.

Spencer Baird has referred to the kingfish as follows:

This species, well worthy of the name which has been given it, and the estimation in which it is held by New York epicures, is certainly savory when taken from the water, and leaves nothing to be desired in the way of a fish diet. . . . It appears quite early in the spring with the squeteague, and is frequently found in company with it. It takes bait readily and affords excellent sport for the fishermen. . . .

They occasionally run to a considerable distance up the rivers, as I have caught young fish of this species at Sing Sing on the Hudson, where the water is scarcely brackish. The kingfish run much in schools, and keep on or near a hard, sandy bottom, preferring the edge of channels and the vicinity of sand bars; and they congregate about oyster-beds, especially when the oysters are being taken up, and may be seen under the boats, fighting for worms and crustaceans dislodged by the operation. They bite readily at hard or soft clams, or even pieces of fish, and are taken most successfully on the young flood. Like the squeteague, they will occasionally run up the salt creeks at night, and may be captured in gill nets as the water recedes.

Spawning of the kingfish commences in June and continues until August, reaching its height in late June or early July. In still waters at a temperature of 68 to 70 degrees F., the period of incubation for the eggs is from 46 to 50 hours.

Upon hatching, the larva of the kingfish is from 2 to 2.5 millimeters in length. The larva floats upside down with its tail inclined upward. Every little while it makes short wriggling dashes, which bring it momentarily into what would be its normal position after its yoke sac is absorbed. Young kingfish, between 1⅛ and 1½ inches in length, already strongly resemble the adults, but the youngster's head and eyes are larger and the body deeper.

The growth of the kingfish during its first summer is exceedingly rapid. Measurements of a large number of young at Woods Hole, Massachusetts, showed that fishes hatched early in June may reach a length of ¾ inch by July 1, 3⅛ inches by August 1, and as much as 5⅞ inches by September 1. During the first winter this species reaches a length of 4 to 6 inches, about 10 inches by the second winter, and by the third winter around 13½ inches.

Maturity occurs at the age of 2 or 3 years. Male kingfish appear to mature earlier than females; many ripe 2-year-old males have been collected, while the females taken usually do not spawn until they are 3 years old.

Flounder rigs are ideal for fishing for kingfish. One should use Chestertown #6 or 1/0 Sproat hooks. Good baits are squid, sand worms, clams, crabs, mussels, and shrimp. Bait should be cut into tiny pieces because the kingfish has a small mouth. Kingfish nibble at first, then they take a strong hold on the bait. Kingfish put up a good fight on freshwater tackle and are an ideal light-outfit fish. They are also tough to beat on the dinner table.

2

Beauties of the Sea

The sleekest, the fastest, and the most graceful always attract the eye. Among these are four species which have outstanding features, placing them among the most fascinating sights to appear in the sea.

The Dashing Swordfish

The following incident was reported in *Forest and Stream* for June 24, 1875:

On Wednesday of last week a Sword-fish attacked the fishing boat of Captain D. D. Thurlow while he was hauling mackerel-nets off Fire Island, thrust its sword clear through the bottom and stuck fast while the fishermen took several half hitches around its body and so secured it. It

was afterward brought to the Fulton Market and found to weigh 390 pounds. Its sword measured three feet seven inches and its entire length was over eleven feet.

G. B. Goode, in a scientific paper published in 1884, gives many instances of swordfish piercing ships and boats. One remarkable incident he mentioned was this:

On the return of the whale-ship *Fortune* to Plymouth, Massachusetts, in 1828, the stump of a sword blade of this fish was noticed projecting like a cog outside, which on being traced, had driven through the copper sheathing, an inch board undersheathing, a three-inch plank of hardwood, the solid white-oak timber 12 inches thick, then through another two and half inch hard-oak ceiling and lastly penetrated the head of an oilcask, where it stuck, not a drop of the oil having escaped.

The earliest record of American swordfish dates back to the discovery of the New World. Among the artifacts that Christopher Columbus brought back from his voyage of discovery was a swordfish sword. This weapon, taken from a slain Indian, was brought to northern Italy and placed in the Church of Siena, where Columbus received his schooling.

Probably the first written account of swordfish in American waters was a passage written by John Josselyn and printed in 1674: "In the afternoon we saw a great fish called Vehuella or Swordfish, having a long, strong and sharp finn like a sword-blade on the top of his head, with which he pierced our Ship, and one of our Sailors dived and brought it aboard."

On August 7, 1887, the schooner *Volunteer*, out of Gloucester, Massachusetts, was off Block Island when it received a strong blow from a 300-pound swordfish that was swimming alongside. When the swordfish was harpooned and taken on board, it was found that the fish had lost its entire sword, no doubt in some previous attack.

The "sword" of the swordfish is legendary in the yarns of seafarers. It is flat and in consequence the fish is often called "broadbill." It is an elongation of the upper jaw and reaches a length of 4 feet. The sword is usually nearly black on its upper surface, and pale underneath. Actually, the sword is a modification that takes the place of teeth in the mature fish, for the mouth of the adult swordfish is devoid of teeth.

"Swordfish to starboard!" shouted the lookout from aloft. The fishing vessel swiftly headed in the direction of a pointed fin on the surface of the flat sea off Martha's Vineyard, near the Massachusetts coast.

"Fish dead ahead," cried the lookout, and the ship slowly approached the fin. Another swordfish was soon on its way to market. Until recently, this scene was repeated many times during the summer months along the New England coast.

Commercial fishermen use a harpoon with a detachable end for capturing swordfish. When the fish is struck, the head of the harpoon usually remains stuck fast in the body of the fish. The harpoon is then attached to a rope that has a keg, barrel, or buoy at the end. Rope and float are towed along by the fish, marking its whereabouts when it gives up the fight.

The swordfish is always harpooned from the end of the bow of the fishing vessel. It is next to impossible to approach this fish in a small boat. Boats engaged in swordfishing are fitted out with a rest, or pulpit, which consists of a narrow platform extending far enough out to enable the harpooner to get above the fish.

In foul weather, swordfish are not available. They come to the surface only in moderately smooth seas. With a lookout stationed at the masthead, the fishing vessel cruises the grounds seeking the telltale dorsal fins of the fish. When visibility is good, a keen-eyed lookout may sight a dorsal fin three miles away. Once a fish has been sighted, the spotter sings out the location, and the vessel quickly overtakes it. The approach must be made as quietly as possible.

The swordfish is no longer sought out by American commercial fishermen. On May 7, 1971, the U.S. Food and Drug Administration found that of 853 swordfish tested for mercury concentration, 811 had levels of mercury above the 0.5 parts per million considered acceptable. As a result of these findings, the FDA banned swordfish indefinitely from interstate commerce in the United States. Swordfish totaling 832,000 pounds were confiscated. Substantial amounts were taken from fish retail outlets, and fish brokers stopped the sale of another 4 million pounds held in cold storage. A fishing industry that comprised 1 percent of the total fish diet of Americans came to a controversial conclusion.

You can occasionally find swordfish selling for $2 to $5 per pound in some fish markets in New England and New York. This swordfish has to be caught and unloaded in the state in which it is to be sold because of an interstate commerce ban.

Americans consumed 26 million pounds of swordfish annually before the reports of mercury in this species. Of this amount, only 4 million pounds were caught by U.S. fishermen off the east and west coasts. The rest was imported, frozen, mainly from Canada and Japan.

The swordfish, *Xiphias gladius*, belongs to the family Xiphiidae. It is an open-water offshore fish found in warm and temperate oceans all over the world. It occurs in the Western Hemisphere from Cuba to Cape Breton Island, off Nova Scotia. During the summer months, swordfish are moderately abundant near Block Island and No Man's Island, off Martha's Vineyard. Broadbills also occur on the Pacific Coast from the Santa Barbara Islands to San Diego.

Plowing through schools of fish, flailing and maiming with quick slashes of its keen, elongated bill, the swordfish is a formidable adversary as well as one of the earth's ancient inhabitants. Fossil evidence dates these fish from the Cretaceous period, some 100 million years ago.

To the Dutch, the fish is known as *zwarrd-fish;* it is *espada,* or *espardarte,* to the Spanish; the Italians call it *pesce-spada;* and the French say *épée de mer.* The swordfish was known to the ancient Greeks and Romans, too. Nineteen hundred years ago Pliny mentioned the swordfish in his *Historia Naturalis,* stating, "The Sword-fish called in Greek *Xiphias,* that is to say in Latin *Gladius,* a sword, hath a beake or bill sharp pointed, wherewith he will drive though the sides and plankes of a ship. . . ."

Swordfish are sometimes confused with the marlins and sailfish since all three groups possess pointed bills. The swordfish has a broader bill than the marlin or sailfish, and it lacks their pelvic fins. In addition, scales are found only on young swordfish less than 30 inches long, while adult marlin and sailfish possess distinct scales. These are all physical features that reduce friction while moving through the water and give the swordfish tremendous thrust while feeding on a school of fish.

Swordfish may have one or more parasitic passengers, internal and external, though no single fish could have too many of them and survive. One species of nonparasitic, hitchhiking suckerfish, *Remora brachyptera,* has a particular affinity for swordfish and attaches itself by means of its adhering disk to the swordfish's sides or gill covers. Several remoras may be found clinging to one fish.

Internally, swordfish may be afflicted with one or another of at least twelve known species of parasitic worms and six species of parasitic crustaceans. These irritating pests have been found in swordfish gills, esophagus, stomach, intestines, and muscles. Tiny crustaceans called copepods also parasitize swordfish both externally and internally.

Veteran swordfishermen say that when you see a swordfish, you know there are mackerel about. In the waters of the North Atlantic, the swordfish feeds on mackerel, menhaden, bluefish, whiting, butterfish, squid, and small, sardinelike fishes. In feeding, the big fish rises beneath a school and strikes vigorously with its sword in all directions. After rampaging through the school, the swordfish devours the victims of its carnage. Captain Benjamin Ashby says he saw a school of herring closely crowded together near the surface of the sea on George's Bank. A swordfish rose through the dense mass of fish and flailed the herring with such telling effect that the captain was able to pick up a bushelful of dead herring.

Swordfish reach a formidable size. According to Bigelow and Schroeder, the heaviest specimen recorded from the Gulf of Maine was caught during the summer of 1921 by Captain Irving King and landed at the Boston Fish Pier. It weighed 915 pounds dressed (that is, with its insides removed), which would place its live weight around 1100 pounds. This specimen was not measured, but its sword was more than 5 feet long, indicating that the total length of the fish must have been about 15 feet.

A swordfish taken in 1931, weighing 644 pounds dressed, was 13 feet long from its tail to the tip of its sword. In 1932, a 925-pound swordfish was taken by commercial fishermen; in fact, every year a few swordfish of 500 pounds or more are taken by harpooners. Currently the world's record *Xiphias* taken by rod and reel is an 1182-pound giant, nearly 15 feet long, taken May 7, 1953, off Iquique, Chile, by Lou Marron.

The average size of Atlantic swordfish is from 100 to 300 pounds. Occasionally very small specimens are taken by fishermen. One weighing 6 pounds 7 ounces was taken by the schooner *Anna* on George's Bank on August 9, 1922; another of 7 pounds was taken by the *Courtney* on a long line on Brown's Bank in 1931. On August 15, 1951, the trawler *Winchester*, on the southeast part of George's Bank, in 46 fathoms of water, hauled up a 5¾-pound swordfish, one of the smallest ever reported off the North Atlantic coast.

The exact mating grounds of the swordfish are still somewhat of a mystery. Taning in 1955 suggested that the distribution of larval and young fish indicated spawning in the western Atlantic and southern part of the Sargasso Sea, from February to April. Swordfish are solitary in habit and only found as paired couples when they are ready to head for shallow waters to spawn.

Juvenile swordfish are common in the Mediterranean, and are frequently captured in the mesh of seines and traps. Swordfish as small as ½ pound are sometimes found in the fish markets of southern Italy.

The meat of the young swordfish is highly prized along the shores of the Mediterranean and said to be perfectly white, compact, and of delicate flavor. Young swordfish possess both teeth and scales, but these disappear in mature specimens.

The swordfish liver contains an oil which, when processed, is exceptionally high in vitamins A and D. And this great fish has a delicate flavor that is different from any other seafood. Perhaps the mercury problem can be solved by science. Already, medical men have stated that no harm can come from an occasional meal of broiled swordfish. In any case, at its present price and scarcity in market and restaurant, few can afford more than an occasional meal of this seafood delight.

Greyhound of the Sea—The Marlin

If you could ask Ernest Hemingway, Michael Lerner, and Zane Grey what they considered the fightingest game fish they ever caught, I'd wager a marlin would be at the top of the list or near it.

Found all over the world, marlins are among the largest and speediest of game fishes. A great deal of confusion has existed among scientists with regard to the various kinds of marlins. The matter of species is not completely cleared up yet, but at the present time ichthyologists recognize five principal kinds of marlins—blue marlin, white marlin, black marlin, striped marlin, and silver marlin.

These large oceanic game fishes received the name marlin because seafarers noted the resemblance of their elongated bill to a marlinspike, the long, pointed tool that is used by sailors in splicing ropes. The marlin is also called spearfish, spikefish, billfish, and skilligallee.

The marlin can be readily distinguished from the swordfish by the shape of its elongated upper jaw, or bill. The swordfish sword, or bill, is broad and flat; the marlin bill is round and somewhat cylindrical. Also, the marlin has small, thornlike scales imbedded in its skin; swordfish over 4½ feet long have no scales. In addition, two rudderlike flat ridges appear on the fleshy, narrow tail of the marlin just before it spreads out into broad-winged fins.

In back of the marlin's spear, just above the edge of its mouth, is a pair of fierce, shiny eyes set in heavy, bony sockets. The formidable eyes on an adult marlin are among the largest in the animal kingdom.

Marlins, like their near relatives the sailfish and swordfish, are

tremendously powerful swimmers. This is because they are hydro-
dynamically among the best-designed fishes in the world. Their powerful, propellerlike tails, beautifully streamlined bodies, and sharply
keeled fins all give them unique water-cleaving abilities. Marlins are
among the swiftest existing fishes. They have been estimated to travel
at speeds of 40 to 50 miles an hour and can travel many hours at such
speeds. According to Norman and Fraser , a torpedo fired from a
battleship would soon be left behind by a marlin going all out.

When the British zoologist Professor Richard Owen was asked to
testify as to the power of one of these fishes, he stated, "It strikes with
the accumulated force of fifteen double-headed hammers; its velocity is
equal to that of a swivel-shot, and is as dangerous as an artillery
projectile." Quite a statement from a man of science.

Blue marlins run larger than white marlins; their weight averages
200 pounds or more. The rod-and-reel record for this species, according
to the International Game Fish Society (IGFS), is a 1153-pound fish

caught on August 21, 1969 by Greg D. Perez off Ritidian Point, Guam. The blue marlin is found in both the Atlantic and Pacific oceans.

The blue marlin differs from its close relative, the white marlin, not only by being larger, but also by having a much darker dull blue color and a more pointed tip on its dorsal fin. The white marlin has a white belly, pale coloration, and a rounded dorsal fin.

During the summer months, white marlins are sometimes plentiful off Montauk, Block Island, and George's Bank. The rod-and-reel record for the white marlin is a 161-pound fish taken by L. F. Hooper of Miami Beach, Florida. South of New Jersey, white marlins are sometimes sighted in small schools of from 10 to 20 fish; off Long Island and New England they are usually encountered alone or swimming in pairs.

A few years back, a record giant marlin was reported harpooned off Grand Banks, the fishermen mistaking it for a broadbill swordfish. This marlin measured 18½ feet long, and its weight was estimated at 2200 pounds. It was most likely an unusually large blue marlin that had strayed from its southern habitat.

The marlins' chief food consists of other fish, but they have been known to feed also on squid and cuttlefish. Mackerel, bonitos, flying fishes, and tuna furnish the bulk of the marlin's diet. These spearfish have been known to pursue schools of fish for days on end. Rising among a school, marlins strike viciously to the left and right with their spears, then feed on the dead and wounded fish at their leisure.

On a recent cruise of the U.S. Fish and Wildlife Service long-line vessel *John R. Manning* in the yellowfin tuna grounds, south of Hawaii near the equator, the capture of a huge black marlin, *Makaira indica*, was reported. Its weight was estimated at 1500 pounds and in its stomach was a freshly killed 5-foot yellowfin tuna weighing 157 pounds. The tuna had been speared twice completely through the body by the marlin, then swallowed head first.

At this writing, more than 30 marlins each weighing in excess of 1000 pounds have been taken by rod and reel. According to the IGFS, the largest marlin captured by an angler was a Pacific black marlin, a *Makaira indica* weighing 1560 pounds taken by Alfred C. Glassel, Jr. It was caught off Cabo Blanco, Peru, August 4, 1953, with fishing line in the 130-pound test class.

The white or blue marlin off our coasts usually puts on an unforgettable performance when hooked at the end of a fishing line. One trick exhibited by these species is known as "tail walking." The fish rises almost entirely clear of the water, thrashing its tail and covering many yards in this position in an effort to rid itself of the hook. Another stunt of the marlin is known as "greyhounding." In performing this feat, the marlin makes a series of long, flat leaps 20 feet or more, barely touching the surface of the water between jumps. This maneuver weakens the fish considerably.

When a marlin is finally subdued and brought alongside the boat, it becomes a potential danger to those on board unless it is handled with caution. The thrashing bill and flapping muscular tail can seriously injure a fisherman if it gets out of control. The usual method of bringing a large marlin aboard a boat is to club it to death, then secure a rope around its tail and haul it in. A few reports tell of marlins putting their bony spears right through the planking on the sides of boats in their final lunge before capture. Caution is the byword when you encounter a marlin.

The natural enemies of the marlin are large sharks, which have been observed chasing marlins in the open sea. On several occasions, the remains of marlins have been taken from the stomachs of tiger sharks or maneaters. Observers say that marlins become furious at the approach of sharks.

Little is known about the life history and breeding habits of the marlin. The American Museum of Natural History and other institutions have sent out expeditions to study the habits of this species. Marlins laden with ripe eggs have been taken off the coast of Cuba. As for young fish, a 5-pound baby marlin has been taken off Miami Beach, Florida; and a 6¾-pound youngster has been found off Cat Cay, British West Indies.

Most marlins taken by hook and line turn out to be females; they seem to be more aggressive than the males because they are somewhat larger.

The white marlin has dark-colored flesh, and the black marlin has light meat; both types are somewhat flaky and not too tasty unless smoked. In the United States there is very little demand for marlin as a food fish. In the fish markets of South America, Hawaii, and Japan, however, marlins are very popular. Cuba has a large commercial fishery for marlins as the fish are smoked and processed there. About five thousand marlins are caught annually by the fishermen of Cuba.

The Daring Flying Fishes

Four miles out past Block Island, Rhode Island, a heavy swell was running, and whitecaps were forming on the waves. At first what seemed like small birds appeared to be skimming the waves; then it was apparent that they were flying fishes. They disappeared into the waves only to appear again.

North American waters contain about twenty-five species of true flying fishes belonging to the family Exocoetidae. In addition, flying gurnards of the family Dactylopteridae sometimes skip out of the sea, but these are not true flying fishes. Flying gurnards are much less numerous than flying fishes, only three or four species having been recorded.

A flying gurnard can be identified immediately because it has a large, bony head armed with spines and two dorsal fins. The true flying fish has a smooth head and only one dorsal fin. Both types of fishes possess the distinctive enlarged pectoral fins that, when expanded, serve as wings for gliding through the air.

Usually found in tropical and subtropical seas, flying fishes occur off the New England coast in late summer and fall. They are very common in the warm waters of the Gulf Stream and have been observed as far north as Newfoundland and Nova Scotia. They are also seen along the California coast.

Frequently seen gliding above the surface of the waves in rough weather, flying fishes prefer a disturbed sea to a calm one for making their aerial excursions. The major reason they take to the air is to escape the jaws of the hordes of marine predators that like to feed on them. Chief among their pursuers is the sleek dolphin, or dorado, which is probably the fastest fish on the open sea (this fish should not be confused with the marine mammal called dolphin). The dorado feeds mainly on flying fishes. Bonitos, tuna, albacore, swordfish, marlins, and porpoises also relish flying fishes.

Generally, flying fishes occur in groups or schools swimming near the surface of the water. Their teeth are small, and they feed on minute zooplankton and tiny fishes. They are difficult to see under the surface because they are metallic blue or bluish green on the back and silvery on the sides and belly. The large pectoral fins, which sometimes reach as far back as the tail, are usually transparent but are sometimes mottled with black or brown blotches.

Flying fishes soar into the air when alarmed by an approaching vessel, or a predator. At other times, they take to the air for no apparent reason. They often fall on board ships, but this never happens during a calm or from the lee side or in daytime. During a breeze, the fish come from the weather side. In the daytime they will avoid a ship, flying away from it; during the night, when they are unable to see, they sometimes fall on deck.

Though they resemble birds in flight, the fish do not fly in the manner that birds do. The fish merely glide through the air, holding their fins rigid, much like a paper airplane. Most flying fishes are two-winged gliders, extending only their pectoral fins. But some use their pelvic fins too, making them four-winged.

The mechanism by which the flying fishes take to the air has been a matter of considerable interest to ichthyologists during the past century. Men such as D. S. Jordan, J. T. Nichols, C. M. Breder, and C. L. Hubbs have made detailed studies on the habits and propelling mechanics of these fishes. Pioneer airplane designers would have benefited more from a careful study of flying fishes than from observing birds. Modern jet planes and rocket ships more closely resemble the streamlined shape of a flying fish in flight than any other flying creature.

Several species of freshwater flying fishes are found in tropic zones. *Pantodon*, a little African fish, flies with its large pectoral fins. In the rivers of South America occurs *Gasteropelecus*, which, by rapid beats of its pectoral fins, cuts across the surface of the water, taking off into a true flight. The smallest flying fish is about 2 inches long and is known as Monroe's flying fish. One of the largest is the California flying fish, a four-winged species, *Cypselurus californicus*, which reaches a length of 18 inches and is a strong flier.

Hubbs has described the flight of *Cypselurus* very vividly. He says they never appear to leap directly into the air, as some species are said to do, but on emerging from the water, they immediately spread their wide pectoral "wings" and smaller pelvic "wings" and move forward on the surface like tiny airplanes for a distance averaging, perhaps, 25 feet. While on the water, their sole source of propulsive power appears to be the normal organ of locomotion of fish—the tail—of which they use the lower lobe alone to provide power. The pectoral fins are seen to vibrate, but apparently with neither sufficient amplitude nor velocity to propel the fishes forward on the surface or to raise them from the water.

The moment the fishes rise into the air, their fins are held taut. They are not flapping wings but planes of support. The flight of these fishes is often straight in direction, but may become semicircular. During flight, the fishes seldom rise higher than 5 feet, except when forced upward by a gust of wind. The length of flight usually varies between 50 feet and 300 feet. When flying with the wind, distances of about one-quarter of a mile are sometimes made. Some observers estimate that a flying fish travels 35 miles per hour when it takes to the air.

In distant parts of the world, flying fishes are of considerable economic importance as food. There is an important fishery for flying fish off the Coromandel coast of India, near Madras. The natives go 12 miles out in catamarans. When they reach the fishing grounds, they throw clumps of densely branched shrubs overboard. These pieces of foliage attract the flying fishes, which congregate under the branches. If the fishes are plentiful, the branches are carefully drawn toward the catamaran. Then the natives quickly take the branches out of the water and scoop up the flying fishes with dip nets. The fishes are eaten fresh or are sun dried without salt and sold in the markets of Penang, Rangoon, and Singapore.

In the Caribbean Sea, Barbados is one of the few places in the world where flying fishes constitute over 80 percent of the fishery. The species most sought is *Hirundichthys speculizer*, which averages about ⅓ pound in weight. Captured by drifting gill nets with 1⅞-inch mesh, or with fine line and small baited hooks, these fishes used to bring from 1.5 to 6 cents each in local markets, depending on their abundance.

In California, from Point Conception to Cape San Lucas, flying fishes are captured in late spring and summer in gill nets, round hand nets, and scoops under lights. Some of the catch is sold in Los Angeles fish markets and some is used for bait fish.

The breeding habits of flying fishes are still being investigated.

Some species deposit their eggs in masses of floating seaweed. The eggs have sticky, hairlike threads that bind them together and hold them to the weeds. Newly hatched flying fishes are yellowish orange and closely resemble the floats of sargassum and other brown algae.

Many people consider flying fishes a great delicacy. Their flesh is very firm and tasty. Fried in cornmeal or bread crumbs, these winged fishes are difficult to beat as a tasty dish.

Bluebacked Bonito

An agile, streamlined fish that visits our coasts during the summer months is the common Atlantic bonito, *Sarda sarda*. *Bonito*, which means "little beauty" in Spanish, was the name given to this fish by the Spanish conquistadors. They encountered this relative of the tuna in the sixteenth century as they sailed to their colonies in South and Central America. The fish was undoubtedly called this because of its beautiful form and the succulent meals it provided sailors who tired of salt pork and stale biscuits. During the American Revolution, one of our men-of-war was named the *Bonitta* after this group of fish.

The bonito differs from school tuna by virtue of the fact that it has from 7 to 20 dark stripes running obliquely along its side. Also, its teeth are larger than the tuna's, and its mouth is relatively wider.

With a beautiful form suggestive of motion, the bonito reminds one of a rocket or a jet plane. The powerful crescent-shaped tail, the fish's chief source of locomotion, propels it at terrific speeds, sometimes pushing the bonito clear out of the water when it is in pursuit of its favorite food, the flying fish. From its custom of occasionally leaping clear into the air before falling back into the water, the bonito has been

given the name skipjack in some places.

Bonitos grow to a length of about 3 feet; they have been known to weigh as much as 12 pounds but generally average about 5 pounds.

The bonito has lovely coloration, its back usually deep indigo blue mottled with lighter shades of the same color and transversed with dark blue stripes. The abdomen is a metallic silver, as are its cheeks and gill covers. The delicate shades of color of this fish change very rapidly when it is taken from the water. It is generally believed that its appearance sometimes changes from blue to green to match the hue of the water.

When swimming in large schools, the bonito frequently becomes relatively easy prey to such ferocious enemies as the swordfish, sharks, and the killer whale. Bonitos themselves often prey on younger members of their own species, according to Frank Bullen.

Bonitos are always found wherever the dolphin and albacore appear, and they quickly respond to a rise in temperature outside of their usual habitat. Semitropical in winter, they are always one of the first species to migrate to the New England coast in late spring. I have observed them in Rhode Island waters as early as June 4.

In New England waters, the bonito and the unrelated bluefish *(Pomatomus saltatrix)* have much in common. Both have insatiable appetites. Together they come and go along our coast and sometimes are taken side by side in the same boat. Both species are attracted to the New England coast in June by the schools of fishes on which they fatten. Stomach contents of bonitos reveal that they feed mostly on menhaden, mackerel, squid, alewives, and flying fishes.

Commercial fishermen take bonitos in traps, gill nets, and seines along with mackerel, menhaden, and bluefish. In 1975, according to Fish and Wildlife Service figures, U.S. fishermen landed 31,744,000 pounds of bonito valued at $3,785,000.

With regard to bonito in the past, on June 21, 1635, Cotton Mather stated in his journal: "This morning our seamen took a bonito [near Newfoundland] and opened him upon the deck; of which being dressed, our master sent Mathew Michel and me part, it was a good fish in eating as could be desired."

J. Hammond states, "This fish used to be quite common in the Stonington, Connecticut, market. I have note of a considerable number in market, July 22, 1842, their first appearance of the season."

D. H. Storer said in 1846: "This species called by fishermen in the Boston market the skipjack and by those on the extremity of Cape Cod the bonito is very rarely met within Massachusetts Bay. It is occasionally taken at Provincetown and even at Lynn. At some seasons it is frequently caught in Martha's Vineyard with trailing bait."

The Providence *Journal* for July 1871 carried the following account by a correspondent:

> Last night I had a fish on my table which they said was a kind of Spanish mackerel; the moment I tasted it I said it was bonito, having eaten it thirty years since, on my first voyage to India and the taste had never been forgotten. It is the salmon of the sea. Mark its solidity of flesh, its weight, its purity of taste, entire absence of the slightly decayed taste all fish has during warm weather. It is as nourishing as beef. We certify from actual experience that bonito is a worthy rival of the Spanish mackerel, the sheepshead and the salmon.

During the nineteenth century, great quantities of bonitos were taken around Block Island. In the summer of 1877, Goode estimates that not less than 2 million pounds of bonito were taken there. During this period, one haul of purse seine by the schooner *Lilian* of Noank, Connecticut, yielded 1500 bonitos, or approximately 75,000 pounds of fish.

In recent times, bonitos have been more plentiful in some years than others. For example, during the summer of 1945, 57,000 pounds of bonito were caught in the waters around Martha's Vineyard and sent to market.

The bonito is believed to spawn off the Middle Atlantic coast in June; Nichols and Breder reported young bonitos 5 to 6 inches in length being found off Orient Point, New York, early in September.

Occasionally, one will find a bonito that is carrying parasites, both internal and external. Tiny shellfishes resembling limpets are sometimes attached behind the pectoral fins and between the ventral fins. Inside the mouth and in the gills may be found small white copepods resembling wood lice. More unpleasant is the fact that several species of nematode worms sometimes infest the muscular tissue. These parasites are killed by cooking.

The bonito is highly regarded by anglers, who catch them by trolling feathers, spoons, and lures behind a boat going at full speed. Bonitos are very powerful for their size and give the angler a game fight.

After being caught, bonitos are usually cleaned and bled immediately; they have a rich supply of blood, and unless it is removed soon after capture, they lose their flavor and deteriorate rapidly. Because of this rich blood supply, their freshly caught flesh looks like beef.

3

Terrors of Mankind

The notoriety of the shark adds greatly to the terror it inspires. Yet other fishes, some of which we may never have heard of but which have been known since Roman times, are far more awesome. Some inflict incredible pain, and others cause death. Here are a few—well known and almost unknown; others appear elsewhere in this book.

"Rough Tooth," the Man-eating White Shark

The scientific name of the man-eater *Carcharodon* originates from two Greek words meaning "rough" and "tooth."

One of the largest and most dangerous forms of life in the world's oceans is the cosmopolitan man-eater shark, known also as the white shark, *Carcharodon carcharias*. This fish is so huge that the renowned Swedish naturalist Linnaeus argued that a man-eater shark, not a whale, swallowed the Biblical prophet Jonah. He thought the ancient writers had mistaken a mammal for a fish.

Found in the tropical waters of all the oceans and the Mediterranean Sea, the man-eater shark has been recorded as far north as St. Pierre Bank, south of Newfoundland, and as far south as the coast of Brazil. Man-eaters of 40 feet or more in length have been reported. The jaws of a specimen 36 feet long are on exhibition in the British Museum; the teeth are nearly 3 inches long. In the distant past, in the early days of the mammals, close relatives of this shark had a mouth gape of up to 7 feet.

Off Cape Lookout, North Carolina, in 1905, a Mr. Coles recorded a

20-foot shark that he believed to be a man-eater that had bitten off the right hind flipper of a large loggerhead turtle. On June 23, 1955, I observed a 7-foot man-eater captured in the Clark fish traps at Jerusalem, Rhode Island. At the time there was also a quantity of butterfish and squid in the trap. The shark thrashed around a good deal in the net. Just before it was taken out of the trap, it bit the tail of a large anglerfish and almost severed it.

On opening the stomach of a man-eater 16 feet long, captured at Port Philip, Australia, Frederick McCoy found a large Newfoundland dog inside. The dog had its collar on, identifying it as one lost the day before. No doubt the dog was swallowed while enjoying a swim at the beach. The stomach of another large man-eater captured near Sydney, Australia, contained such sundry items as a number of mutton bones, a tin can, the hindquarters of a pig, the head and forequarters of a bulldog, a quantity of horseflesh, and other things too numerous to mention. It is possible that most of them had been jettisoned from passing ships.

The man-eater can be readily identified by its large, triangular, serrated teeth. Large specimens are generally white, while smaller ones are blue-gray on the back and white on the belly.

During the summer months, man-eaters are found scattered along the New England coast. Trap fishermen and seiners frequently encounter the toothy monsters among catches of butterfish or mackerel. On rare occasions they come inshore along beaches and cause quite a panic among bathers. It is generally believed that it was a man-eater shark that caused fatalities among swimmers at a Sandy Hook, New Jersey, beach in 1916. A fatal attack on a swimmer in Buzzard's Bay at Mattapoisett on July 25, 1936, was also thought to have been caused by a man-eater.

There are also several records of this shark making unprovoked attacks on fishermen's dories. On July 12, 1830, Joseph Blaney, aged fifty-two, went out in a small rowboat to fish near Swampscott, Massachusetts. A man-eater overset his boat and killed him. In November 1928 a 15-foot man-eater overturned a dory with two fishermen in it off Monomoy Point, Massachusetts. The fish was later killed.

The food of the man-eater consists of almost anything that it can sink its razor-sharp teeth into. D. S. Jordan reported a man-eater 30 feet long that was captured off the coast of California in 1880. It had a whole young sea lion in its stomach.

The modes of attack by sharks on people have been classified by Gilbert Whitney of the Australian Museum in five categories: (1) taking of swimmers along ocean beaches; (2) taking of bathers in harbors or well upriver; (3) bumping of boats that are often viciously attacked; (4) biting of hands, legs, or bodies of bathers in shallow waters; and (5) net fishermen bitten when hauling in their catch.

A long and critical study of shark stories has been made by F. A. Lucas of the American Museum of Natural History. Dr. Lucas states that there are many well-authenticated records of fatal attacks in tropical seas, but he adds that the dangers of being seriously molested in temperate waters are very small.

The man-eater is of little economic importance at present. Its fins are very rich in gelatin, and in China they are used in making gelatinous soups that delight the souls of Chinese epicures.

The natives of many Pacific Islands eat man-eater flesh, generally considered the best tasting of the shark family. On some tropical islands, the man-eater shark's liver is looked upon as a luxury. The large liver is hung on wooden boards in the sun until all the oil has drained away, then the dried liver is carefully wrapped up in leaves and preserved.

Anglers have captured the man-eater around the globe on rod and reel. A large specimen 12 feet long, which weighed 998 pounds, was reeled in off Brielle, New Jersey, in June 1935. The present world record taken on fishing tackle, according to the International Game Fish Association, is a 2664-pound monster 16 feet 10 inches long, caught April 21, 1959, by Alfred Dean at Ceduna, Australia. This fish is believed to be the largest ever taken by rod and reel.

The Terrible Candirú and Piranha

Among the most unusual fishes that dwell in the waters of our planet are a group of small, slender South American catfishes known collectively as candirú. They are unique in being the *only* vertebrate parasite of man—and a nasty one at that. These slender, almost trans-

Candirú / Piranha

parent catfishes with patches of hooks on the back of their heads and with suctorial mouths possessing rasping teeth have been held in great fear by the natives along the banks of South American rivers for centuries. They have the incredible habit of penetrating the penis of male and the vulva of female bathers . . . especially when these are passing urine in the water.

Perhaps the smallest species of fish dangerous to man, this catfish was called *canero*, or *carnero*, by the Spaniards of Peru. *Carnero* means "flesh eater," and this small catfish is uniquely suited to scrape the skin like a rasp, suck blood, and hold other fish with its barbs and spines.

One of the earliest recorded descriptions of this dangerous fish was given in 1829 by C. F. P. Von Martius in his preface to J. B. Spix and Louis Agassiz' volume on selected genera and species of Brazilian fishes. He states:

> The Brazilians call this fish *Candirú*, the Spaniards living in the province of Maynas (Peru) name it *Canero*. By a singular instinct it is incited to enter the excretory openings of the human body when it can get at these parts in those who are bathing in the river. With great violence it forces its way in and desiring to eat the flesh it unfortunately brings danger to human life. These little fishes are strongly attracted by the odor of urine and consequently the dwellers in these parts, when about to go into the river Amazon, in whose bays this pest abounds, constrict the prepuce with a string and refrain from urinating.

In 1836 E. Poeppig, writing about a Peruvian plant called Xagua that was used to ward off insects, goes on to say:

> The fresh juice of the Xagua is rightfully claimed to be the surest means of killing and getting rid of these two-inch long little fishes which slip into the outer openings of the bodies of careless (unprotected) bathers and bring about the most dreadful accidents. . . . In Maynas as *Canero* and on the Solimoes (Amazon) as *Candirú*, it is known and feared. The attack of such a fish is such an extraordinary thing that one can scarcely believe it. . . . I myself have been an eyewitness of such a case. An Indian woman, after the penetration by a *Canero* into the vagina, suffered such frightful pain and loss of blood that she was given up to die. However, after both internal and external applications of Xagua, the little fish was gotten out and the woman came through alive.

In 1855 Castelnau described another amazing characteristic of specimens only 9 centimeters, or 3.6 inches, long. His account states:

> This species is, on the part of the fishermen of the Araguay, the object of a most singular prejudice. They claim that it is very dangerous to urinate in the river, because, they allege, this little animal launches itself out of the water and penetrates the urethra by ascending the length of the liquid column.

Steiner, the ethnologist who traveled throughout the region of the lower Amazon and its tributaries, encountered candirú and writes about it in 1884 about the region of 12 degrees south latitude:

We were cautious when bathing. Candirús had been found here. One of them was two centimeters long, a transparent little fish with a yellow iris. They like to push into any available body opening. If, as is said to occur often, they slip into the urethra, the situation is very critical because of the hooks around the head that bury themselves in the mucus membrane. If a hot bath does not bring the disturber out, then the only thing left is an operation. The Sertanejo at that time are said not to have known how to perform urethrotomy, and in many cases death resulted from their heroic treatment.

Interest in this unusual catfish became very great among biologists. In 1897, at a meeting of the Zoological Society of London, G. A. Boulenger, curator of fishes at the British museum, exhibited specimens of the South American catfish known scientifically as *Vandellia cirrhosa*, collected by J. Bach in a tributary of the Amazon. Dr. Bach, a South American physician, transmitted information about the fishes, which Dr. Boulenger summarized as follows:

> The "Candyru," as the fish is called, is much dreaded by the natives of the Jurua district, who, in order to protect themselves, rarely enter the river without covering their genitalia by means of a sheath formed of a small cocoanut-shell, with a minute perforation to let out urine, maintained in a sort of bay of palm-fibres suspended from a belt of the same material. The fish is attracted by the urine, and when once it has made its way into the urethra, cannot be pulled out again owing to the spines which arm its opercles. The only means of preventing it from reaching the bladder, where it causes inflammation and ultimately death, is to instantly amputate the penis; and at Tres Unidos, Dr. Bach had actually examined a man and three boys with amputated penes as result of this dreadful accident.

Another firsthand account of the candirú was given in 1922 by Paul Le Cointe, an authority on the Amazon Valley and director of the Museo Commercial de Para. He described the candirú as very small and uniquely occupied in doing evil. He reported that it grows no longer than 5–8 centimeters (2.–3.2 inches). It often becomes entangled in the meshes of the net and makes bad wounds by means of the spurs on the angles of its gill covers.

Dr. Ammerman, a U.S. naval surgeon stationed in 1910–11 on the Madeira River in South America, said he had operated to remove candirús two or three times. In one instance he tried to pull a fish out of the patient's penis, but the tail pulled off and he had to operate, making a suprapubic opening into the bladder to remove the fish, which had penetrated into that organ.

The South American physician Alfredo da Matta of Manaos reported two cases of accidents due to candirús. The first concerned a girl who, while menstruating, went naked to bathe herself in the Cambixe, Rio Solimoes. Girls were in the habit of staying quietly in rather shallow water, only their heads out of the water, and thus bathing themselves. The candirú introduced itself partway into the vagina, causing a hemorrhage when it was pulled out, and a subsequent severe inflammation. The girl had to stay in bed some days. The other case the doctor recorded was of a candirú that swam into the urinary canal of a naked fisherman who was working in the water in the Rio Solimoes at Boa Vista. The fish was pulled out of the penis with considerable pain.

Not only does the candirú penetrate genital apertures but it also has a voracious appetite for blood and flesh. J. Pelligren in 1911 described the grotesque habits of this fish as follows:

> Some of the species of the *Pygidiidae* called "Candirú" attach themselves to any kind of fish or animal including man. By means of suction, for which their mouths are adapted, they fasten themselves on their victim and then painlessly cut the skin, and gorge themselves on its blood. The fishes brought into the market at Manaos often show many wounds inflicted by the Candirús. Below the first fall in the Madeira River it is difficult to take a catfish which has not been bitten several times by the Candirús.

W. R. Allen of Indiana University made expeditions to South America in the 1920s and wrote that he had seen a candirú attacking another fish. It had its head and forward part of the trunk inserted through a perforation of the body wall into the body cavity. One man pointed to a scar on his abdomen that he told Allen was due to an attack by a *canero*.

The fact that candirús will attack bathers and waders leads to some confusion of its habits with that of the most dangerous of fishes, the piranha, as both species are sometimes found in the same rivers. Edward Bancroft gives a vivid account of the dangerous characin South American fishes, which he calls *peri*, and of which there are actually four different species that vary in color.

> It is extremely voracious and bites everything which hangs in the water. The feet of ducks swimming in creeks are frequently amputated; as have been the breasts of women and the privates of men swimming in the rivers; for this reason the White Inhabitants never bathe themselves in the upper part of these rivers without tying a napkin or handkerchief about the waist.

A. Hamilton Rice of New York City, an Amazonian explorer of long experience and wide knowledge, stated in 1930:

> I have seen most deplorable results of mutilations by the piranha, and my own men have from time to time suffered from attacks of these fish. . . . The piranha is a voracious bloodthirsty fish of a foot to 20 inches in length, not unlike a tautog (blackfish) in conformation, and with jaws similar to a circular saw in power and sharpness. . . . In May 1920 at the Portuguese Beneficente Hospital in Manaos, I saw a boy of ten or eleven years of age whose entire penis had been snipped off. He had been bathing in a river at a spot where the water reached only to his knees. A piranha jumped suddenly, seized his penis, amputating it at the base.

Many accounts tell of horses and cattle fording streams being literally eaten alive by piranhas. Oddly enough, there are just as many accounts of neither beast nor man being attacked while in the midst of a whole school of piranhas. Nonetheless, it would be very foolish to try to predict this potential killer's behavior and to venture into waters where they are known to occur.

There is no question that these two groups of South American river fishes—the candirú (or *Vandellia*) and the piranha (or *Serrasalmus*)—are among the most dangerous of finned creatures.

The Shark That Looks Like a Bulldozer

Some sharks literally use their heads. The family Sphyrnidae is composed of species that have flattened and expanded heads. In pursuing prey they frequently use their grotesque fronts like a rudder, to make sharp turns in catching elusive prey.

Hammerhead, shovelhead, shovelnose, and bonnethead are descriptive names given to members of this family by commercial fishermen. In New England waters two species, the smooth hammerhead *(Sphyrna zygaena)* and the Atlantic bonnethead *(Sphyrna tiburo)* are sometimes captured in fishing nets. They immediately create a weird impression on whoever encounters them because the widely separated cowlike eyes bulge out on either end of the broad head.

Hammerheads are cosmopolitan, being found in the warm regions of all the oceans and the Mediterranean Sea. In the Western Hemisphere they have been recorded from southern Brazil to Nova Scotia.

Swimming with their dorsal and caudal fins protruding above the water searching out prey on the surface or in the depths, these sharks have a highly developed sense of smell with elongated nostrils running out along the edge of the "bonnet." Some ichthyologists feel that these sharks can "triangulate" by smell and can pinpoint potential prey in that fashion.

Another feature is their strange dietary habits. They seem to prefer feeding on smaller sharks, including their own species, and attack even stingrays armed with poisonous spines, if only to prove to the world that they are the most dangerous. Gudger has reported taking an almost perfect skeleton of the stingray *Dasyatis sayi* from the stomach of a hammerhead. He found over fifty stingray spines imbedded in various parts of this shark, which was harpooned while it was chasing a stingray.

Numerous observers have watched hammerheads chasing huge stingrays in shallow water. The ray is driven round and round in a circular path as the shark bites out large chunks of the ray's "wings."

These sharks should be handled with extreme caution by fishermen and avoided at all costs by swimmers and skin divers—considerable evidence bears out that they are man-eaters. In 1805, an 11-foot hammerhead was netted at Riverhead, Long Island, that contained parts of a man in its stomach. On September 21, 1913, a large hammerhead *(Sphyrna tudes)* about 8 feet long viciously attacked a bather at Palm Beach, Florida, resulting in lacerations that required over two hundred stitches. Attacks on bathers have also been reported off the beaches of British Guiana and Australia.

Hammerheads are grayish brown, shading to white on the undersurface. They reach a maximum length of 18 feet, but being slender, generally weigh less than other sharks the same size. On March 21, 1919, a 17-foot great hammerhead weighing about 1500 pounds was harpooned off Miami, Florida.

They are viviparous, giving birth to live young. There is a record of an 11-foot hammerhead containing 37 well-developed embryos!

In some areas hammerheads are hunted for their skin, which is very thin and makes a durable and handsome leather. The flesh has a fine grain and is considered to be a fine dish by the Japanese.

The Blowfish and the Poisonous Tetraodon

"Look here, the fish I just caught is growing bigger and blowing itself up like a balloon!"

The little boy at the end of the dock was proudly displaying the white-bellied, orange-brown fish he had just caught that was gulping in air and growing larger till it looked as though it was going to burst.

The boy has caught a common puffer, *Sphoeroides maculatus*, known also as globefish, blowfish, swell-belly, and balloonfish, which is found along our Atlantic coast from Florida to the Bay of Fundy. They are very common off the New England coast in the summer months, frequenting the bays, mouths of rivers, and sandy beaches. Commercial fishermen find them plentiful in pound nets, haul seines, and traps.

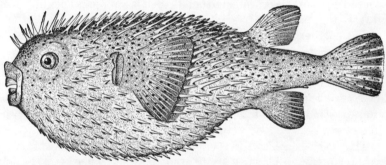

Persons wading or swimming on sandy beaches frequently step on a puffer without realizing it. The puffers push themselves along the beach bottom half covered with sand; they are looking for small clams, worms, and crabs, which constitute the bulk of their diet. Against the sand background the puffer is very difficult to discern because of its protective coloration. The puffer quickly changes color to match the hue of sand, pebbles, seaweed, or whatever element surrounds it.

The most fascinating characteristic of the puffer is its unique method of defense. When in danger of attack from a larger fish, or disturbed by being tickled on the stomach, it draws water or air into its belly and expands as much as three times its normal size. The air or water is held in the fish's belly by a special valve in its throat. When the puffer feels that the danger has passed, it opens the valve and expels the air or water. There have been several eyewitness accounts of puffers being picked up by seagulls or ospreys, after which the fish would inflate itself and slip out of the bird's grasp.

The blowfish has a very small mouth at the tip of its snout and is toothless. What appear to be teeth are really the upper and lower edges of its jaws, which possess sharp cutting edges.

In feeding on small crabs the puffer takes particular care, according to J. T. Nichols and C. M. Breder, to first bite the front part of the crab so as to sever the frontal nerve ganglion, which paralyzes the crab. It then becomes an easy matter for the puffer to tear the crab apart. The claws of the crab are flexed so as to protect this vulnerable spot, and the attacking puffer usually receives many nips around the mouth before it can put the crab out of commission. If a large blue crab is to be attacked, usually a half dozen or so swellfishes gather around it, each taking repeated nips at its less protected points till it is crippled. Then all join in and feast together on the remains.

The northern puffer on our Atlantic coast usually spawns between June and August with the female laying about 176,000 eggs. The female is always larger than the male of the same age. W. W. Welch and C. M. Breder wrote that among mature puffers, those over 8½ inches long are almost surely females while those under 7 inches are nearly all males. Puffers are said to grow to a length of 14 inches but usually average from 6 to 10 inches.

The flesh of the blowfish is very tasty and free from bones. Considerable quantities of blowfish are filleted and sent to market to be sold under the names of sea squab and chicken of the sea. In cleaning the fish, the fish seller takes great care to separate the two small fillets of meat that run along the fish's backbone from the puffer's liver, air bladder, and gonads, as these organs may contain the poison tetrodotoxin. There is no known antidote for this type of poison. In Palm Beach, Florida, a few years ago, an elderly man died soon after eating a supper of blowfish livers.

The northern puffer belongs to the family Tetraodontidae of which there are about sixty different species scattered all over the world. One relative of our blowfish, *Tetraodon hispidus*, which is found along the shores of the South Pacific and Japan, is considered by many ichthyologists as the most poisonous fish. Persons who eat the flesh of this species of *Tetraodon* usually die within five hours. The gall of this fish was used by natives of some South Pacific isles to make poisonous spears and arrows. Strange at it may seem, one species of puffer may be edible in one locality and poisonous in another. This odd phenomenon is

A pen of blowfish on a fishing boat

believed to be caused by the puffers' feeding on poisonous planktonic dinoflagellates in certain areas, and also to the development of ovaries during the females' egg-laying time. No one seems to know for certain. It is easy to see how people can make fatal mistakes in identifying and cleaning these fish properly. There is even a special school that trains chefs how to prepare *fugu*, or Pacific puffer, considered a delicacy, so as to assure a savory and nondeadly meal. Despite these precautions, over two dozen deaths occur each year in Japan because of unfortunate mistakes.

4

The Great Migrators

Migrant movements of fishes are linked to celestial bodies. The moon and the sun, with their regular tidal pull on the waters of our planet, govern feeding movements of most coastal fish species. Seasonal changes in the degree of sunlight alter water temperatures below limits tolerable for some fishes, which then move on to warmer seas. And continual shifting of ocean currents bring fishes into new realms of the sea.

The search for food usually compels movement. Finally, reproductive urges governed by instinct of countless generations send eels, grunion, salmon, shad, tuna, and others to their distant ancestral spawning grounds.

Eels and Their Elvers

The ancients regarded the eel not only as a sacred fish but also as an epicurean delight. Herodotus wrote that it was held as a god by the Egyptians, being sacred to the Nile. Other Greek classicists proclaimed the eel "the king of fish," "a very goddess," and "chief of the fifty Virgins of Lake Copais."

Oppian, a second-century Greek poet, relates the following method of capturing eels:

> The eeler from a high bank of the river Eretaenus, where the eels are the largest and by far the fattest of all eels, lets down at a turn of the stream some cubits length of the intestines of a sheep. An eel seizing a bit of it at the nether end, tries to drag the whole away. The fisher places his mouth on the long tubular reed attached to the near end and blows into the sheep's gut. The gut swells and the eel receiving the hair in his mouth swells too and being unable to extricate his teeth from the intestine is hauled out adhering to the inflated gut.

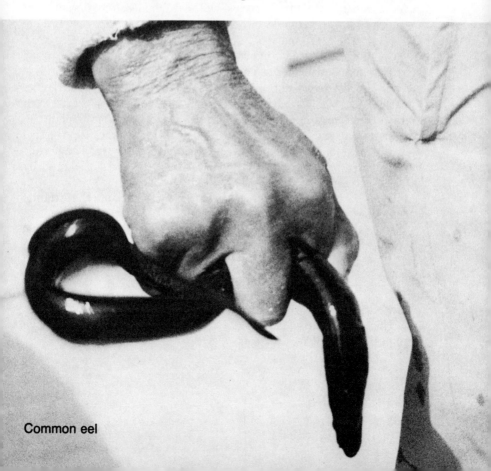

Common eel

In addition to this pneumatic method of Oppian, other old-time methods were employed in the capture of the slippery eel. Stirring up the mud in which eels were known to lurk was a common practice. From this activity came the expression "to fish in muddy waters."

The Romans built large fish ponds in which to raise conger eels, which they relished. According to Pliny, one Hirius gave a party at which six thousand conger eels each measuring over a yard in length were placed before his guests. Crassus was the owner of a large conger eel over which he displayed so much affection that when it died he gave it a stately funeral and wept over its grave. When mocked in the Senate by Eneius Domitius Ahenobarbus for having cried at the death of an eel, Crassus scored heavily by retorting that it was more than "Old Brazen Beard" (Hirius) had done for any of his numerous deceased wives.

Eels form a distinct order of fishes under the classification Apodes, which is from the Greek meaning "without foot" and refers to the absence of ventral fins on the elongated belly of the fish. Eels, which include the conger eels and morays, make up about twenty families and include over three hundred species. Of these families, only the common eels of the family Anguillidae are freshwater forms during most of their lives—the others are marine.

One misbelief held by many people is that the common eel can jar you with an electric shock. This is entirely without foundation. The electric eel, *Electrophorus electricus*, is one of the most powerful electric fishes, but it is not an eel. More closely related to the sucker or carp families, the electric eel looks superficially like an eel and is found in the rivers of Brazil and Guiana. Some scientists believe that it uses the two electric organs in its tail for protection against alligators. The organs are also used to stun prey. Electricity is built up and discharged by masses of specialized cells.

The American eel, *Anguilla rostrata*, occurs all along the Atlantic coast in the brackish waters of rivers where they meet the sea, as well as in freshwater ponds, lakes, old wells, and quarry holes. The commercial eel fishery of the United States extends from Maine to North Carolina and has an annual catch of over a million pounds. Eel fishing on a large scale is generally carried on in or near the mouths of rivers and is sometimes regulated by the individual state's division of fish and game. A few states charge commercial fishermen a small eel-fishing fee.

The eel is captured in a variety of ways—traps, eel pots, seines, on set lines, or by bobbing for eels.

Electric eel

Every common eel ever caught in rivers, bays, and ponds on the Atlantic coast was hatched from a microscopic egg 650 to 1800 feet below the surface of the Sargasso Sea, southwest of Bermuda. The eel's method of reproduction has been a classical biological mystery for many centuries. Aristotle in his *Historia Animalium* mentioned that eels have no milt or roe and seem to come from the entrails of the earth. Pliny stated that eels reproduce by rubbing themselves against rocks and scrapings come to life. Von Helmont attributed the birth of eels to the dews of May mornings. Other authorities deduced eels originated from the hairs of horses or the gills of fishes, while the renowned Izaak Walton insisted upon spontaneous generation.

The procreation of eels remained an unsolved problem until a Danish biologist named Johannes Schmidt unraveled the mystery. Director of the Danish Commission for the Exploration of the Sea, Schmidt sailed in 1906 on the first of many expeditions to locate the spawning grounds of the eel. For over fifteen years he towed nets up and down the Atlantic Ocean from Greenland to Puerto Rico and the English Channel to Chesapeake Bay collecting specimens of leptocephali, which are the transparent, ribbonlike larval stages of eels later known as elvers. (At one time, leptocephali were considered a separate species of fish since no one imagined that they eventually turned into adult eels.) He correlated the sizes of the larval forms with their locations and reasoned that the smallest larvae would be closest to the breeding area. In 1925, after long and intensive research, Schmidt finally worked out that the spawning grounds of American and European eels are found in the Sargasso Sea in latitudes 20 to 30 degrees north and longitudes 60 to 78 degrees west, or about midway between Puerto Rico and Bermuda. He also determined that the spawning beds of the European eel overlapped those of the American eel.

Schmidt did not find the eel's eggs. That discovery is credited to Marie Poland Fish of the Narragansett Marine Laboratory staff, who was a member of the *Arcturus* expedition to the Sargasso Sea in 1926. Marie Fish determined that three fish eggs attached to a crab shell dredged from the bottom were really the first ripe eel eggs known to science. They were later hatched in the ship's laboratory. Eels, it was discovered, are among the most prolific of fish; large females release between 15 and 20 million eggs.

Spawning of the eel begins in late winter or early spring. Mature fat eels from the rivers of North America and Europe set off on their long journey to the Sargasso Sea. On their trip to the spawning grounds they do not feed; in fact, their gut disappears. Other changes also occur. Their eyes grow increasingly bigger until they spread over most of each side of the head. No one has yet determined exactly what the large eyes are for. They cannot be for finding food as eels do not eat on their trip back to their birthplace. It is also a mystery whether the parents live or die after they mate, for they are never seen again.

Newborn eels are entirely transparent, about ¼ inch long, and ribbon shaped. They are called leptocephali until they take on the appearance of miniature adults. The leptocephali drift upward from the depths feeding on microscopic algae, then slowly drift toward the latitude of Bermuda where a separation takes place. The European larvae head eastward across the Atlantic, and the American eels head northeast in the Gulf Stream toward the haunts of their parents. In the brackish river mouths of the East Coast the young eels lose their transparency and turn into elvers, taking on the coloration and proportions of the adult form.

American eels remain in the leptocephalus stage for about a year; their European cousins take three years to transform into elvers because of their longer homeward journey. The American eel averages 107 vertebrae in its backbone, while the European species has 114. This is the major physical difference between the two groups.

The common eel is unique in the fish world by virtue of the fact that it spends most of its life in fresh water and migrates to the sea to lay its eggs. Because of this characteristic, it is called a catadromous species. Catadromous means "down running." Eels tend to grow rather slowly. By tagging them, it has been determined that European eels attain average adult size anywhere from 5 to 20 years of age. H. M. Smith found a female eel in the Potomac River that was in its twelfth year.

When kept in captivity, eels are known to have great longevity. The celebrated Eel of Ross was caught as an elver in a small Scottish river in 1895 and kept in an aquarium until it died in 1949, having lived a total of 57 years.

The eel is chiefly a scavenger, feeding voraciously on small fishes, insects, crayfishes, and aquatic plants. In addition, eels destroy quantities of marketable fish. D. S. Jordan in 1903 stated that the destruction of shad and herring by eels in the Susquehanna and other Atlantic rivers was enormous. He mentions that, not infrequently, when a gill net would be lifted out, the catch consisted largely of heads and backbones; the greater part of the catch had been devoured by myriads of eels in the short time the net was left in.

Eels also consider the spawning shad a special delicacy. Many female shad are found empty at the vent and completely gutted of their ripe ovaries. Sometimes a shad apparently full of roe is found to contain several eels of considerable size. In turn, many game fish such as the striped bass and the bluefish prey voraciously on these snakelike fish.

The common eel generally averages between 2 and 3 feet. Unusually large specimens have been recorded up to 4 feet in length with a

weight of 16½ pounds. As a rule, all eels in the headwaters of large
streams are females; males remain in the mouths of rivers. Male common eels never grow larger than 2 feet.

During the winter months eels tend to hibernate in the muddy
bottom of inlets. Frequently, eels are speared with gigs through holes
chopped in the ice. Commercial eel fishermen generally trap their catch
in pots set out in river mouths and salt ponds. One man can operate as
many as 300 pots, but the average is usually about 150 per man. The best
bait for the trap includes horseshoe crabs, chopped squid, herring, and
alewives. The caught eels are usually kept alive in a car-tank placed at
the end of a dock until they are shipped to market. During the Christmas holidays live eels bring a price quite out of proportion to their actual
value during the rest of the year because of the custom of persons of
Southern European extraction to eat eels at Christmas.

Except in the yuletide season, the eel is a rare item on American
menus. Farmers and city dwellers alike associate the eel with the snake
and tend to shy away from it. Orthodox Jews avoid it because it appears
to fit under the precept stated in Deuteronomy that "all that have fins
and scales shall ye eat: and whatsoever hath not fins and scales ye may
not eat." Although common eels appear slimy and smooth, they do have
minute scales embedded in their skin.

Because of the widespread distribution of eels around the globe,
countless recipes have been devised for cooking them. They should be
prepared for cooking when freshly caught or when bought alive from the
fish dealer. There are two principal methods of skinning eel; one starts
from the head, the other from the tail. In the first method you make a
shallow incision around the head, and grasping the head with a cloth or
gloved hand, you pull the skin off with pliers in a rapid outward motion.
With the second method, you nail the tail to a board, and after making a
shallow cut around it near the end, you pull the skin out over the head,
somewhat like taking off a stocking. When preparing eel, you must be
careful if you have any open wounds on your hands. This fish's blood can
be a powerful nerve poison if it enters the bloodstream.

Many recipes call for cooking eels in red or white wine, and some
state that it is better to boil eels in beer than in water. The tastiest eels
are the so-called silver eels, which are actually the familiar yellow-
bellied eels that have reached sexual maturity.

Among the famous continental delicacies are smoked eels. The
finest of these come from Holland and Germany. During England's

Victorian era one observer wrote of London: "From one end to the other the city teems and steams with eels." Not having hot dogs at that time, the people ate hot eels. "Everywhere smoking away, with many a fragrant condiment at hand to make what is in itself palatable more savoury; and this too at so low a rate that for one half-penny a man may fill his stomack with six or seven long pieces."

Eels are delectable fried, stewed, smoked, or pickled. Any good seafood cookbook will provide suitable recipes. Fried eels served with a seasoned sauce are an especially tasty dish.

The Long Journey of the Bluefin Tuna

In ancient Rome, the capture of the first tuna of the season precipitated the festival of Thunnaeum, which was a joyous pageant during which the fish was sacrificed to Neptune, the god of the sea.

Today, as their forebears have been doing for centuries, fishermen along the shores of the Mediterranean capture the giant bluefin tuna *(Thunnus thynnus)* in massive traps as they pass by on their annual migrations. Along the coasts of Portugal, Sicily, Sardinia, and several areas off North Africa, there are locations where one can find huge trap nets where the giant tuna are captured for canning.

One trap off Paro, Portugal, has been described in detail by Alan Villiers, marine historian. This trap, owned by Manuel Francisco La, was several miles offshore in the unprotected sea. Set out in May for the spring migration of thousands of tuna, the trap is L shaped with each of its arms some 9000 feet long. The nets are supported by corks, and the netting is kept in place by a series of moorings that include over 600 anchors. The arms of the trap lead to a heavily netted corral about 1200 feet long and 50 feet wide. Tuna travel in large schools that may number from 60 to 200 members; frequently, a whole school will be ensnared in the corral.

When all the tuna are imprisoned in the corral a signal is given; the floor of the heavy netting is raised, and the surrounding boats close in. The giant tuna massed together in the enclosed space are clubbed and speared by the fishermen.

As soon as the slaughter is over, the 200- to 800-pound fish are dragged into the boats and taken ashore. They are then hung up in sheds

A 673-pound tuna taken off the Rhode Island coast

to allow the blood and some of the oil to drain out of their bodies. After hanging and draining for several hours, the flesh is cut up and soaked in brine or packed in boxes to be cooked and canned.

In North American waters the same species of giant bluefin tuna is found at various times of the year along the Atlantic from the northern Bahamas to Newfoundland. The bluefins that head up from locations south of Bimini pass this island, usually in large schools, during May and June on their northern migration. They appear off New Jersey in June and July, off Rhode Island in July and August, and from Massachusetts northward to Nova Scotia from July to October. On the other side of the

Atlantic the bluefins range from the Mediterranean to Norway. Some ichthyologists believe there are physical differences between the populations on opposite sides of the Atlantic. (Along the Pacific, bluefins occur from Guadalupe Island to Oregon, but are seldom taken north of Point Conception—the West Coast giant tuna is somewhat different again.)

In Massachusetts waters off Ipswich Bay and Cape Cod, anglers usually get good catches of tuna or horse mackerel. Maine boasts excellent tuna fishing off Bailey Island. But the world's finest tuna fishing area is off Wedgeport, Nova Scotia.

The waters off Wedgeport are full of rips and eddies where tuna find abundant food from the first week of July till the middle of October. The first sportsman to test the quality of Nova Scotia tuna was Thomas Pattilo, a schoolmaster, who tackled them from a dory in Liverpool harbor about 1871. He took 32 fathoms of ordinary cod line, wound it on a swivel reel, fashioned a steel hook ⅜ inch thick and 8 inches long with a 3-inch shank, and set out with a single companion in a fisherman's dory. He soon hooked a monster tuna that towed his boat across the harbor and hurtled it merrily into a fleet of herring netters, swamping one and creating havoc among the rest. One of the irate herring fishermen cut the line, and thus Pattilo's first tuna got away. His second attempt was rewarded with success, for he brought to gaff a mighty tuna that weighed 600 pounds.

A giant bluefin tuna was taken on rod and eel off Wedgeport, Nova Scotia, in 1950 by Commander Duncan M. Hodgson while he was fishing in an open 16-foot dory pulled by the veteran guide Percy MacRitchie. This record bluefin towed the small craft approximately 12 miles in 80 minutes. The fish was beached, and when weighed 9 hours later, after considerable loss of blood, weighed 977 pounds. A 1120-pound bluefin was hooked by Lee Coffin in Canadian waters in 1973.

Reliable sources, however, have reported tuna of 1600 pounds. Even today, commercial fishermen frequently harpoon 1000-pound tuna. On August 15, 1956, Captain Mark Connally harpooned an 1100-pound tuna a short distance southwest of Block Island, Rhode Island. The largest Rhode Island tuna on record was one taken in 1913 that weighed 1225 pounds but, again, not on sporting tackle. There also is the record of one giant bluefin taken off Narragansett Pier, Rhode Island, in the 1890s that weighed about 1500 pounds. This fish was divided among the various hotels at the pier, and fed to more than a thousand people.

Sometimes termed the torpedoes of the fish world because of their streamlined bodies, tuna unquestionably rank high among the speed fishes. They have been reported traveling alongside a ship logging eight knots without any apparent exertion. Their bullet-shaped heads and oblong bodies cut through the water with a minimum of drag. Dorsal and pelvic fins fit into grooves as the fish propel themselves forward by their powerful crescent tail. A tough, mucus-covered skin with minute scales slides easily through water.

Being pelagic fish, ranging from coast to coast in dense shoals, tuna are constantly chasing the smaller migratory fishes such as herring, mackerel, and dogfish. A favorite article of the tuna's diet is the acrobatic flying fish. When chasing one, the tuna will frequently estimate the winged fish's trajectory and capture it as it reenters the sea.

The tuna's fondness for flying fishes led to the development of a unique way of angling—the tuna-plane or kite-fishing technique. This method of fishing was devised by Captain George Farnsworth off Avalon, California, in 1912. A kite, with a baited flying fish suspended from it, is flown from the stern of the boat. The action of kite and wind is supposed to give the suspended bait the realistic actions of a flying fish, if conditions are right. Tuna weighing up to 200 pounds have been taken by this method.

At present, the most universally used method of angling for giant tuna is chumming for them. Menhaden, herring, and mackerel are ground up into an oily brew and slowly spilled over the transom of a boat into the sea, luring the big tuna up to the boat's stern. When giant bluefins are hooked, they will take terrific runs trying to free themselves. Frequently they'll tow a boat for miles—or snap the angler's rod and line with their tremendous power.

Tuna occasionally become troublesome to commercial fishermen by ripping holes in the netting of traps to get at the mackerel and herring they contain. Captain N. E. Atwood gives an interesting account of tuna off the Cape Cod area in the latter part of the nineteenth century.

> They [tuna] don't come till the weather gets warm. We don't see them at first when we begin setting mackerel nets, but about June they are liable to appear, and we find holes in the nets. My brother had forty-seven holes through one eighty-yard net in one night. When they strike a net, they go through it, and when they go through it the hole immediately becomes round. It looks as if you could put a half-bushel basket through it. . . . The tuna remain through the summer and early autumn, when they are killed for oil. When they are here, they feed on any small fish, and when menhaden were here I have seen them drive the harbor full of them. I

have seen the horse mackerel swallow a whole dogfish weighing eight pounds. There was a great deal of whiting here at that time. They have almost totally disappeared. The horse mackerel seems to be the enemy of all kinds of fish. There is nothing to trouble the horse mackerel until the killer (whale) comes, and then they know it, I tell you. Then the horse mackerel will run! Some fishermen say they have seen a killer poke his head out of the water with a horse mackerel in his mouth. I have known a horse mackerel to yield twenty-three gallons of oil. The average size is about eight feet in length.

Sprightly Striper—The Coastal Bass

The striped bass is found on the Atlantic coast northward to the St. Lawrence River and southward to the Escambia River in western Florida. It also occurs in the Gulf of Mexico from western Florida to Louisiana.

In the 1870s, S. R. Trockmorton, who was chairman of the California Fish Commission, came up with the idea that Atlantic striped bass might be transplanted to the waters around San Francisco Bay, where conditions seemed ideal for spawning. During 1879, 107 stripers were shipped from the Navesink River area of New Jersey and released in the Carquinez Straits near San Francisco. The length of the fishes in this first shipment ranged from 1½ to 3 inches. Three years later, 300 bass from 5 to 9 inches in length were shipped from the Shrewsbury River area in the East and released in Suisun Bay, California. Ten years after their introduction to California, stripers were taken in nets for the commercial market on the West Coast.

Twenty years after the transplanting, the West Coast commercial catch had risen to over a million pounds per year. Sport fishermen were alarmed by the increasing size of the commercial catch, and in 1935 the Cronin-Fisher-Andreas Act was passed. This act prohibited all commercial fishing for stripers in California waters, despite the findings of biologists that the striped bass population could support both a commercial and sport fishery. The striper is now found along the Pacific coast from San Diego County in southern California to Oregon, the Columbia River, and Vancouver in the north. There have even been reports of striped bass reaching Alaskan waters.

Because of its wide range, the striper is known in different locales by a variety of names, including greenhead and squid hound. South of New Jersey it is commonly called rockfish or rock.

Today striped bass are caught commercially on the Middle Atlantic coast by three principal methods. The first of these is the pound net, which consists of a leader, heart, and pocket. The fish travel along the leader to the heart and ultimately reach the pocket. When the net is emptied, the fish are removed from the pocket by a scoop net.

Fish are also captured, or "gilled," by having their heads stuck in the meshes of the twine of a gill net. Three common types of gill nets are known as drift, anchor, and stake nets, depending on the way they are set up in the water.

The most widespread commercial method used in capturing striped bass is the haul seine. During the last century seines were used in New England and the Middle Atlantic region. Today most beach seines range

in length from 600 to 1800 feet with widths of 9 to 11 feet. The mesh size is usually 3 or 4 inches. From 400 to 500 haul seines are operated yearly in the Chesapeake Bay region.

The striper is migratory. Along our Atlantic coast a great many striped bass move northward and eastward into New England waters in late winter and early spring from Chesapeake Bay, New Jersey, and New York. During the summer months this migrating group remains rather stable in New England waters until about mid-September when they begin their southward trek back to the Chesapeake. In certain rivers and inlets from Maine to Long Island small local groups of stripers overwinter. This is known to occur in the Parker, Thames, and Niantic rivers.

The Atlantic striped bass is most abundant from Cape Cod to northern North Carolina. The center of this abundance is the Chesapeake Bay region, the most important area for the production of striped bass along the entire Atlantic coast.

An anadromous fish (i.e., spending most of the time in the sea but spawning up the coastal rivers and streams), the striper is coastal in habitat and seldom goes more than 3 miles offshore. However, there have been authenticated records of stripers taken in waters as deep as 70 fathoms 60 miles south of Martha's Vineyard, Massachusetts.

The striper spawns in the fresh water of rivers between April and July, depending upon the location. The immature bass stay in the rivers and coves until they are nearly 2 years old.

Most female bass are able to spawn when they are 4 or 5 years old but do not spawn every year. A 3-pound female will produce about 14,000 eggs, while a 50-pounder will release about 5 million. All male stripers are mature at 3 years of age, most at 2. Observations of spawning in the Roanoke River showed that large ripe females, from 5 to 50 pounds, were surrounded by 20 to 50 small males weighing no more than 2 pounds each. The eggs are spherical and green in color. If the proper food is not available for them, the larvae die when they reach a length of 6 millimeters. The eggs usually hatch 2 or 3 days after fertilization. Young stripers reach a length of 1½ inches when they are about a month old.

Striped bass feed on a wide variety of smaller fish and invertebrates including menhaden, alewife, anchovy, herring, eel, shad, mullet, launce hake, white perch, shrimp, clam, sand worm, lobster, crab, mussel, and squid. E. H. Hollis, after examining the stomachs of 1736 stripers taken from Chesapeake Bay, found that anchovies and menhaden were the most common foods in the summer, and spot and croaker were important in the winter months.

Stripers are long-lived. According to Daniel Merriman (1941), striped bass 40 inches long average about 25 pounds and are 11 or 12 years old; those 50 inches in length weigh about 50 pounds and are roughly between 20 and 25 years old. A specimen 54 inches weighed 65 pounds and was about 30 years old.

H. M. Smith reported that several striped bass weighing 125 pounds apiece were taken in a seine near Edenton, North Carolina, in 1891. G. B. Goode reported a striper captured at Orleans, Massachusetts, that weighed 112 pounds and one from Cuttyhunk that weighed 104 pounds. The present record for rod-and-reel fishermen is the 73-pound specimen taken by C. B. Church in August 1913 in Vineyard Sound. The largest striper taken by a skin diver with a spear is believed to be a 48-pounder captured by Kenneth Parrilla off Watch Hill, Rhode Island, in June 1957.

The striper played an important part in the early economy of the New England colonies. Just nineteen years after the pilgrims landed at Plymouth Plantation, the Massachusetts settlers, realizing the value of the striper, sought to conserve the supply. In 1639 a general court order of the Massachusetts Bay Colony prohibited the use of cod or bass as fertilizer.

Few people are aware that the first public schools in the New World were made possible, at least in part, by the sale of stripers. Plymouth Colony in 1670 granted that all income accumulating from the striped bass, mackerel, and herring fisheries at Cape Cod go to the establishment of schools.

Stripers were plentiful in the seventeenth century. Captain John Smith of Virginia, who in 1614 voyaged to New England and mapped the coast from Penobscot, Maine, to Cape Cod, wrote the following in his *New England's Trials:*

> The Basse is an excellent Fish, both fresh & salte, one hundred whereof salted (at market) have yielded 5 pounds. They are so large, the head of one will give a good eater a dinner, & for daintinesse of diet they excell the Marybones (marrow bones) of Beefe. There are such multitudes that I have seene stopped in the river close adjoining to my house with a sande at one tide so many as will loade a ship of 100 tonnes. I myselfe, at the turning of the tyde have seene such multitudes passe out of a pounde that it seemed to me that one mighte go over their backs drishod.

William Wood's *New England Prospect,* written in 1634, describes the striper as follows:

> The basse is one of the best fishes in the Country, and though men are

soon wearied with other fish, yet are they never with basse. It is a delicate, fine, fat, fast fish, having a bone in his head which contains a saucerful of marrow sweet and good, pleasant to the pallat and wholesome to the stomach. . . . Of these fishes some may be three and four foote long, some bigger, some lesser; at some tides a man may catch a dozen or twenty of these in three hours. . . . When they use to tide in and out of the rivers and creeks the English at the top of high water do crosse the creeks with long seanes or bass nets, which stop in the fish; and the water ebbing from them they are left on the dry ground, sometimes two or three thousand at set, which are salted up against winter, or distributed to such as have present occasion either to spend them in their homes or use them for their grounds.

Since colonial times there has been a gradual decline in the numbers of striped bass except in certain years, such as 1934 and 1941–43, when ideal conditions were suitable for the development of large-year classes. Pollution, dam building, and possibly overfishing can be blamed for the continued decline of this valuable natural resource.

The various states today are attempting to preserve their stripers, as California's 1935 law attests. In North Carolina waters it is unlawful when fishing to keep a striped bass under 12 inches long. In all other states except Maryland it is against the law to keep stripers that are less than 16 inches long. Because Maryland and Virginia have large spawning populations of stripers, these states have regulations that prevent the taking of large productive bass. In Maryland stripers over 15 pounds, and in Virginia bass over 25 pounds, have to be put back in the water.

Striped bass make excellent quarry for spearfishermen, and it is a skillful sport to stalk and spear a striper. In California and Connecticut laws have been passed that prohibit the spearing of striped bass. In New Jersey waters it is unlawful for spearfishermen to spear stripers under 18 inches or to take more than 10 specimens per day.

Anglers use a variety of lures and methods for stripers. Surf casters use tin jigs and artificial plugs resembling mullet and eels. Many fishermen use fresh bait such as eels, squid, or crabs. Trollers have elaborate spinner rigs and lures known as "jigit eels," "upperman bucktails," and "atom plugs." The striped bass is one of the chief attractions for tourists along the coasts of Massachusetts, Rhode Island, Long Island, and New Jersey.

Both commercial and sport fishermen on the Atlantic and Pacific coasts of North America hold the striped bass, *Morone saxatilis*, in high esteem. It is an exciting game fish, and its flesh makes a delectable dish when broiled or baked.

5

Weaponry of the Deep

Teeth are not the only weapons among fishes—even among sharks. Here are four highly developed weapons, each as different as nature could devise them. But the most vicious weapon is purely defensive.

Practically every fish in this book has a weapon of some sort; some are beyond our imagination.

Tail Weapon—The Thresher Shark

Among the unusual fishes occasionally appearing off our northeast Atlantic coast is a distinctive shark with a stretched-out tail, *Alopias vulpinus*, the common thresher shark. Widely scattered around the globe, it is also found in European waters, the Mediterranean, and the Pacific, and known by the names of swingletail, whip tail shark, long tail shark, sea ape, sea fox, and fox shark. The latter two names are derived from its scientific name, *Alopias*, the Greek word for "fox," and *vulpinus*, the Latin word for "fox."

There is little difficulty in identifying a thresher shark because of its extremely long scythe-shaped tail, as long as the shark's head and body together. A short, blunt snout and small mouth are provided with rather short, triangular smooth-edged teeth. The thresher generally has a brownish gray color on its back and upper parts of the sides. The color has a sharp line—changing abruptly to white on the bottom side. Though 20 feet or more in length, this shark is relatively lightweight because of its thin, elongated tail.

On September 3, 1956, the Stonington, Connecticut, fishing drag-

ger *Jane Dore* brought up two thresher sharks in one drag of her otter trawl net 4 miles southeast of Watch Hill, Rhode Island. One thresher was 7 feet long and weighed 65 pounds; the other whip tail was 12 feet long, and weighed approximately 450 pounds. Captain T. Silva said this was the first time he had ever dragged up one of this species. Trap fishermen occasionally capture threshers, when they chase schooling fishes to inshore areas. They generally feed on most schooling fishes, including mackerel, herring, and menhaden.

Although a formidable-looking fish, the thresher is relatively harmless to man because of its small mouth and short teeth. I have been unable to find any reference to any attack on swimmers or fishermen, but one has to be careful not to be slapped by this shark's powerful, flapping tail in a boat when he is freshly caught and still alive.

In the water, the tail proves to be a formidable weapon for the rounding up as well as the stunning of prey. The thresher is a speedy swimmer and glides around the perimeter of a fish school, thrashing the water and chasing the helpless fish into a compact mass where they can be easily stunned by the whip tail, and eaten. Sometimes two threshers will pair up and combine their efforts in attacking a school of fish. A Mr. Coles described a thresher that was feeding in North Carolina waters. He said the shark was "throwing the fish to its mouth with its tail and one fish which it failed to seize was thrown for a considerable distance clear of the water." There is also an account of a thresher shark in Irish waters rising and killing a wounded sea bird with a stroke of its tail, and swallowing it.

W. E. Allen gives a graphic description of an attack by a thresher shark on a small fish about 10 inches long in *Science* magazine (1928).

> While taking my plankton collection at about 7:25 A.M. April 14, 1927, I heard a splash nearby. Turning I saw a swirl in the water . . . a moment later a long slender compressed tail (about three feet long) flashed above the surface and lashed about like a coach whip. About 7:45 . . . it was coming diagonally toward the surface and swinging rapidly. Almost immediately I noticed a small fish frantically swimming just in front of it. A moment later the pursuer, a six-foot thresher shark passed partly ahead

of the victim (a fraction of its own length), when it turned quickly and gave the coach whip lash with the tail which I had seen before. The victim was very much confused, if not actually injured by the whip-lash movement which seemed to be very accurately aimed. The whip stroke was instantly repeated with very confusing speed and it became evident that the victim was seriously injured.

Thresher sharks are one of the few fish known to attack schools of bluefish. The breeding habits and life history of threshers are not too well known, and studies are being carried out with observations and tagging experiments.

The thresher has some economic value, as its flesh is tough and moderately good, tasting slightly similar to swordfish. It is occasionally sent to fish markets in our Midwest. In some places in France, the species is sold under the name white tunny. In ancient times, Greek fishermen also used it for food.

Stingray—Assassin of the Sea

Did you ever hear of a fish that stabs, possesses poisonous venom, and is as deadly as a rattlesnake? Most likely one of those tropical species from the South Pacific?

Well, be prepared. These fishes that will not only knife you but poison the wound as well are found from Maine to Florida, in the Gulf of Mexico, and on our Pacific coast. Whip-tailed stingrays are found all over the globe, even though they do have a preference for warm cli-

mate. They range in size from the giant stingarees of Australia, which attain weights of over 750 pounds, to small tropical freshwater species no bigger than a pancake. Common in the summer off the northeastern coast of the United States, the stingray *Dasyatis centroura* can reach a length of 12 feet and measure nearly 7 feet in breadth. On the California coast there is the round stingray, *Urolophus halleri*, whose venom affects the circulatory system.

Commercial fishermen sometimes refer to the stingray as clam-cracker, devilfish, fair maid. North and south, fishermen give a wide berth to the powerful tail and stiletto.

Many painful attacks on bathers and fishermen could have been prevented if the victims had known more about the habits of the at-tacker. Stingrays are usually encountered along sandy beaches and in the shallow waters of bays and estuaries. Unlike other bottom fish, such as the sea robin, puffer, flounder, and croaker, which almost always flee from an approaching bather, the camouflaged stingray lies still and unnoticed on the sandy bottom, partially covered with silt or sand. When an unsuspecting bather steps on its broad back the fish has the leverage it needs to whip its tail into a quick, cruel arc. This lashing is enough to cause a nasty wound, but the ray has an erected spine that stands out from the tail itself. The spine has venom cells near it that contain the poison, and when driven into the victim's foot or leg, ex-cruciating pain begins.

Waders could go unharmed if they would slide their feet along the bottom in the upper layer of sand or silt. By dragging the feet in this way, the toes would strike the side of the resting ray, and the fish would move elsewhere without any fuss. They don't mind being nudged, but they hate to be stepped on.

The stinger of the sharp, knifelike spine with its jagged sawtooth edges may be anywhere from 3 to 15 inches long. When it is worn out, the old stinger is replaced by a new one that grows up behind it. Sometimes two or three stingers are present at the same time.

Frequently people were stung by stingrays without apparent ill effects, so the question of whether these fish had a true poison ap-paratus had long been debated. It is now known that they do—mice and rabbits injected with extracts from the poison cells die within minutes. The reason for some stingrays' harmlessness is due to the fact that the venom gland is often pulled out along with the protective sheath of the spine, leaving an impotent stinger capable only of mechanical injury.

The Roman naturalist Pliny wrote in his classic work, *Natural*

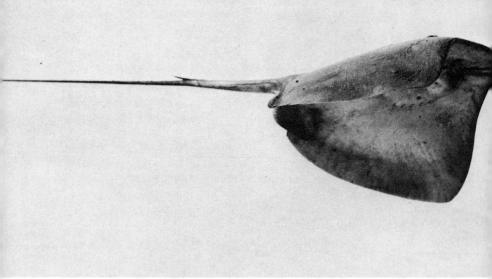

History: "Nothing is more terrible than the sting in the tail of a stingray. . . . Driven into the root of a tree it will kill the tree. It pierces armour like an arrow, and to the force of steel it adds the venom of poison."

The arrowlike tip and backward pointing teeth of the spine penetrate skin and flesh with ease, but removing the barb is another matter—lacerations of the tissue frequently occur when the spine is withdrawn. When the sting penetrates the foot, the venom is released from glandular tissue in a narrow groove on each edge of the stinger. As it goes deeper, the venom is squeezed out of the tissue, down the groove, and into the wound.

Intense pain is the predominant symptom, and it usually begins immediately. The pain has variously been described as sharp, shooting, spasmodic, throbbing, localized, and radiating. The area about the wound has an ashen appearance at first; later it becomes bluish, to be followed by redness and swelling. In some cases the patient develops convulsions and dies. Shock may also be present in the victim, indicated by faintness, nausea, clammy skin, loss of consciousness, a rapid and weak pulse, and difficulty in breathing.

First aid promptly and correctly administered will help to alleviate the severity of an attack. The following are good rules for treating stingray injuries: (1) irrigate the wound with the cold salt water at hand; (2) immerse the foot or leg in hot water for 30 to 60 minutes; (3) apply an antiseptic dressing and consult a physician for further treatment.

From time to time it has been rumored that persons have been stung by stingrays while actually swimming; there is no proven case of this kind. When stingrays swim, they keep within inches of the bottom, which makes it unlikely that a swimmer would come into contact with a ray's stinger.

Another misconception, one commonly held by old-time ichthyologists, is that the stingray strikes and poisons other fishes to get its food. Pliny wrote in his *Natural History*, "the *Pastinaca* [Mediterranean stingray] lies lurking in ambush and pierces the fish as they pass with the sting with which it is armed." The French ichthyologist Rondelet said that "when a ray has stung a fish the spine holds it like a hook." Both these statements are unfounded; as a bottom dweller, the ray feeds almost entirely on small animals living in the sandy bottom, such as clams, crabs, worms, and sea snails.

It is quite evident that the stingray uses its armed tail only as a defensive weapon. Hammerhead sharks, the stingrays' chief adversaries, have been found with numerous stingray spines impaled in the head, jaw, and stomach. When a shark attacks a stingray, it bites off pieces of the ray, gradually swallowing the whole ray—sometimes including the tail.

The stingray is usually a dark mottled brown on its back and white on its belly side. All species of stingray are ovoviviparous, which means that their eggs are hatched within the body of the mother.

Since their flesh is generally rank and unpalatable, none of the species is of any value as food. The rough skin of some of these rays is used to make a good-quality shagreen, a kind of untanned leather. Years ago in Ceylon, stingray tails were dried, treated with oil to make them more supple, and used as whips for punishing criminals, a practice now forbidden by law.

The stingray should be feared by all who venture into the sea. It can drive its spine to the bone and cause the worst pain imaginable. I know because I was stung by one! My advice? Watch your step.

The Destructive Sea-Lamprey Eel—Not an Eel

Probably the most bloodthirsty fish found along the Atlantic coast is a circular-mouthed creature that resembles a 2-foot piece of garden hose that was left out in the yard all winter. The scaleless, jawless sea lamprey derives its name from the Latin word *lambere*, which means "to lick." It is also known by the local names of suckerfish, lamfree, stone-sucker, nine-eyes, and lamper.

The sea lamprey is found along the Atlantic coast of North America from the St. Lawrence River to Florida. Recently it has been found in Greenland, and it is known to have been in European waters from ancient times.

In Lakes Huron and Michigan the sea lamprey has become land-locked and does not run down to the ocean. Here they became a serious problem when they almost totally destroyed the lake trout and whitefish commercial fishery by their vicious parasitism. To cite an example, the catch of lake trout in Lake Michigan was 5.5 million pounds in 1946 and fell to 402 pounds in 1953 due to the rampages of the lamprey. U.S. Fish and Wildlife biologists have waged a determined battle to rid the Great Lakes of the lamprey and have made good progress toward this end.

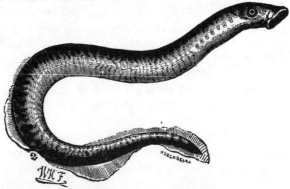

The principal item of food of the lamprey is the blood of other fishes, which it obtains by means of its suckerlike mouth, sharp teeth, and sandpaperlike tongue. The lamprey attaches itself to the belly of its victim by a suction action of its mouth and then rasps through the scales and skin with its horny teeth to extract the blood. The victim will thrash around violently but is unable to shake off the parasite. The lamprey will stay with its prey until its gut is filled or its victim dies. Frequently a small fish is killed while a larger one becomes so badly scarred that it would be unmarketable.

In the Atlantic Ocean lampreys have been found preying upon mackerel, shad, cod, menhaden, haddock, pollock, herring, swordfish, hake, salmon, and eel. As many as three or four lampreys have been found on a single shad at one time. Near the mouth of rivers large amounts of shad and herring are attacked by lampreys. In January 1955 I found lampreys among a net full of sea herring in Block Island Sound off southern New England.

All mature sea lampreys migrate into fresh water to spawn like the shad and salmon. During April, May, and June the lampreys head up into streams to lay their eggs. In New England large lampreys go up many if not all the rivers to spawn. They are found in the spring in the Kennebec, Penobscot, Merrimac, and Connecticut rivers and their tributaries.

During the mid-nineteenth century there was quite a fishery for the lamprey in New England rivers. The records show a catch of 3800 lampreys taken on one spring night in 1840 at Hadley Falls on the Connecticut River. It was then the habit for some families to salt down several barrels of lamprey for winter use. Lampreys were caught at night because they did most of their traveling in the dark. G. B. Goode describes men catching lampreys in the Connecticut River in 1884 with just a gloved hand. He states: "On a dark spring night men might be seen in the river clasping now and then with one hand a squirming lamprey and in the other a birch bark torch, which threw light on the river and all the objects on its borders." Lampreys not used for human consumption in Connecticut and Massachusetts were fed to the hogs. Lampreys were sold in New Jersey fish markets as late as 1868. After they are cleaned, rolled in flour, salted, peppered, and fried in sections they are said to taste quite a bit like bullheads. It was once the custom in Europe to drown the lamprey in wine and then stew it. This was supposed to give a better taste to the fish. However, because of their extreme susceptibility to fungus infection and the softness of their bodies, lampreys are not at present popular in the kitchen.

In ancient times the lamprey was a favorite dish of the Romans, who kept the fish in special ponds at great expense. The best lampreys were brought from Sicily as presents to reigning emperors and high officials. A gruesome story is on record about a friend of Augustus Caesar, named Pollio, who believed that lampreys fed on human flesh had a more delicate flavor and ordered his disobedient slaves thrown

A sea lamprey attached to a whitefish

into the lamprey pond for fish food. The Roman emperor eventually heard of this barbarity and ordered the lamprey ponds filled in.

There is a century-old tradition in England that the reigning monarch is presented with a lamprey pie during his coronation year by the citizens of Gloucester, England. In 1953 a twenty-pound lamprey pie was presented to Queen Elizabeth by the mayor of Gloucester; it had been made from lampreys taken from the Severn estuary. Historians tell us that Henry I was an ardent fancier of lampreys and that he died right after eating an excessive amount of them. Even today, in France and Germany, lampreys cooked in earthenware jars with vinegar and spices are sometimes seen among the hors d'oeuvres and relished at banquet tables.

While en route to spawning sites the lamprey does not prey on other fish. When a suitable place for spawning is reached, the male and female begin to build a nest in which they deposit their spawn and milt. The ideal nesting site of the lamprey requires a bottom of coarse gravel and pebbles with a moderate current. Then the male and the female begin to grasp pebbles and stones, some as big as your fist, with their mouths and move them into crescent-shaped piles. The eggs are released in the gravel by the female and fertilized by the male. As many as 236,000 eggs may be produced by one female. The sea lamprey spawns only once, and both parents die soon after the eggs are deposited.

In 10 to 20 days, depending on the water temperature, the eggs hatch into toothless, eyeless larval forms called *ammocoetes*. They then gradually drift downstream until they reach mud or silt where they burrow into small holes that they make in the soft mud. The larval stage is believed to last from 3 to 4 years. During this time they are not parasitic; they take in mud and filter it for tiny organisms on which they live. When they reach a length of from 4 to 6 inches they begin to resemble adults in form and structure. They then turn down to the ocean to live and grow for one or two years more until they are mature.

The parasitic adult lamprey has no jaws, true backbone, or ribs and is considered one of the most primitive fishes. It is a specialized, degenerate survivor of the first vertebrates, the mudgrubbing jawless fishes that began to appear in the world's oceans some 450 million years ago. Later fishes all developed true grasping jaws.

Today in New England the lamprey fishery is no more than a memory. A few lampreys might be taken occasionally by commercial fishermen and used for home consumption or sent to supply the laboratories of educational institutions. There these fish are studied because of their interesting biological background. Along some rivers and streams where baby lampreys are found, they are taken in considerable numbers and sold as bait for bass and other fish.

U.S. Fish and Wildlife biologists directed by Vernon C. Applegate made excellent progress in their efforts to rid the Great Lakes of the lamprey. They attacked this parasite by building traps, mechanical weirs, and barrier dams to block off its spawning migrations up the streams that flow into the lakes. The fishery biologists have learned from extensive surveys that lampreys inhabit 90 U.S. streams of Lake Superior, 107 streams of Lake Michigan, and 33 streams of Lake Huron.

Although effective, the traps and weirs had many disadvantages. They were expensive to construct and maintenance was quite a job as they blocked up rapidly and had to be cleaned out frequently. During floods they broke down, and the few lampreys that got by the barriers to spawn produced enough progeny to maintain the population.

When the faults of the mechanical barriers showed up, the Fish and Wildlife Service turned to electricity. Single, double, or triple rows of electrodes were suspended from cables into the streams. The electrodes hang a few inches from the bottom, creating electrical fields strong enough to stop lampreys moving upstream to spawn. With regular 110-volt alternating current, the electrical devices are much more economical to construct and maintain than the purely mechanical traps and weirs.

Another successful method of attack has been the development of a chemical substance that kills lamprey larvae. The problem here was to find a compound that would kill lamprey larvae and not harm other fish species. The Fish and Wildlife Service obtained approximately 5000 organic chemical compounds from 65 chemical firms and tested them at their Hammond Bay, Michigan, laboratories. After considerable testing, a group of chemicals called mononitrophenols were found suitable for killing larval lampreys, and by the end of 1960 all streams on Lake Superior were treated with the larvicide TFM (3-trifluoromethyl-4-nitrophenol). From 1962 to 1966 intensive larviciding of lamprey spawning streams on Lake Michigan and Lake Huron was carried out.

Combating the sea lamprey in the Great Lakes has been an expensive proposition. In 1953 Canada spent more than $300,000 fighting the parasite. In May 1955 a joint U.S.–Canada agreement was drawn up for eradicating the lamprey on both sides of the Great Lakes with the two countries investing nearly $3 million, 69 percent of this contributed by the United States and 31 percent by Canada. The lamprey research and control program is carried out under contract with the Great Lakes Fisheries Commission established by treaty with Canada in 1956.

Eradication of the lamprey from the Great Lakes seems unlikely, but the larvicide has proved effective, and the parasites have been reduced to a point where the natural productivity of the Great Lakes is coming back. Coho salmon have been introduced into Lake Michigan and have become successfully established in recent years without any major threat from the sea lamprey.

The Anglerfish—The Fish That Fishes

Familiar to almost every commercial fisherman on our northeastern coast is a somewhat grotesque, conical-shaped fish. It has received many names since the first description of its habits was given by Aristotle some 2300 years ago. Some of its more common names are anglerfish, goosefish, molykite, bellyfish, frogfish, all-bellows, monkfish, sea-devil, all-mouth, and by the French, *baudroie* and *poisson-pecheur*.

The common anglerfish, *Lophius americanus*, ranges from Newfoundland to Brazil. In the North Atlantic, it is regularly taken by draggers with otter-trawl nets in both inshore and offshore waters. The anglers are seldom shipped to market in any great quantity. Indeed, they are usually put in with trash fish by fishermen, or thrown overboard.

Having a distinctive and grotesque appearance, the angler can be easily recognized. Unusual features are its large, gaping jaws with four rows of sharp pointed teeth directed inward; its conically shaped body, tapering toward the tail; its strange pectoral fins that, instead of rising from the sides of the body as in most bony fishes, take the form of fleshy arms formed by an elongation of the wrist bones and project out from the base of the head. On the lower jaw, and extending in a straight line along the sides of the body, are a fringe of barbels, or fleshy projections, resembling small pieces of seaweed. These are best developed on the lower jaw, where some of them may be 2 inches long. Located on top of

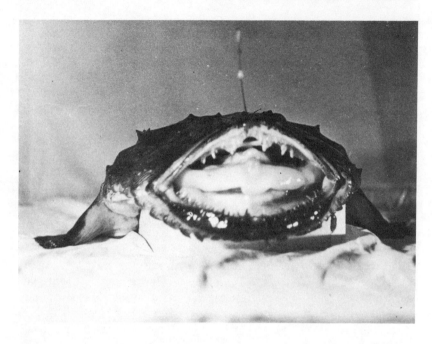

the head are three individual spines that are modified rays of the dorsal, or back, fin. The first of these has a fleshy tip that is used as "bait" to lure fish up to the angler's mouth.

Descriptions of the angler using the spines or rods on its head to attract fish have been given by W. F. Clapp of Duxbury, Massachusetts, and by Chadwick in *Nature,* vol. 124, 1929, p. 337 and Wilson in the *Journal of the Marine Biological Association of the United Kingdom,* Vol. 21, Pt. 2, 1937, pp. 486–490. Wilson, who made quite a study of the angler's habits, states:

> An angler when hungry erects the first spine immediately when any suitable fish comes anywhere near and endeavors to attract one of them close enough to be caught. The lure is jerked quickly to and fro and, since the spine is almost invisible, the bait, which is "fly like," simulates some tiny creature darting about. An attracted fish rushes up in an attempt to catch it; the bait is skillfully flicked out of its way just in time, and with a final cast, is dashed down in front of the mouth, which may open very slightly. The intended victim, still following the bait, turns slightly head downward; it is now more or less directly in front of the angler's mouth.

The jaws snap faster than the eyes can follow, and the tail of the prey is next seen disappearing from sight through the firmly closed mouth. . . . When the moment comes to strike the prey it seems that the angler suddenly thrusts itself a short way upward and forward with the aid of the pelvic fins against the ground. Little assistance appears to be given by the pectorals, at the same instant the mouth opens and presumably the mouth cavity is rapidly enlarged, sucking in water and the fish at the same time. The jaws snap and the angler sinks back into its sandy hollow to swallow its captive in leisurely fashion.

The molykite will eat almost anything. It is known to have swallowed wooden buoys attached to lobster traps, and there have been reports of persons hauling up an anchor that had hooked a molykite. The sixteenth-century French ichthyologist Guillaume Rondelet tells of finding an angler along the shore holding a fox fast by the leg.

There have been quite a few accounts of anglers swallowing water birds. Seven wild ducks are said to have been found in the stomach of one angler, and six coots in another. This fish is sometimes called the goosefish because it is known to have swallowed some geese that were floating on the surface of the water.

However, the usual food of the angler in New England waters appears to be herring, flounder, whiting, sculpin, cod, haddock, skate, and sandshark. In other words, it likes any fish it is able to sink its teeth into.

Prent Lamphere of Watch Hill, Rhode Island, while out handlining for cod on the reef off Weekapaug, Rhode Island, was hauling up a fish when he found the line had suddenly grown a lot heavier. He hauled it up as quickly as he could and saw that he had hooked a cod that was swallowed by an angler while he was pulling it up. There have been several accounts of similar circumstances by other fishermen.

When large anglers are captured in otter trawls, they are likely to be found with the tails of three or four fish sticking out of their mouths. It seems that when they find themselves among thousands of fishes they promptly take advantage of the situation and eat as many of their companions as they have capacity to hold. I have even seen a small molykite, with several small fishes in its mouth, trapped in the mouth of a larger member of its own species.

Anglers are most common in New England waters during the summer months, when they spawn in inshore waters. The eggs of mature anglers are extruded in a mucuslike mass that extends for about

30 or 40 feet and is about 12 inches wide. The eggs are violet-gray in color and float near the surface. Frequently they are attached to lobster and fish traps. Estimates of the number of eggs released by a large female run from 1 to 3 million.

There is not any doubt that the angler is a tasty food fish. The flesh is firm and white and especially suitable for frying or baking. European countries have been utilizing the angler as a staple food fish for many years. In some places it is even regarded as a delicacy. It was introduced on the New York market in the summer of 1918 and has been sold there in comparatively small quantities ever since.

The average adult angler is about 42 inches long and weighs about 28 pounds. Of this weight about 10 pounds are marketable. There is a great deal of waste because of the fish's large head. If the head is cut off as soon as it is caught, what is left can be easily handled, and most of it is good meat. The flesh on both sides of the backbone is entirely free of bones and can be cut up into delicious steaks. Anglers reach a length of 5 feet and have been recorded as heavy as 70 pounds. Occasionally a large angler will get stranded by the tide on the beach. Frequently beach-combers encounter anglers' skulls and jaws.

Normally the anglers are found on the bottom, but occasionally they appear on the surface. Old-time fishermen say that they usually come during a storm. European fishermen believe that the appearance of an angler heralds a storm. This idea is also found on this side of the Atlantic for, according to D. H. Storer, a saying prevalent among old-time Massachusetts fishermen is, "When you catch a goosefish, look out for an easterly storm."

The deep-sea anglerfish, which differ from other anglerfishes by the absence of fins on its undersurface, dwells in the abyss miles deep, where light never penetrates. There are some 12 species, and they make good use of their fleshy fishing rod because so little life exists for them to feed upon. Or rather, for her to feed on. Because here, in the blackest environment imaginable, there are many deep-sea anglers where only the female ever eats. For decades, marine biologists were puzzled that only females of certain kinds were ever brought up from the deep. Where were the males? Finally it was discovered that the males were dwarfs, spending the greater part of their lives as parasites of the female. In such darkness, where courtship could easily prove futile, once the male finds his mate, he attaches himself to her, never to let go. The site of the attachment appears to be a random choice—

sometimes on the abdomen, the sides, the head, or even the gill cover.

The male grips the female with his strong teeth, and his lips and tongue grow into her skin. His mouth, jaws, teeth, fins, and gills degenerate. Only his reproductive system remains independently active. The two blood systems become fused, and the male is nourished by her blood, literally becoming part of her, his body merging into hers. He never grows; if anything, much of the male disappears into the female.

An angler female taken near Iceland was 40 inches long, and the attached male only 4 inches. The female was judged to be a thousand times the weight of her mate.

6

They Run in Millions, Billions

Fishes outnumber all other vertebrates on our planet both in numbers and in species. They are often astoundingly prolific in the number of eggs they release into the waters during their spawning season. A mature herring will lay up to 50,000 eggs, a 21-pound lumpfish 279,620 eggs, a 17-pound turbot 9 million eggs, a 75-pound cod 9.1 million eggs, a 54-pound ling over 28 million eggs, and a giant oceanic sunfish may release 300 million eggs. Only a fraction of one percent of the released eggs survive to maturity. Predation and lethal environmental factors produce a staggering mortality among the developing young.

Countless Fillets—Ocean Perch

A brilliantly red fish of great importance to commercial fisheries is the ocean perch, *Sebastes marinus*. Found on both sides of the Atlantic Ocean in northern waters, this species is called by a great variety of names: red sea perch, red bream, rosefish, redfish, Norway haddock, and bergylt.

In its general appearance, the ocean perch resembles the bass or perch but is not related to either group. Its brilliant coloration makes it easy to identify, for it is a vivid orange to flame red with the belly a paler red. The large black eyes stand out markedly on the spiny head.

With meat that is firm and of a rich flavor, the ocean perch makes an excellent food fish. It was well known as a table fish in Europe long before it became popular in North America. The ocean perch occurs from Greenland and Davis Strait as far south as New Jersey in deep water. In European waters it is taken from the northern part of the North Sea to the southwestern coast of Iceland.

Long familiar to New Englanders fishing in 50 to 125 fathoms, the ocean perch was of no major economic importance there until the mid-1930s when the haddock catch dropped to its lowest level and fishermen had to turn to other species to make ends meet. Ocean perch were available in large quantities and were found to yield attractive fillets of a rich and agreeable flavor suitable for shipping to inland markets. A consumers' demand for the fillets developed, at first in the Midwest and later in other sections of the country. Catches increased from 257,000 pounds in 1933, to nearly 67 million pounds in 1936, reaching a peak of more than 258 million pounds in 1951. In 1933 ocean perch ranked 106th in volume of production among the U.S. fisheries. By 1959, the ocean perch catch ranked fifth, with only menhaden, Pacific salmon, tuna, and shrimp landed in larger quantities.

During the early years of the ocean perch fishery, most of the catch was at Boston, Massachusetts; but soon landings at Gloucester, Massachusetts, grew rapidly, and in each year since 1938, it has been the principal port for this species. In 1951, nearly 178 million pounds of fish were brought in at Gloucester. In 1975, U.S. Atlantic coast landings totaled 32,054,000 pounds, valued at $3,304,000.

The average market-size ocean perch is about 11 inches long and about ¾ pound in weight. The largest ocean perch of recent record, according to the *Maine Coast Fisherman*, was landed in Gloucester and weighed 5 pounds 11 ounces, and was 22 inches long. Goode (1884) mentions a record specimen brought in by one of the Gloucester halibut schooners that was about 2 feet in length and weighed about 14 pounds.

The ocean perch matures sexually when 9 to 10 inches long, with the male always staying somewhat smaller than the female. Unique among our food fishes (although by no means unusual among fishes in general), it gives birth to living young. Actually, the eggs of the ocean perch develop and hatch within the oviduct of the mother. According to H. B. Bigelow and W. C. Schroeder (1953), the number of living young produced by large ocean perch may run as high as 40,000 yearly. This is a small number of progeny compared to many other marine fishes, but the protection given the eggs by being retained in the mother's body during incubation gives the newborn fish a better chance of survival than eggs floating helplessly in the sea.

The larvae are about 6 millimeters long at birth, with a small bit of the yolk sac visible. Soon the juveniles develop many recognizable characteristics of the species—large spiny heads, large eyes, and relatively short, tapering bodies. The fins are fairly well developed by the time the little fish reach a length of 1 inch, and usually about this time the characteristic red color appears. During the first few weeks of their existence, the larvae, later called fry, live near the ocean's surface. When they attain about ¾ inch in length, the little fish travel down to the lower regions of the ocean.

The food of the ocean perch consists of a large variety of crustaceans—especially various species of shrimp, mollusks, and small fishes. Ocean perch bite on almost any bait; in turn, they are devoured by larger predaceous fishes such as cod and halibut.

A typical bottom fish in the western Atlantic, the ocean perch is captured chiefly by the otter trawl, although a few are taken on lines on the Banks and in South Channel. Beginning in the 1939 season, the deep channel known as the "Gully," off eastern Nova Scotia, became important as a source of ocean perch. In 1951, important catches were made in the Gulf of St. Lawrence and on the Grand Banks of Newfoundland, and this trend continued through the decade.

Fishing for rosefish is carried on throughout the year, during the daylight hours. It seems that they scatter and rise off the bottom at night, which makes trawling ineffectual during that time.

Almost the entire catch of ocean perch is used in the production of fillets, most of which are frozen. Waste materials from the filleting process are utilized in the manufacture of fishmeal and oils and for lobster bait. Goode, back in 1884, mentioned that native Greenlanders prized the spines of the fins of the ocean perch for use as needles.

In recent years, the imports of ocean perch and groundfish fillets from Iceland, Greenland, and other European countries have been steadily climbing. The lower prices of these imports have caused considerable concern in our domestic fishery.

Armies of the Sea—Herring, Sardines

According to some geographers, herring were responsible for the migrations of the Vikings into American waters. Dependent on a fish diet, the Norsemen simply followed the great hordes of these fish.

Marine biologists estimate that there are at least a trillion (1,000,000,000,000) herring in the Atlantic Ocean. *Heer* means "army"

Boatload of sea herring

in Dutch. With the present world catch about 4 billion pounds per year, we can easily see that they were and are the most numerous fish in existence. As food, herring are more important than any other species of fish.

The greatest quantity of the world's herring catch is taken in the northernmost half of the Northern Hemisphere around all three continents, the European waters being the most productive. The most cosmopolitan and widely utilized is the Atlantic sea herring, *Clupea harengus*, a species that gathers in tremendous schools in the North Atlantic and was actually responsible for the rise and fall of nations.

In the fourteenth century, the Hanseatic League, which had controlled the vast Baltic herring trade for 200 years, lost most of its power when the herring stocks declined in that area. The Dutch in the North Sea were next to exploit the industry, when the fish became abundant there. In 1610 Sir Walter Raleigh estimated that the Dutch had 3000 ships and 50,000 people employed in their herring fishery. The Baltic stock probably declined as a result of a change in temperature or salinity, which halted successful reproduction of herring, although some historians say that the herring suddenly left the Baltic and migrated to the North Sea. At any rate, about the time that the Hanseatic merchants lost their herring trade in the Baltic, the Dutch developed a North Sea herring fishery with an improved method of curing the fish. Holland's fortunes prospered; only the Spanish conquest brought an end to this Dutch prosperity. Interestingly, a century before this, the two great political parties of Holland called themselves the Kabeljaauws (codfish) and the Hocks (hooks). Holland to this day remains an important fishing nation.

When tremendous schools of this species were discovered in the waters off North America, the herring's exploitation became cosmopolitan. On the western Atlantic, it occurs from northern Labrador and the west coast of Greenland to Cape Hatteras, with the greatest abundance in the Gulf of St. Lawrence and the Gulf of Maine. Relatively cold water and an available food supply of minute crustaceans called copepods, which are part of the plankton, are the chief attractions for herring.

During the nineteenth century, herring hostilities raged between the fishermen of New England and those of British Newfoundland, culminating in 1878 in the infamous incident known as the Fortune Bay Riot. Under the Halifax Commission Treaty of 1877 the United States paid Great Britain $5.5 million for the privilege of fishing for 12 years within the 3-mile limit in the St. Lawrence gulf and off Newfoundland. Defending what they considered their natural rights, Newfoundland fishermen, on a bitter cold Sunday morning in Fortune Bay, cut to shreds the seine nets of the Gloucester schooners *New England* and *Ontario*, letting the herring catches escape. The crew of the *Moses Adams* defended their catch at gunpoint, but the entire American fleet (22 vessels) soon set sail for home with only a partial cargo.

A device that helps locate herring fishing grounds is the plankton indicator, developed by Sir Alistair C. Hardy, the English biologist, and his colleagues. By finding areas rich in certain kinds of plankton, scientists can predict that herring will be attracted there to feed.

Herring feed by simply gulping down the tiny plankton. As they swim through the ocean, seawater passes through their gill filaments, in which the blood is oxygenated. The plankton organisms carried in this stream of water are sifted out by comblike structures called gill rakers, of which there are approximately 60 per inch at the back of the mouth. The rakers allow the water to pass out but hold back the food, which passes into the gullet. One scientist counted as many as 60,000 copepods in the stomach of a single herring. To feed the billions of herring in the Atlantic the copepod requirements must be astronomical!

Almost every large fish and many medium-size ones prey upon the defenseless herring. Cod, haddock, hake, pollack, salmon, dogfish, shark, bluefish, striped bass, swordfish, and tuna are among the predators. Squid and other invertebrates eat immature herring, and mammals such as porpoises, seals, and finback whales join in the hunt.

Through the centuries man has used a variety of techniques to catch herring. The weir, employed by American Indians and still in use, consists of leaders of brush or netting extending from a pocket. The fish encounter the leaders, their path is blocked, and they are detoured into the pocket from which they cannot escape. In 1958 over 25 million pounds of herring were caught in weirs off the coast of Maine.

Another early American fishing method was "torching," attracting fish to a light at night. In this method a rowboat carries a torch in its bow, and a fisherman at the stern scoops up the herring in a dip net. Despite laws against it, fishermen all over the country indulge in night fishing with a light.

A few years after the first weirs were built, gill nets were used. These were suspended at various depths between the surface and the bottom by buoys and anchors. The size of the mesh ranged from 2 to 3

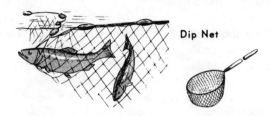

Dip Net

Menhaden Vessel

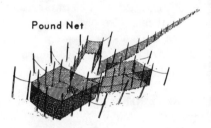

Pound Net

The long wall--up to a mile long--directs fish into the trap. Later the fish are removed by dipping into a carrier vessel

Gill Net

An upright fence of netting that "gills" fish swimming into it. Meshes vary in size; some nets let smaller fish pass through them (gilled fish at right)

Gear Used to Catch Finfish

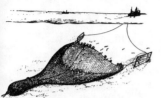

Otter Trawl

A funnel-shaped net pulled along the bottom. "Otter" boards at ends of wings spread mouth to greatest width. Also used for shrimp

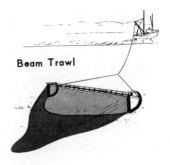

Beam Trawl

Bag-shaped net without wings, towed along the bottom. A rigid beam holds the mouth open

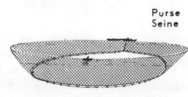

Purse Seine

Surrounds fish which run in schools near the surface. A drawstring pulled through rings in bottom closes it

Fyke Net

A conical, winged net, supported on poles and used in shallow water

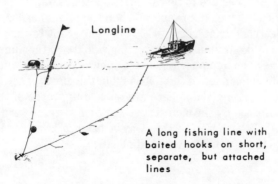

Longline

A long fishing line with baited hooks on short, separate, but attached lines

inches, which snared only the larger herring. Between 1887 and 1898 gill nets took about 16 percent of the herring catch, but this method had declined in importance.

In Maine today, the stop seine is the dominant herring gear. This small mesh net, generally used at night, prevents the herring from leaving a cover or inlet. When a school is spotted, the net is spread around it, and the net ends are taken ashore. The school is then concentrated into a compact mass and taken into the boats by dip nets. The stop seine is essentially a small-boat operation, with most of the boats under 50 feet long and the seines carried from dories.

The purse seine, where a net is entirely manipulated from boats, is another method. After the fish have been encircled, the bottom of the net is closed, preventing their escape.

In 1950 a Danish netmaker developed a floating trawl that makes it possible to drag a net for herring and to fish for them at any depth. Echo sounders locate the depth of schools, and nets are set at the depth at which the fish are swimming.

Another application of modern technology employs electricity in a more direct manner. It is known that at certain low voltages, fish will rapidly swim away from an electric field. If, however, the voltage at which this occurs is doubled, the same fish will obligingly swim in the direction of the lines of force of the field, toward the positive electrode. The fish will do so even in the presence of a pulsed current, provided the frequencies are above a certain minimum.

This fact is exploited in the fishery for herring and also menhaden (a close relative of the herring). Normally, these fish are pumped from the bottom of a purse seine into a boat. It is necessary to raise the catch, either mechanically or manually by the crew, so that the fish cannot escape the suction of the pump. This is quite difficult when nets of 200,000 fish or more are to be raised. Sometimes, entire nets are lost.

Electricity solves the problem when the pump head is used as the positive electrode that attracts the fish to swim toward it. All the herring do not do so simultaneously; this would clog the pump. The first fishes to reach the pump form a dense sphere around it which partially insulates the remainder of the fishes from the effect of the charge. As the fishes comprising the sphere are sucked up, more of the outlying fishes are affected by the charge; they in turn swim toward the pump, replenishing the sphere. In this way a balance is achieved between fishes attracted and fishes pumped aboard.

One of the most interesting ways to control movements of herring schools was recently demonstrated by U.S. Bureau of Commercial Fisheries researchers. Flexible plastic pipe, perforated at regular intervals, was laid across the ocean bottom and compressed air pumped into the pipe, with a resulting curtain of bubbles, which proved to be an effective barrier against the herring. In this way the herring can be herded into designated areas.

During the last half of the nineteenth century, an important industry developed on the Maine coast, using herring that were too small for smoking or pickling. These herring were called sardines. The true sardines came originally from the vicinity of Sardinia in the Mediterranean, but the term is now applied to various members of the herring family in the Eastern and Western hemispheres including the Atlantic sea herring. The sardines canned in Maine are young fish that are caught in huge numbers when they appear in inshore waters during the spring and summer.

The idea of packing small fish in oil under the name sardines originated in France in 1850. The demand for this product increased enormously during the first decade of its existence, and other countries—Spain, Portugal, Italy, Germany, Sweden, Norway, and Japan—began to pack small herring and other fish with oil in metal containers.

In America the sardine industry was developed by George Burnham of Portland, Maine, who visited France to familiarize himself with the operation of French canneries. Having purchased equipment and olive oil, he returned to Eastport, Maine, where in 1867 he obtained a plant and began to experiment with canned herring. Unable to rid his product of a herring-oil flavor, he abandoned his herring business on the threshold of success. Still, his work had called the attention of others to this resource, and he is credited with being the originator of the sardine industry in the United States. Today the Maine sardine industry supports about 5000 fishermen and packers in 34 canneries. The yearly production often exceeds $15 million.

A female herring may deposit from 20,000 to more than 40,000 eggs; 30,000 is average. Herring generally reach maturity during their third year and come to inshore waters to spawn on pebbly or gravelly bottoms. When herring eggs are deposited, they sink to the bottom and stick in clumps to the sand, seaweed, or pebbles. They may be as large as 1/20 inch in diameter and take from 10 to 15 days to hatch in the Gulf of

Maine. The sea herring are about ¼ inch long at hatching and have a yolk sac attached that is absorbed by the time they grow to approximately ½ inch. North Sea herring reach a length of about 4 inches by the end of their first year and 10½ inches at the end of their sixth year. Some have been found to live 20 years or more.

Fresh herring without salting, pickling, smoking, or canning are among the most delicious fish; but the American public rarely get to know the great treat of small raw herring as they are consumed in Holland for dinner, much as we eat oysters.

Because of the seasonal nature of the herring fisheries, processing industries must handle large quantities of fish over short periods of time. As a result, many high-capacity cleaning and boning machines have been developed. One German machine, for example, is operated by a single skilled person and can process 2800 herring per hour. The fish is automatically headed and measured for length and thickness. All tools of the machine are set according to these measurements so that there will be a minimum waste. Next, the herring is seized by the tail and pulled through the machine, which first removes a narrow strip along the belly and the ventral fins. A rotating knife opens the fish, and the viscera, including roe and milt, are removed, often to be marinated later. A special device removes not only the backbones but also the side ribs, and then the herring goes through a washing section.

There is no fear at present that the march of progress will endanger the world herring stock. Today in Central Europe, herring, salted and packed in barrels of brine (the process developed by the Dutch in the fourteenth century), are still in great demand. Kippered and "bloatered" herring are popular in the British Isles, while young herring packed as sardines are enjoyed the world over. In the United States, recent figures show herring the fourth-ranking fishery species, with most canned as sardines, pet food, or manufactured into meal and oil products. Ready to meet weirs and seines, pumps and bubble curtains, those trillion herring are waiting in the sea.

The Menhaden—A Billion Pounds a Year

The king of the industrial fish-processing world is the menhaden, or pogy, found in Atlantic waters from Nova Scotia to Brazil, a fish whose products are used today in the manufacture of candles, soap, printing inks, paint, insect sprays, and many other products.

Although this species is edible, it is not well regarded as food for humans because of its high oil content.

Probably the first person to utilize menhaden oil in Maine was Mrs. John Bartlett, of Blue Hill. About the year 1850, while boiling some fish for her chickens, Mrs. Bartlett noticed a thin scum of oil on the surface of the water. She bottled some of this oil and on her next trip to Boston showed samples of it to E. P. Phillips, one of the leading oil merchants of that city. Phillips said the oil was marketable at $11 a barrel and encouraged her to produce more. The following year the Bartlett family sent thirteen barrels of menhaden oil to Boston, and the next year produced a hundred barrels.

The silvery, greenish blue menhaden may be identified easily by its large scaleless head, deeply forked tail, and toothless mouth. Though averaging from 10 to 14 inches in length, the largest specimen on record appears to be one taken in 1876 off Woods Hole, Massachusetts, which was 18 inches long.

Menhaden usually travel on clear, calm days in tremendous schools in the millions, coming up near the surface and even leaping out, slapping the surface with their tails. As they swim, their wide mouths are kept constantly open, gulping in seawater and the nutritive plankton it contains.

Great quantities of water are filtered in this unusual way, according to James I. Peck of Williams College, who calculated by the width of the mouth opening and rate of speed of swimming that a feeding small menhaden forced water through its gills at the astonishing rate of 6.8 gallons per minute. Menhaden therefore do not have to feed continuously—extracting as they do nearly a pint of microscopic food an hour. In turn, they are preyed upon by virtually every carnivorous species of fish that inhabits the same waters.

Menhaden have been known since early colonial times, when the Indian chief Squanto, who was friendly with the European settlers, taught the Pilgrims to fertilize their crops by placing a fish in the soil with their hills of corn.

Because of its extensive migratory range along the Atlantic coast,

A catch of menhaden on the deck of a fishing vessel

the Atlantic menhaden, *Brevoortia tyrannus,* probably is known among fishermen by more local names than any other fish. Down East, north of Cape Cod, we find the names pogy and hard-head, in southern New England, bony-fish and menhaden, and a little farther south, in New York and New Jersey, mossbunker, or bunker. The name mossbunker is a relic of the Dutch colony of New Amsterdam, where the Hollanders originally called this fish "marshbanker," the common name of a species that visited northern Europe in large schools.

In Delaware and Chesapeake bays and the Potomac River we find fishermen calling this species bay alewife and green-tail. In Virginia, it is sometimes known as bug-fish and bug-head because of a parasitic crustacean that quite frequently infests the mouths of southern members of the species. From North Carolina to Florida, fishermen generally use the name fatback because of the smooth, fat back and oiliness of the flesh. Other names sometimes used along the coast include yellow-tail shad, shiner, old wife, chebug, white fish, and pilcher.

The catch is controlled by its seasonal appearance. According to J. G. Ellison, pogies generally make their appearance from Virginia to Maine as the water warms, the main schools appearing when the water reaches nearly 60 degrees F. They appear in the Chesapeake Bay region in March and April; in New Jersey, New York, and southern New England in April and May; Cape Ann, Massachusetts, in mid-May. If they appear on the Maine coast, it is usually in the latter part of May and June. The fish generally stay in New England waters until fall, when they migrate south to join those who remain off the Florida coast throughout the year.

Menhaden mature during their third or fourth years, and generally spawn in the summer or fall. They increase in oil content with age and size, although northern menhaden tend to have a higher oil content than their southern counterparts.

The chief method used in the capture of menhaden is purse seining, the fish usually being removed at the processing plant by suction pipe or conveyor belt. As with herring, there are now electrical means of attracting many thousands of menhaden to surface seines. It is necessary to process the catch as soon as possible, as the stale fish putrefy rapidly.

While there seems to be a seasonal variation in the yield of oil per fish, the menhaden is always larger and fatter in the fall than in any other season. According to D. K. Tressler, northern factories sometimes get as much as 20 gallons of oil from 1000 fish, while the Floridian fish rarely yield more than 8 gallons per 1000 fish.

Today the manufacture of menhaden oil, scrap, and meal is an important part of our marine industry. Thirty-six plants, located along the Atlantic and Gulf coasts from Massachusetts to Texas, process menhaden for fishmeal and industrial products. The centers of this widespread industry are Virginia and Louisiana, where the greater poundage of menhaden are landed. The total catch of menhaden in the United States is worth some $50 million a year to fishermen, and the overall value for the oil and meal obtained has been known to run as high as $75 million.

The first commercial attempts to extract menhaden oil were made in 1817, according to Goode and Clarke. During the War of 1812 paint oils became so scarce and expensive that the people of southern New England conceived the idea of using fish oil for the purpose. Among the first to go into the business was the Gardiner family living on the shore of Mount Hope Bay, Rhode Island. Say Goode and Clarke:

> The first method was to drag the pogies ashore with seines and put them in large casks or hogsheads brought down to the water for the purpose. After filling the casks with fish, salt water was added to cover them and boards—weighed down with stones—were put on top of the fish to press them down. The fish were left to rot for a few days, after which they were thoroughly stirred with a long stick daily to break up the fish and liberate the oil so that it could come to the surface of the putrid mess. This process was kept up from two to three weeks, the oil being dipped off daily, after which the barrels were emptied into the water.
>
> About 1820 they commenced boiling the fish in large kettles, stirring them frequently and skimming the oil off by hand. Among the first to do this was John Tollman at Black Point, East River, Portsmouth, R.I.
>
> Soon the business reached such dimensions that the kettles were too small and they were obliged to build large cooking tanks, and with these steam was introduced for cooking, the pipes being laid at the bottom, but wholly unprotected. The fish were thoroughly cooked and stirred, and after standing for a time the oil was skimmed off. A plug was then pulled from the bottom of the tank, and the whole mass allowed to run off on the ground near by. Quantities of scrap or chum accumulated in this way and found a ready sale for manure to the farmers. The cooking by steam was introduced about 1830 by John Tollman at Black Point, John Herreshoff at Prudence Island, and others in Long Island Sound. The next great improvement was the introduction of the press for taking the oil and water from the chum between 1855 and 1860 by a Charles Tuthill of Greenport, New York.

In Poquonnock Bridge, Connecticut, Elisha Morgan was reported to have made oil from bony fish prior to the year 1850. He owned seines with which he captured the fish, and spread them on the ground fresh. When he could not sell all his fish to the local farmers, he boiled the remainder and extracted their oil.

From 1873 to 1875, young menhaden were canned under the names shadine, ocean trout, and American sardine, but the developing Maine sardine industry based on herring soon put an end to canned menhaden.

During the Second World War, food shortages caused the menhaden to be canned in fairly large quantities, but most of the pack was put up for export; little was consumed in this country. Today, only the roe is sometimes saved for freezing, salting, or canning as food for human consumption.

Much menhaden oil is utilized in the manufacture of soaps. When properly hydrogenated, a solid, odorless and almost colorless fat is produced, which is used extensively for making laundry soap and the lower grades of toilet soap. Some of the oil also is used in the preparation of lard substitutes and in the manufacture of candles, lubricating oil, and leather dressing. Menhaden oil is sometimes used in the preparation of heat-resistant paints and as an ingredient in the manufacture of certain types of linoleum.

Many questions are yet to be answered by fishery biologists about the habits of the menhaden. What are the causes of the fluctuation in their abundance? Where are the exact locations of their spawning grounds? How can we control a parasite that sometimes sterilizes the male menhaden? What is the relationship of the menhaden's diet to its oil content? In view of the economic importance of the menhaden, it is not surprising that several marine research organizations are conducting extensive studies of this fish.

Mackerel Never Sleep

A sleek, iridescent fish that periodically travels along our North Atlantic coast in dense schools is the Atlantic or common mackerel, *Scomber scombrus*. Next to the large herring family, the mackerel family takes second place in economic importance around the world. Scattered throughout the oceans are 12 genera and approximately 60 species belonging to the family Scombridae.

Mackerel are among the swiftest fish known. They have been estimated to travel as fast as 70 miles an hour when disturbed. They propel themselves with powerful muscular tails, making short, sideward strikes. According to A. E. Hall, strange as it sounds, the mackerel, like the menhaden, has to keep swimming constantly in order to stay alive! Mackerel require a great deal of oxygen for their vital functions, so when the water is warm and the oxygen content low, they must keep swimming to bring a sufficient flow of oxygen to their gill filaments. The common mackerel also differs from most fish in that it does not have an air bladder, an anatomical device used for buoyancy regulation.

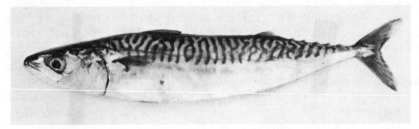

Mackerel vary greatly in their abundance. There have been numerous firsthand accounts of encounters with tremendous schools of mackerel. One of the greatest magnitude was a school seen in South Channel in 1848 by Captain King Harding of Swampscott, Massachusetts. He described it as follows: "It was a windrow of fish; it was about a half mile wide and twenty miles long, for vessels not in sight of each other saw it at the same time." Captain Harding saw another school off Block Island in 1877 that he estimated to contain a million barrels of fish; he could only see one edge of the school at a time.

Records of the commercial landings of mackerel have been made each year from as far back as 1804, and there have been great ups and downs in the annual landings of this species—from 23 million to 179 million pounds. These fluctuations are due chiefly to the success or failure of the young. Recent studies made by Oscar E. Sette of the U.S. Fish and Wildlife Service show that mortality during the early period of the mackerel's life may be extremely high. During years in which conditions in the spawning grounds are unfavorable, such as in 1932, as few as four out of every *million* eggs spawned survive the larval period. The unfavorable direction of the prevailing winds and currents, which carried the young mackerel away from their usual nursery grounds, along with a scarcity of suitable food for the young, were the probable causes of the 1932 disaster, according to Sette.

From 1804 to 1831 the catch gradually increased to a level of about 70 million pounds per year. The next nine years saw a gradual falling off to 23 million pounds in 1840. Again a change occurred, and there was a rise in landings ranging from 80 million to 100 million pounds per year. In 1884, the greatest year ever for mackerel landings, the catch totaled a record 179 million pounds. After 1884 a period of low catches began, which continued until 1926. The annual catch still varies from year to year, but we now appear to be experiencing a new abundance of this species. During 1975, the Atlantic coast catch of mackerel amounted to 4,402,000 pounds, with the largest quantity taken in purse seines. The remainder of the catch was captured by gill nets, pound nets, weirs, otter trawls, floating traps, and hand lines.

Each spring the mackerel travel toward land from the deep waters off the Atlantic coast where they have spent the winter. Grouped together in schools that may be miles in length, the mackerel approach the coast in two great divisions. One arrives off Chesapeake and Delaware bays in April, and a northern group comes inshore in the vicinity of southern New England in late May. Both groups then head up the coast in a northeasterly direction.

This springtime migration of the mackerel brings them to their chief spawning ground, an area from 10 to 50 miles offshore extending from the vicinity of Chesapeake Bay to the region off Cape Cod. The buoyant eggs, about 1¼ millimeters in diameter, are released from May to July. A 1⅛-pound mackerel has been recorded as producing 546,000 eggs. These eggs usually take about 5 days to hatch at a temperature of 56 degrees F. Young fry grow to a length of 2 inches the first two months, and may reach a length of 5 to 6 inches by September or October.

From colonial times until the present, mackerel have played an important part in our fishing economy. Large mackerel schools were observed with great admiration by colonial trawlers. Francis Higginson, in his *Journal of a Voyage to New England* (1629), writes of seeing "many schools of mackerel, infinite magnitudes on every side of our ship." In Governor Winthrop's *Journal*, speaking of the year 1639, he remarks: "There was such a store of exceedingly large and fat mackerel upon our coast this season as was a great benefit to all our Plantations, since our Boat with three men would take in a week ten hogsheads, which were sold at Connecticut for three pounds, twelve shillings per hogshead."

Because of the variations in abundance of mackerel, as early as 1670 laws were passed by the Massachusetts Bay Colony regulating the length of the mackerel season and the use of seines in their capture.

The chief method used by the early colonists of New England in capturing mackerel was the drag seine. As early as 1626 we find mention of the establishment of a fishing station by Isaac Allerton, at Hull, Massachusetts, where mackerel were seined by moonlight. The practice of fishing with baited hooks was also common at this time. During the early 1800s, it was usual to attract the fish around an anchored boat by throwing overboard great quantities of fish cut in small pieces. The mackerel were taken with short lines held in the hand, and drawn in with a swift motion of the arm. The fish could also be taken on cloudy or wet days with the hook. It was found that the fish were partial to red, so small strips of red cloth were used sometimes on a line. Pout, the best bait, was a small strip of flesh taken from the mackerel's tail.

The mackerel jig is said to have been invented between the years 1810 and 1814 by Edward Caiss, a fisherman of Hingham, Massachusetts. The jig was a simple hook that had a piece of lead, pewter, or tin cast around the shank. The weighted piece was somewhat globular at its upper end, tapering slightly toward the bend of the hook. The weight of mackerel jigs has varied from ¼ ounce to 4 ounces at different periods. Early mackerel jigs were much heavier than present-day ones. Today, heavy lead drails are sometimes used with the mackerel jigs in trolling.

The old-time fishermen made their own mackerel jigs in molds improvised in buckets of sand or ashes. After being cast, the rough metal was beaten into shape, and a hole was bored for the fish line. Since the 1850s, fishermen have become very critical of their mackerel jigs, and are not satisfied unless the jigs are elegantly shaped and brilliantly polished. It was the usual practice to bait the jig with two or three small circular pieces of pork rind placed on the hook.

The food of mackerel consists of plankton (which it filters from the seawater with its gill rakers), fish eggs, small herring, squid, and even small members of its own species. Frequently, 3- and 4-inch baby mackerel have been found in the stomachs of mature adults.

The large schools of mackerel attract numerous predators. Herring gulls, gannets, and squid feed on great quantities of young mackerel.

Fresh-caught mackerel are considered choice food fishes. Mackerel is rich in fat content, and when properly baked, broiled, or fried can be a gourmet's delight. Mackerel should be cleaned and dressed as soon as possible after they have been caught as they tend to soften and lose their flavor if not eviscerated.

Our Atlantic mackerel, *Scomber scombrus*, receives its name from the Greek *scomber*, which is the ancient name for this fish. It can be identified by the five little finlets on the lower and upper edges of the peduncle (the fleshy part of the tail). It has a large mouth equipped with small, slender teeth on each jaw and an elongated, streamlined body. The mackerel's scales are minute, reducing resistance through the water. The color of the upper surface is a dark greenish blue to blue-black, and the belly is a silvery white. Along the upper portions of the fish's sides are usually from 27 to 30 dark vertical, wavy streaks.

Smaller mackerel have several names among commercial fishermen. The 5- or 6-inch ones are called tacks or spikes; they are 5 to 11 months old. Next are the blinkers, or blinks, which range from 6 to 9 inches long and are 1 to 2 years old. Tinkers are the next group; they are from 10 to 12 inches long and 2 to 3 years old. So-called full-grown mackerel are generally about 17 or 18 inches long and weigh from 2 to 3 pounds. Occasionally they reach more than twice that size.

7

The Diminishing: Threatened with Extinction

Delicate parameters control the existence of life both on land and in the sea. Ideal temperature, adequate oxygen, sufficient nutrition, survival from predation, and the absence of toxic chemicals are critical in the survival of all living organisms. Many species of fish have declined in recent times.

The main causes of fish decline are overfishing; lack of successful reproduction; lack of adequate nutrition; toxic environmental factors such as lethal temperature, red tide, raw sewage, eutrophication, insecticides, and other toxic chemicals. The key to the survival of endangered fishes is the development and enforcement of adequate conservation action and the elimination of water pollution.

Sturgeon and Their Caviar

Sometimes human activities can put an end to creatures that have survived millions of years of geological stress. The sturgeon belongs to a primitive group of fishes dating back to the Devonian period of about 300 million years ago. But, in spite of such long ancestry, and although in recent centuries very plentiful in North American waters, it has shown an incredible decline.

In ancient Rome the sturgeon was accorded a high place. It alone was reserved the high honor of being served at banquets accompanied by the music of flutes and pipes, crowned in flowers and carried by slaves likewise ornamented. Cicero makes at least four references to the sturgeon and states: "Lo! This is a fish fit only for a few choice palates."

Edward II of England, who assumed the throne in 1307, took a great liking to this fish and issued the following edict: "The King shall have the wreck of the sea throughout the realm, whales and great sturgeons." At one time any sturgeon captured above London Bridge belonged to the Lord Mayor of London; all others belonged to the king by royal decree. Henry I is said to have banned the eating of sturgeon at any table except his own.

Early colonists to America marveled at the abundance of sturgeon in the rivers of the New World. An old report states: "In some rivers of Virginia, sturgeon are found in such numbers that six hundred have been taken in two days with no more trouble than putting down a pole with a hook at one end to the bottom and drawing it up again on feeling it rub against a fish."

During colonial times in New England, pickled sturgeon was an important article of commerce, and considerable quantities were exported to the West Indies. In 1629, Governor Endicott of Massachusetts was ordered to send home to the company in London "two or three hundred firkins" of sturgeon and other fish. By 1693, a considerable export trade existed in pickled sturgeon, most of which was caught in the Merrimac River. Pickling is the process of boiling the flesh and preserving it in weak vinegar flavored with suitable spices.

In the early 1700s there was a flourishing sturgeon fishery in the Kennebec River area in Maine. Thousands of kegs of cured sturgeon were put up every season, and they were declared as good as any that came from Hamburg or Norway.

During 1841, N. K. Lombard, representing a Boston fish firm, came to the Kennebec and set up a sturgeon business in the town of Woolwich, between Bath and Merrymeeting Bay. He proposed to put up the roe for caviar and also boil down the bodies for oil. He paid 25 to 50 cents for each fish, and a large number of local fishermen became engaged in sturgeon fishing to supply him. An old record states that during the first year, Lombard obtained 160 tons of sturgeon, which yielded a lamp oil said to be superior to sperm-whale oil. This fishery appears to have flourished until 1851, a year in which the species became scarce.

The name sturgeon originated either with the Anglo-Saxon *stiriga,* meaning "a stirrer," the Swedish *stora,* "to stir," or the German verb *storen,* which means "to poke" or rummage around, which the fish does on the bottom. In very old books we find this species referred to as storgin or sturjourn.

Sturgeons include about 15 species in the Northern Hemisphere, seven of which occur in American waters. The most abundant species along our east coast is the Atlantic sturgeon, *Acipenser oxyrhyncus,* found from the St. Lawrence River to the Gulf of Mexico. A second species, less abundant and smaller, is the short-nosed sturgeon, *Acipenser brevirostrum,* recorded from Provincetown, Massachusetts, to Charleston, South Carolina.

Sturgeon hold the lofty position of being also the largest species of freshwater fish. In the United States a sturgeon 18 feet long was recorded from Pacific coast waters. A white sturgeon, *Acipenser transmontanus,* taken at Astoria, Oregon, weighed 1900 pounds. Probably the largest sturgeon on record is a beluga, or Russian, sturgeon, *Acipenser huso,* which weighed 3210 pounds.

The beluga, which makes the best-quality caviar, is found in the Volga and Dnieper rivers and the Caspian and Black seas. Many Russian sturgeons weighing over a ton have been recorded. One 2680-pound female contained over 320 pounds of eggs, enough to make canapés for a regiment.

Like salmon and shad, sturgeons enter coastal rivers in the late spring on their spawning migration. During the early summer months, the female forces out her eggs by rubbing her belly over rocks, submerged stumps, and other firm objects. A mature female may produce as many as 2 or 3 million eggs during a single breeding period.

The ripe eggs are blackish in color, and each egg is enclosed in a sticky, gelatinous envelope that causes it to adhere to nearby objects. Sometimes the eggs clump together in a large, dark mass. They usually hatch in 3 to 7 days, and the larvae when they emerge are less than ½ inch long.

The roe from ripe sturgeon is relished around the world by gourmets. To prepare the expensive caviar, the fresh roe is placed in large masses on a small-meshed screen. The processor gently rubs the mass of eggs back and forth over the screen, separating the eggs from the enveloping membranes.

The eggs are washed in vinegar or white wine, and afterward spread out. The best-quality Luneburg salt is then rubbed in well by hand. After adding the salt, the eggs at first become dry, but in ten to fifteen minutes the water from the eggs gets drawn off into the salt and a copious brine is formed, which is discarded. The salted eggs are poured into very fine mesh sieves, which hold about 10 pounds each, and allowed to drain for 8 to 20 hours. They are then packed in oaken kegs or cans for market as caviar.

The word *caviar* is not of Russian origin but comes from either the Turkish word *khavyah* or the Italian *caviale* and applies only to sturgeon eggs after they have been salted. There is a so-called red caviar, which are salmon eggs of far larger size, that is also relished.

The majority of the caviar served in American restaurants today comes from the Caspian Sea region of the Soviet Union. Russian caviar occurs in three sizes. Beluga is the largest and best quality, coming from fish weighing up to a ton or more. A medium-size caviar called osetra is taken from fish weighing up to 300 pounds. The smallest size, sevruga, is from sturgeon under 150 pounds.

The best caviar is generally made in the winter months and must be refrigerated at a temperature of from 41 to 46 degrees C. or it will spoil. Difficulties in preparation and transport, along with unique flavor, have made caviar an expensive delicacy around the world. It has been known in Western Europe at least since the sixteenth century, when Shakespeare first used the word in *Hamlet:* "His play . . . 'twas caviare to the general."

Caviar is best appreciated as an hors d'oeuvre with dry champagne, kümmel, or vodka. A coarse-quality caviar, strongly salted in brine and known as *pajusnaya*, forms a staple article of food in many parts of the Soviet Union.

Most species of sturgeon are found both in salt and fresh water, spending much of their adult life in the sea and entering the rivers only for spawning, like the shad and salmon. In some of the rivers and lakes of North America and Europe, certain species of sturgeon have become permanent residents of fresh water. The largest sturgeons are among these.

Off the New England coast, fishing draggers occasionally capture sturgeons in their otter trawls. One of the most notable catches (recorded by Bigelow and Schroeder) was an Atlantic sturgeon weighing 600 pounds, caught by the steam trawler *Fabia* on George's Bank in December 1932. In the winter of 1954 the trawler *Phantom* landed a 374-pound sturgeon taken 35 miles off Cape Breton Island, Nova Scotia. Numerous smaller sturgeons are caught each year by trap fishermen and draggermen.

In 1975, the *New York Times* said that sturgeons were once again appearing in the Hudson River, though shad fishermen despise them for tearing up the shad nets there. This is a far cry from the turn of the century when the sturgeon catch of the Delaware River just south of the Hudson alone totaled 5,023,175 pounds. The decline of these great fisheries can be traced to several factors—overfishing, pollution, and the opposition of the competing shad fishermen. At the beginning of this century there were no conservation measures such as size limits regulating the fishery, and it was soon exploited to the utmost. Industrialization, especially steel smelting, along the Great Lakes and coastal rivers created waste pollution, which made vast stretches of water unsuitable for fish reproduction of any kind. The sturgeon diminished, died out, or went elsewhere.

Sturgeons are formidable-looking, with large bony plates or scales on the head and body. There are five distinct rows of them along the sides of the fish. The sharp-edged plates along the muscular tail make sturgeons a considerable menace to fishermen handling those freshly caught. The plates have been known to cut a man's leg to the bone. The end of the tail and caudal fin resemble those of a shark.

The mouth is rounded and small and is located on the underside of the head. The sturgeon has the unusual ability to pucker its mouth and extend it forward when it wants to suck in a choice morsel of food. The mouth is also unique in that it is toothless in all stages except the larval.

Immediately in front of the mouth, arranged in a transverse row, are four short sensory barbels, like those of the catfish, which aid in searching for food in muddy waters where the eyes are of little use. The eyes and respiratory openings are relatively small and found in the sides of the snout, which serves to keep them free of mud.

The sturgeon is usually a slow-moving creature rooting in the bottom muck for small organisms that it draws up into its protruding mouth. It eats mainly worms, mollusks, crustaceans, aquatic plants, and small fishes. On rare occasions sturgeons have been known to leap clear out of the water.

One product of the sturgeon formerly of considerable trade importance was made from its air bladder. As early as 1525, Dutchmen produced semitransparent, plasticlike sheets from these bladders, calling them *huisenblas*, which literally means "sturgeon's bladder." Users of this material came to call it isinglass, which was a little easier for non-Dutchmen to pronounce.

In the preparation of isinglass, the air bladders are split open, thoroughly washed to remove the blood and membranous tissue, and spread out to dry on wooden boards. The silvery white inner lining, which is nearly pure gelatin, is then stripped off, and after being specially treated, is dried to form the commercial product. Common forms of Russian sturgeon isinglass are long staple, short staple, leaf book, and cake.

Today the most important use of isinglass is in the clarification of wines, particularly white wines. Formerly used as a fining agent for beer, it has been superseded by more modern filtration methods. A single ounce of isinglass will usually clarify 200 to 300 gallons of wine in 8 to 10 days. Isinglass was formerly used in the preparation of jellies, but other gelatins have taken its place. Isinglass is still used to a limited extent in the manufacture of court plaster, special cements, and waterproofing compounds.

The flesh of the sturgeon is firm but somewhat coarse compared to filet of sole or trout. Much depends on the nature of preparation, cooking, and accompanying sauces. One gastronomic authority has stated that an experienced cook can turn sturgeon meat into beef, mutton, pork, or poultry!

Perhaps with increasing interest in marine science and national means of managing our water resources, such versatile products as those of the sturgeon may be kept from vanishing. After surviving 300 million years, it would be ironic for this group of fishes to succumb to man, a species that has only existed a few million years.

Smelts for Breakfast

One member of the true smelt family, the eulachon of the Pacific Northwest, is so oily that the Indians of the Northwest call it the candlefish. After drying it out, they stick the head into a crude candlestick and set the tail afire. The fish burns for a considerable time, and rivals candlelight.

It is also used as a substitute for cod liver oil, yet the oil flavor is extremely attractive to the palate. The widespread acclaim of this small fish makes it one of the most favored delights of our table (it happens to be a relative of the salmon). When eaten fresh from the water, even the candlefish *(Thaleichthys pacificus)* is said to surpass all other fish in delicacy of taste.

Of the thirteen species of true smelt of the family Osmeridae, four are found in our northeastern waters. One of the most abundant is the capelin, or lodde, which is most plentiful north of Cape Cod. The eggs of the capelin that visit the Arctic shores wash up along the beaches there; as they hatch, the beach becomes a quivering mass of eggs and sand. The most widely known species of the smelt family is the common, or rainbow, smelt *(Osmerus mordax)*, which occurs naturally on the Atlantic coast from Labrador to Virginia and in the St. Lawrence River, Lake Champlain, Lake Ontario, and their associated streams.

About 1912 the smelt was introduced into the other Great Lakes where it thrived and became abundant. At first it was feared that the prolific little fish would eventually outnumber most of the native fishes

of the lakes and become a pest. Its damaging effect on fishes such as lake trout is still debated. Soon, however, a valuable commercial and sport fishery developed in the Great Lakes, and many millions of pounds of the fish are harvested.

Suddenly, in the early 1940s, almost all the smelts of the upper Great Lakes disappeared. The cause of the disappearance still remains somewhat of a mystery among fishery biologists, as there was little evidence of epidemic wiping them out at the time. Today we find that the smelt is slowly making a comeback in the Great Lakes.

Two limited local varieties of smelts occur in the New England area where they are landlocked in two small lakes. Wilton smelts are found in a pond of that name in Kennebec County, Maine. This is a smaller fish than the common smelt but with larger eyes. The second is the Cobessicontic smelt, found only in Cobessicontic Lake, Kennebec County, Maine. A stouter fish with smaller eyes than the smelts previously described, it was given the scientific name of *abbotti* in honor of C. C. Abbott, an ardent naturalist.

Smelts enter our rivers and brackish streams during the winter months for the purpose of spawning, and at this time they are sometimes caught in large quantities by seines and dip nets.

Today the smelt population has been reduced to a mere fraction of former times as a result of the large number of bays, rivers, and streams that have been made uninhabitable by industrial and municipal pollution. Yet the smelt fishery has long been an active one in New England. Captain John Smith wrote in 1622: "Of smelts there is such abundance that the Savages doe take them up the rivers with basket-like sieves." John Josselyn in 1677 remarked: "The Frostfish [smelt] is little bigger than a Gudgeon, and are taken in fresh brooks; when the waters are frozen they make a warm up hole in the Ice, about a half yard or a yard wide, to which the fish can go for air in great numbers. Then with small nets bound to a hoop with a staff fastened to it, fishermen take them out of the hole."

In the nineteenth century smelt fishermen were quite successful in New England waters during the winter and spring months. In 1853, D. H. Storer stated that in Watertown, Massachusetts, alone, about 9 million smelts were taken annually in scoop nets from the first of March to the first of June. Perley, writing in 1852, stated that on the Gulf coast of New Brunswick large quantities of smelts were used every season as manure, while at the fishing station at the Bay of Chaleur smelts were taken in seines and used as bait for cod.

Fisherman removing smelts from a gill net

According to a Massachusetts Fishery Report for 1870, smelts were so plentiful in the Back Bay area of Boston that distinguished merchants of Lower Beacon Street could be seen during early hours eagerly catching their breakfasts from their back doors.

The smelt is mostly an inshore fish. It is never found in waters more than a few fathoms in depth and never encountered beyond a mile or two from the nearest land. Confined to shoal waters, many smelts spend the whole year in river estuaries.

Smelts feed greedily on shrimp, copepods, and very small fishes. Bigelow and Schroeder (1953) describe smelts taken in the Sheepscot River in May packed full of young herring. Cunners, anchovies, sand launces, sticklebacks, and alewives have been identified from smelt stomachs at Woods Hole, Massachusetts.

Like shad, salmon, and alewives, smelts mature in salt water. In the fall they gather in river mouths and estuaries. During the winter months they generally stay in the lower regions of the rivers. In the early spring, as soon as the ice breaks up, mature smelts make their migration to freshwater streams to spawn. An adult smelt is about 7 to 9 inches in length and usually weighs from 1 to 6 ounces. A 2-ounce mature fish may deposit up to 50,000 eggs.

Efforts have been made for years to replenish the diminishing smelt population by using hatchery-reared stock. The Palmer Massachusetts Fish Hatchery has had some success in attempts to stock certain rivers and streams with eggs or fry.

During the cold winter months, a few hardy anglers still attempt to catch smelt with hook and line. Very small hooks are used, and the best baits are shrimp, angle worms or sea worms, and small mummichogs.

Almost translucent with an ash-colored back, white sides and belly, feeding smelts are easily captured by a quick but not too forcible jerk to set the hook. The fishes are too small to make a long fight and too feeble to require a heavy reel. However, they offer invigorating sport on a cool brisk day.

The smelt's meat is soft, white, and sweet with no bones but the spine and ribs, which are so small and tender that they are sometimes eaten too. Some fishermen say that smelt has a slight cucumber smell.

The best way to prepare smelts is to have them split and broiled and garnished with butter, salt, and pepper. If fried after being cleaned, scaled, and dried, smelts should be lightly rolled in powdered cracker crumbs or meal and turned rapidly in hot butter.

The Day the Tilefish Died: March 1, 1882

Of all the fish caught off our coasts, the large and brilliantly colored tilefish probably has the most incredible history.

Strangely enough, the tilefish was unknown until May 1879, when Captain William H. Kerby of the schooner *William V. Hutchins* caught the first specimen south of Nantucket Lightship in 150 fathoms of water while working cod lines. When his crew found that the plentiful fishes made an unusually tasty meal, some of the specimens were salted down and taken to Gloucester where a portion of the catch was smoked.

Gourmets quickly recognized the fish's merits; some rated it the equal of pompano. It is delicious baked, boiled, or fried, and makes a fine steaming chowder. The tilefish was on its way to becoming a favorite. Nobody imagined that within a few years after its discovery, it was to be knocked almost completely out of existence.

Since neither Captain Kerby and his crew nor the fishermen at the dock in Gloucester had ever seen the fish before, Kerby sent a specimen to the U.S. National Museum. The museum declared it to be a new genus and species belonging to a tropical family inhabiting the Gulf of Mexico. George Brown Goode and Tarleton H. Bean gave it the name of *Lopholatilus chamaeleonticeps*, which means "the crested tilus with a head like a chameleon." Fishermen understandably shortened the name to tilefish.

Catches of the "new" fish by other boats prompted the U.S. Bureau

of Fisheries to send out the newly commissioned 157-foot research vessel *Fish Hawk* to study it off southern New England in the summers of 1880 and 1881. The coal-burning, twin-screw *Fish Hawk* made four survey trips to the edge of the continental shelf in 1880 and nine in 1881. Tilefish were found to be plentiful along the shelf from George's Bank to Delaware and as abundant as cod on the northern banks. There were enough tilefish to support an important new fishery. Everyone was happy.

Those who studied its habitat found that the fish occupied a very specific part of the ocean—a narrow band along the outer edge of the continental shelf where the sea floor is bathed by warm water from the Gulf Stream. The temperature of the water here ranges from 47 to 50 degrees F., with very little variation from season to season. As far as is known, the tilefish never leaves this limited strip off the coast to venture into the cooler water of the landward shoals or the frigid depths of the Atlantic abyss.

Apparently this inability to tolerate changes in environment brought near-annihilation to the tilefish just three years after its discovery. On March 3, 1882, Captain Lawrence of the bark *Plymouth* of Windsor, Nova Scotia, sailing to New York, recorded the following description in a report to the Fisheries Commission Board:

> We were sailing off George's Bank, and about daylight on Sunday morning the mate came down into the cabin and said that the bark was passing through a lot of dead tilefish and wanted to know if we should get some of them. I went out on deck and saw that the water all around us and for miles back of us was filled with these fish. Their gills were red, and upon scooping up some of them I found that they were hard, showing that they had not been dead very long. From six o'clock in the morning until five o'clock in the evening, we were passing through this school of fish, and as we were sailing at the rate of six knots we went through 69 miles of them.

A week later the brig *Rachel Coney* sighted the dead fishes 75 miles south-southwest from the lightship on the south shoal of Nantucket and sailed through them for 40 miles. Ole Jorgensen of the Norwegian bark *Sidon* reported that in latitude 40 degrees north and longitude 71 degrees west there were dead and dying fish as far as the eye could see—"thousands of them, even millions." This was on March 14. A week later, the schooner *Navarino* sailed through them for a distance of 150 miles.

Tabulating these and other accounts, the range of destruction was found to extend over an area 170 miles long and 25 miles wide, covering at least 4000 square miles! The Bureau of Fisheries estimated that almost 1½ billion tilefish perished. It was then believed that the entire species had been wiped out.

The disappearance of the tilefish was so devastating that fish surveys by the U.S. Fish Commission off southern New England in 1882 through 1887 did not yield a single tilefish! In 1884 the government search was especially diligent but met with no success.

Scientists offered this explanation: Tilefish are bottom dwellers in about 100 fathoms of warm water. In 1882, the Gulf Stream, near the edge of which the tilefish dwell, moved farther out to sea, leaving them in cold water. They could not follow the shifting stream, as the bottom of the ocean drops abruptly near the 100-fathom line. Consequently, almost the entire population, unable to remain in the Gulf Stream, was killed.

Whether this explanation is correct is not certain. In any case, no tilefish was caught anywhere for approximately ten years, although frequent searches were made. Then, in 1892, they were found again. In that year, the *Grampus* took 8 fish; in the following year, 53 others were caught. As the years passed, tilefish reestablished themselves rapidly, and by 1915 they were plentiful enough to become popular again on the market. From July 1, 1915, to July 1, 1918, 11.5 million pounds were landed. In 1950, almost 2.5 million pounds were landed on the Atlantic coast, with a value of more than $150,000. Annual landings now average about 2 million pounds.

Tilefish have been reported up to 50 pounds, but they average between 15 and 25 pounds and are from 2 to 4 feet long. They have been found from the Banks of Nova Scotia down to the Gulf of Mexico, although they are most plentiful in water from 50 to 80 fathoms in the region from Nantucket to Cape May, New Jersey.

The tilefish is easy to recognize because its dazzling hues call to mind a tropical fish. It feeds on a variety of bottom-dwelling invertebrates, chiefly crabs. It will take almost any kind of bait but apparently prefers cut menhaden. Mature females taken in July and August are full of ripe eggs at spawning time.

Recent observations of the fishery resources at the edge of the continental shelf in the Woods Hole submarine *Alvin* resulted in an interesting discovery with regard to tilefish habits. Richard A. Cooper of the National Oceanic and Atmospheric Administration's lab at Woods Hole, Massachusetts, observed from the minisub that tilefish at the edge of the shelf lived in small caves that the fish had dug into the sea-floor sediments.

The tilefish has been doing well in its delicately balanced watery climate since the devastating year 1882, but no one can predict when the vagaries of the Gulf Stream will play another fateful trick on it.

The Coelacanth—Fossil Resurrected from the Dead

One of the greatest biological discoveries of this century occurred on December 22, 1938, in the Indian Ocean, three miles off the African coast near the mouth of the Chalumna River, twenty miles southwest of East London, Union of South Africa. The fishing trawler under Captain Goosen had a meager catch; while heading into port for Christmas, it decided to trawl on a 40-fathom bank they were passing over. Their catch was mostly sharks, some marketable food fish, and a strange, blue, 5-foot-long fish that became one of the greatest catches of all time.

Captain Goosen and his crew noted that the 127-pound fish was unlike any they had seen before. It had large bony scales and strange lobed fins. After it was emptied from the trawl net, the fish became a vicious brute, snapping its jaws fiercely. When Captain Goosen examined it and touched its side, the fish heaved itself up and snapped its formidable tooth-lined mouth at the captain's hand. The hardy fish lay twisting on the deck in the hot African sun for three hours before it expired.

As was his custom with strange fish, Captain Goosen ordered the crew to put the curious creature on one side of the deck for the East London Natural History Museum.

When the fishing boat tied up to the dock in East London, a phone call was made to the young curator of the East London Museum,

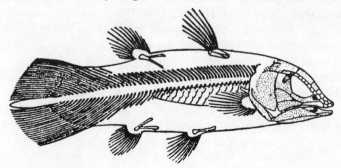

Marjorie Courtenay-Latimer. The youthful curator summoned a taxi and went down to the wharf several miles away with Enoch, her native assistant. When she arrived at dockside, the Captain had already left the boat, but the crew showed her the large, heavily scaled blue fish. She examined its mouth and fins and asked one of the old fishermen if he had ever seen a fish like this before. He said that in his thirty years of fishing he had never encountered a fish like this with its armlike fins. Latimer thought it somewhat resembled the air-breathing lungfish and realized that it was a significant find.

The problem was now to get the strange fish to the museum. It was a hot day, and the heavy fish was starting to smell. Latimer had a difficult time persuading a taxi driver to take the odorous fish into his cab even though she had brought along old bags to put on the cab floor. Imagine the female curator and native assistant struggling to get the most valuable biological specimen of the century into a taxi! They managed to get the fish to the museum; unfortunately, there were no jars or tubs to hold such a large fish. Adequate formaldehyde or alcohol to preserve it was not available. The local cold-storage company and funeral parlor refused to store it because of its odor. The fish was unlisted in all the reference books at the museum. Realizing that the find must be preserved for science at all costs, Latimer and her helper took the fish in a wheelbarrow to an elderly taxidermist nearby, who mounted specimens for the museum. The fish's skin and skull were saved and stuffed, and the smelly internal organs were discarded.

Latimer sent a letter with a description and sketch of the fish to the late J. L. B. Smith of Rhodes University. Smith was honorary curator of fish for the East London Museum and a world authority on African fishes. Unfortunately, Professor and Mrs. Smith had gone to their cottage laboratory at Knysna, 350 miles away from East London, for the holiday season. Smith received Latimer's letter over a week and a half after it was sent. He immediately recognized the significance of the discovery from Latimer's sketch and description. Smith recognized that in East London was a recently caught fish that had been believed to have been extinct for millions of years.

From his out-of-the-way location Smith sent a cable to Latimer to preserve the whole fish. The next day, after a three-hour wait, Smith was able to speak with Latimer, only to find that the head and skin had been saved by the taxidermist but that the gills and internal organs had been discarded. Smith thought the soft parts ought to be salvaged from the city rubbish heap, but was dismayed to learn that the garbage had already been dumped at sea.

Mr. Center, the taxidermist, had done a reasonably good job of mounting the remains of the fish with its lobed fins outstretched and its mouth open. On February 8, 1939, Smith left Knysna a week early and got his first glimpse of the mounted fish in Latimer's study on February 16, 1939. Professor Smith's description of his first face-to-face contact with the living fossil is as follows:

> We went straight to the Museum. Miss Latimer was out for the moment, the caretaker ushered us into the inner room and there was the —Coelacanth, yes, God! Although I had come prepared, that first sight hit me like a white-hot blast and made me feel shaky and queer, my body tingled. I stood as if stricken to stone. Yes, there was not a shadow of doubt, scale by scale, bone by bone, fin by fin, it was a true Coelacanth. It could have been one of those creatures of 200 million years ago come alive again. It's true! A real coelacanth! And yet all coelacanths died out sixty million years ago!

The remarkable living fossil confronting Smith and his wife was a direct descendant of an ancient lobe-finned group of pikes that had split off from the main freshwater stock and become marine. Coelacanths developed 300 million years ago in Devonian times and were believed to have died out with the dinosaurs 60 million years ago at the end of the Cretaceous period. The freshwater lobe fins, to which the coelacanths are closely related, were the direct ancestors of the first four-legged vertebrates, the amphibians. And the amphibians then gave rise to reptiles, birds, and mammals.

Paleontologists first described fossil coelacanths in 1839 from specimens preserved in rocks from strata found six miles south of Durham, England. Fossil coelacanths have been discovered during the past century in the sedimentary rocks of Scotland, Germany, Greenland, the Connecticut River valley, and in excavations for a new Princeton University library in New Jersey.

For Smith, who had identified and named more than 100 new species of fishes, this was his greatest discovery. It was an event that could be likened to seeing a dinosaur walk down the street—for here was a contemporary of the dinosaur that was thought to have become extinct with them, found swimming in the Indian Ocean. This close cousin to the direct ancestors of land animals, a fossil living relatively unchanged for almost 300 million years, was given the scientific name *Latimeria chalumnae*.

The genus name *Latimeria* was selected to honor Marjorie Courtenay-Latimer, who in spite of considerable difficulty preserved the fish for posterity. The species name *chalumnae* was chosen to commemorate the river near which the fish was captured.

Smith wrote a description of the new fish that he sent along with photographs to scientific circles in London. A special meeting of the Linnaean Society was called at Burlington House. The world's leading experts on recent and fossil fishes were present to examine the evidence. The scientists included J. R. Norman, curator of recent fishes, and E. I. White, keeper of fossil fishes at the British Museum, D. M. S. Watson of University College London, an outstanding authority on early vertebrates, and Sir Arthur Smith Woodward, a world authority on fossil fishes. The scholars verified and authenticated Smith's account and approved its publication. The event soon became a major scientific discovery from London to Boston to Australia. Textbooks on fishes and fossils had to be updated and revised around the world as a result of the discovery of this fish.

The first modern coelacanth specimen left many unanswered questions about its structure. Significant questions regarding its respiration, digestion, and reproduction were left unresolved.

Smith began a fourteen-year quest off the eastern coast of Africa to obtain additional coelacanths. Thousands of illustrated leaflets promising rewards to fishermen in Portuguese, French, and English were prepared and distributed by Smith. A reward of 100 pounds sterling served as an added incentive to report the strange fish when it took a hook or appeared in the nets.

Eventually, on December 20, 1952 Ahmed Hussein, a fisherman of Comoni, a port of Anjouan Island in the Grand Comoro archipelago, caught a strange 5-foot-long fish. Ahmed was fishing in 120 feet of water about 200 yards from shore. He took the fish home and brought it to the fish market the next day. He was about to sell the big fish when another fisherman exclaimed that this was *Le Poisson*, the fish with the great reward that everyone was looking for. On the other side of the island was Captain Eric Hunt, a friend of Professor and Mrs. Smith, who had passed out the reward leaflets. The fish was hauled that long, hot day 25 miles over the mountainous island to the other side where Captain Hunt had anchored his schooner. Hunt immediately recognized the fish as the second coelacanth to be caught in modern times. Hunt had only salt as a preservative, so he had the natives make incisions in the fish into which salt was placed. The fish was then totally immersed in salt. Hunt immediately set out for a nearby physician, Dr. LeCoteur, who helped him inject 5 liters of formalin into the fish. The following telegram was sent off to Smith:

> *Have Specimen Coelacanth Five Feet Treated Formalin . . . Advise or Send Plane Reply—Hunt Dzaoudzi Camores.*

Smith flew to Anjouan on a plane supplied by the South African prime minister. He obtained the second coelacanth, smelly but with all the soft parts preserved for anatomical studies.

Worldwide publicity greeted the discovery of a second coelacanth. The French government was dismayed at having foreign scientists visit their oceanic possession and usurp the rare fish specimen. To counter the activity of the renowned South African professor who was "stealing" scientific glory from the French Republic, the French minister of overseas territories notified the administrator of the Grand Comoro Islands that *all* future coelacanths captured in French territorial waters would henceforth be exclusively under the control of French scientists. The French government went further and designated Jacques Millot, a specialist in spiders and other arachnida of the Paris Museum of Natural History and the marine laboratory at Nosey-Be off the northwest coast of Madagascar, to be in charge of all future coelacanths taken in French territorial waters. All foreign scientists were refused access to Comoran waters by the French.

On September 24, 1953 Houmadi Hossani, an Anjouan fisherman, caught *notre coelacanthe*, as the triumphant French called it. Hossani's specimen, coelacanth #3, weighed 83 pounds and was 4 feet 3 inches long. Hossani caught the fish on hook and line at 11:00 P.M. He recognized the coelacanth immediately by the native name *Kombessa*. He abandoned the rest of his catch and rowed to shore with his prize as fast as he could. He carried the fish home. Leaving his wife to guard the fish, which was still alive, he went to get the village physician, Dr. Garrouste. Garrouste hurried to the fish in the town ambulance. At 1:00 A.M. the fish was carried alive into the doctor's laboratories where it died and was preserved with formaldehyde. At 6:30 the next morning the preserved fish was flown from Anjouan to the Oceanographic Institute of Madagascar. It was a flawless specimen, well preserved, and was sent on to Paris for further study.

Coelacanth #4 was captured on January 29, 1954. The next day an even larger fish was brought into Grand Comoro Island Administrator Georges Savignac. Two days later an additional coelacanth was obtained. It turned out that the living fossil was caught on rare occasions by local fishermen under the name of *Kombessa*, or *Combessa*. After it was dried and salted, the natives considered it a good food fish. The thick, armorlike scales of the coelacanth were used as abrasives by residents of Anjouan in the repair of flat bicycle tires and tubes.

The capture of additional coelacanths prompted Millot to double the reward for the capture of a living fish. His efforts resulted in the capture of the eighth specimen, a live female, on November 12, 1954.

This fish was pulled in from waters 840 feet in depth by Zema Ben Said Mohamed, assisted by Madi Bacari, fishing in a canoelike pirogue. The fish was taken about 3000 feet offshore with a baited line. It took a half hour to haul in, and great care was exercised in keeping it alive. A rope was passed through the fish's mouth and gill cover before the creature was towed to shore. When the fish was brought into inshore waters, it was decided to sink a whaleboat in several feet of water by removing its bung. The fish was placed alive into the 22-foot-long water-filled boat. A net covered the top of the whaler to prevent the fish from escaping. The greenish yellow luminescence of its eyes was very pronounced and could be seen at considerable distance. The color of the 90-pound, 56-inch-long fish was grayish blue. The fish swam in the sunken hull for 17½ hours before it died. Observers of the living coelacanth noted the remarkable mobility of its lobelike fins, which appeared to move with ease in all directions. It was believed that the change in the depth of its habitat, the struggle when it was captured, and the bright sunlight led to the fish's death. Another female coelacanth was captured January 1, 1960.

Examination of female coelacanths revealed about sixty birdlike eggs. The gravid females contain clusters of eggs in various stages of development, such as are observed in a chicken. One observer who tasted a coelacanth egg said that it tasted like a chicken's egg.

In 1955 the French refused to grant permission to an expedition from the San Francisco Steinhart Aquarium to try to capture a living coelacanth. When the French withdrew politically from Madagascar and the Grand Comoro Islands in 1960, Mrs. L. B. Smith estimated that they had collected about forty coelacanth specimens. The French had offered the Comoran natives monetary rewards for each specimen caught. To the natives, catching a coelacanth was like winning the Sweepstakes.

By 1976, 86 coelacanths had been captured from the waters of the Indian Ocean. These living relics of ancient epochs ranged in size from 43 to 209 pounds. They were taken in waters from about 120 to 2000 feet in depth in the Indian Ocean, between the months of September and February.

One Comoro fisherman, Ahmed Hussein, has caught several coelacanths. His first fish was coelacanth #2 taken in 1952 and almost sold for food at the local fish market. On December 11, 1964, using a hook and line baited with octopus, in 450 feet of water almost a mile

offshore from Anjouan, Hussein caught a 4½-foot-long coelacanth that weighed 78 pounds. This fish was preserved with formalin and deep frozen. Arrangements were made with grants from the U.S. National Science Foundation, U.S. Atomic Energy Commission, and U.S. Public Health Service so that this perfectly preserved fresh specimen could have chemical analysis tests made of its tissues at the Department of Biophysics and Nuclear Medicine of the University of California at Los Angeles. Examination of the coelacanth's muscles, liver, and spleen showed a chemical similarity to the organs of certain deep-water fish that were in no way related to coelacanths.

Scientists are still trying to unravel the mysteries of the coelacanth's durability through millions of years. Evidence indicates its armorlike scales have helped it evade predators. Its ability to adjust to variations in sea depth and water temperature have proved valuable in survival. Its agility in using its lobed pelvic and pectoral fins like legs or flippers in order to walk or creep on the sea floor to stalk food has also been of advantage.

At the beginning of the last quarter of the twentieth century, marine scientists look forward to obtaining new knowledge of ancient life forms by obtaining fertile coelacanth eggs. Observation of the developing eggs and juveniles would provide not only insight into coelacanth development, but also clues to the structure and form of its freshwater lobe-fin ancestors.

In September 1975 a startling discovery in coelacanth life history unfolded at the American Museum of Natural History in New York City. A dissection of the museum's 5-foot 3-inch, 150-pound coelacanth, captured in January 1962 off Anjouan Island, revealed that the preserved specimen was a pregnant female. Careful dissection by Curator James W. Atz and his associates uncovered five advanced young baby coelacanths, each about a foot long, lying free in the right oviduct. The five baby coelacanths resembled miniature adults, and their location confirmed the fact that coelacanths give birth to living young.

Around the world, icthyologists look forward to the time when captured coelacanths can be raised in captivity to learn more about their habits by direct observation. Coelacanths living in captivity would also ensure that this survivor of the dawn of animal life will not be destroyed in our lifetime.

Cod, a Story of Overkill

On March 17, 1784, John Rowe, a Boston merchant, introduced a motion in the state legislature: "Leave be given to hang up the representation of a cod-fish in the room where the House sits, as a memorial of the importance of the Cod-Fishery to the welfare of the Commonwealth." The motion was carried. The effigy of a codfish, carved out of pine, was exhibited opposite the Speaker's chair in the chamber of the House of Representatives in the Massachusetts statehouse in Boston, where it hangs to this day. Many years later, an aluminum codfish was placed in the senate chamber, also as an emblem of the state's fishing industry.

Probably no other item of commerce played a more important part in the early economics of the United States and Canada than the cod. In fact, during the century prior to the landing of the Pilgrims on our shores, over 300 French, Basque, Portuguese, Spanish, and English fishing vessels traveled across the Atlantic to Newfoundland waters to catch codfish. Captain John Smith, trying to entice settlers to the New World, wrote, "And is it not a pretty sport to pull up two pence, six

pence, and twelve pence as fast as you can haul and vere a line; he is a very bad fisher who cannot kill in one day one, two or three hundred cods, which dressed and dried be hold for ten shillings a hundred. . . . Therefore honorable and worthy countrymen, let not the meanness of the word fish distaste you, for it will afford as good gold as the Mines of Guiana or Potassie, with less hazard and charge, and more certainty and facility."

The principal location of cod fishing in North Atlantic waters is a great shoal known as the Grand Bank, lying about 100 miles off the southeast coast of Newfoundland. The Grand Bank is also known as the Great Banks and covers an area about the size of Pennsylvania. The Bank is about 300 miles long, lying less than 100 fathoms below sea level, and projects southeast from Newfoundland toward the center of the Atlantic. This region is rich in plankton brought in by oceanic currents, making the area one of the favorite haunts of the capelin, a sardinelike fish that is a favorite food of the cod. Many invertebrates, such as mollusks and crustaceans, also abound in this region.

The Atlantic cod, *Gadus morhua*, described by Linnaeus in 1758, is found in the North Atlantic around Greenland, Iceland, and Spitzbergen, and south to our North Carolina coast. It is especially abundant on banks and ledges such as Grand Bank, George's Bank, Brown Bank, Grand Manan, Jeffrey's Ledge, Cashes Ledge, and varied rocky areas off the coast.

The cod is omnivorous, feeding on both plant and animal organisms. Young cod browse on Irish moss and other algae in addition to their regular diet of copepods. Mollusks form a large part of the adult cod's diet, and if both large and small shellfish are available, the cod appears to choose the large mollusk. Sea clams are eaten in large numbers, being swallowed whole. The acids in the fish's stomach digest the meat. Empty clam shells have been found in piles of six or seven, stacked like empty dessert dishes in the stomachs of cod or expelled and stacked on the ocean bottom. Cod sometimes eat crabs, shrimp, lobsters, sea urchins, brittle stars, sea cucumbers, sand worms, and squid. Also they feed on almost any small species of fish they encounter, including herring, shad, mackerel, launces, capelins, menhaden, alewives, whiting, and even young cod.

The *Gloucester Telegraph* for May 6, 1857 tells of James Osborne, who, on dressing a 60-pound codfish, found it had swallowed two full-grown ducks that still had most of their feathers.

Many foreign objects, which could hardly be classified as nutritious, have been taken from cod stomachs, including old books, rope, oil cans, scissors, rocks, corncobs, rubber dolls, parts of old boots, a cigarette case, and false teeth. The *Boston Journal* for July 9, 1871, tells of a St. Johns, Newfoundland, fisherman who found a wedding ring in a cod's entrails that belonged to a woman who was lost on the steamship *Anglo Saxon*, which had been wrecked off Chance Cove, Newfoundland, ten years earlier. The lucky fisherman received a reward of 50 pounds sterling for returning the highly prized memento to the missing lady's son.

The coloration of cod generally ranges from greenish to red-brown, depending on the habitat of the individual. Cod living in the vicinity of kelp and other seaweed generally tend to have a darker color resembling that of the weeds. Cod are distinguished by mottled spots on their sides, three dorsal fins, two anal fins, a broom-shaped tail, a pale lateral line, and a distinctive barbel on the chin. They are found in depths to 250 fathoms, but most fishing for them is done between 10 and 75 fathoms.

Codfish vary greatly in size and weight. According to Jordan and Evermann (1896), the largest cod recorded from New England waters weighed 211½ pounds and was over 6 feet long. This enormous cod was taken on a trawl off the northern Massachusetts coast in May 1895. Another codfish, which weighed 136 pounds when eviscerated, and probably 180 pounds alive, was taken in 1838 on George's Bank. Goode (1884) mentions five codfish taken off the Massachusetts coast during the nineteenth century which ranged between 100 and 160 pounds. In the twentieth century I have been unable to find any record of codfish over 90 pounds taken off the New England coast. Today, in the Gulf of Maine, a large codfish is one in the vicinity of 40 pounds.

Cod are marketed in three distinct size categories: scrod are generally young cod weighing from 1½ to 2½ pounds; so-called market cod run from 2½ to 10 pounds; and large cod may be any weight over 10 pounds. Sometimes cod 40 pounds and over are classified as whale cod.

The codfish turns out to be one of our most prolific fishes. The ovaries from a 21-pound cod have been computed to contain 2,700,000 eggs, and those of a 75-pound cod 9,100,000 eggs. The eggs are small, about 1/18 inch in diameter, with about 227,000 eggs making a quart.

After fertilization, the eggs hatch in about 17 days, and in 3 years the cod are fully mature. On George's Bank young cod grow to about 7½ inches their first year, and reach about 15 to 16 inches at 2 years of age. There is generally a spawning migration to inshore waters during the winter months. Tagging has shown that cod that spend the summer on Nantucket Shoals have a mass migration to the coasts of southern New England, New York, and New Jersey for spawning. In the spring they return to Nantucket Shoals. The longest cod migration on record is that of an individual tagged in Iceland that crossed the Atlantic and was recaptured in Newfoundland 2000 miles from its point of origin.

Today, in addition to cod landed by otter trawlers, they are taken with lines, gill nets, floating traps, and pound nets. Cod are marketed principally as fillets, either fresh or frozen. We also have shredded codfish, codfish flakes, salt cod, pickled cod, green or smoked cod, and pickled cod tongues. Although cod are still relatively numerous, their populations in no way compare to the vast hordes harvested in the nineteenth century.

St. Peter's Thumbprint on the Haddock

Long familiar to fishermen on both sides of the Atlantic, haddock was known as *haddoke* in fifteenth-century Middle English. Irish for haddock is *codog; hadot* and *hadon* are old French names for this species, and sometimes it was given the name of *egrefin;* the Scotch know this fish as *haddie;* the Germans call it *schellfish.*

Haddock occur in greatest abundance in the North Sea, off Iceland, Newfoundland, Nova Scotia, and George's Bank. In North American waters, they occur generally from the Gulf of St. Lawrence to Nantucket Shoals. In a few isolated instances they have appeared as far south as Cape Hatteras.

Preferring a bottom made up of smooth hard sand, gravel, pebbles or broken shells, the haddock, *Melanogrammus aeglefinus*, is a purplish gray on its back and lighter on its belly and lower sides. A member

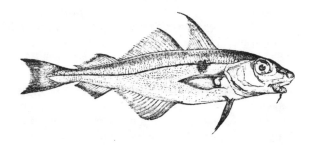

of the cod family Gadidae, the haddock differs from the codfish by virtue of the fact that its lateral line, which runs along each side from head to tail, is dark, while the cod's is light-colored. In addition, the haddock possesses a dark blob of coloration on each side just over the pectoral fin, which adds to its distinctiveness.

This blotch on the fish's side has given rise to the superstition among certain European fishermen that this species was the one from which St. Peter took tribute money, the dark spots resulting from the impression of the Apostle's thumb and fingerprint. This superstition is also associated with the dark spot on the European John Dory, *Zeus faber.* Nevertheless, the haddock and its relatives do not occur in the Sea of Galilee. For some reason, the dark spots are also known as the "devil's thumbmark."

The haddock is strictly a bottom-dwelling fish, rarely rising more than a fathom or two from the bottom; its close relative the pollack swims at all depths, chasing small food fishes. Haddock generally live in deeper water than the codfish, with the greatest abundance occurring at from 150 to 450 feet. Haddock are extremely rare in shallow or shoal waters.

Food for the haddock consists chiefly of the bottom fauna of the area in which they dwell. Bigelow and Schroeder report haddock feeding on such varied organisms as brittle starfish; bivalve mollusks; small worms; amphipods; hermit, spider, and common crabs; shrimp; sea urchins; sand dollars; and sea cucumbers.

W. F. Clapp has reported 68 different species of mollusks found in the stomachs of 1500 haddock from George's Bank. Haddock also prey on squid and various small fishes such as herring, mackerel, and silver hake when the opportunity presents itself.

In New England waters, haddock mature at 3 or 4 years of age and weigh 2 to 3 pounds. The principal spawning grounds appear to be the eastern end of George's Bank and South Channel. Spawning occurs from February to May. The number of eggs produced range from 150,000 to 2 million, depending on the age and size of the fish. The eggs are about $1/16$ inch in diameter and usually hatch in 2 to 4 weeks, drifting with the tide and currents. The fish are about $1/10$ inch long when they hatch. When they are 3 months old and reach a length of $1\frac{1}{4}$ inches, they resemble adult haddock and head to the ocean bottom for the rest of their life span.

Haddock are much smaller fish than cod. The largest on record is an Iceland specimen that was 44 inches long and weighed 37 pounds. In the autumn of 1949, a 30-pounder was caught on Le Havre Bank and landed at the Boston Fish Pier. In New England waters, the fish average about 20 inches, weighing from $2\frac{1}{2}$ to 3 pounds.

In recent years, considerable effort has been made by U.S. Fish and Wildlife Service researchers to chart the migration of haddock through tagging. Results of these studies indicate a seasonal migration from the South Channel area in the springtime north along the Massachusetts and Maine coasts, some fish going as far as the Bay of Fundy. A reverse movement back down the coast to South Channel, and from there out to George's Bank, occurs in fall and winter. These seasonal movements appear to follow the fish's search for favorable feeding, spawning, and temperature conditions. Haddock avoid water colder than 33 degrees F. and stay away from waters warmer than 52 degrees F.

The George's Bank–South Channel area, extending for 200 miles east of Cape Cod, has been the most productive haddock ground since the beginning of the U.S. haddock fishery in the mid-1800s. In 1930 over 80 percent of the New England catch came from these grounds, with about 16 percent coming from Nova Scotia. In 1940 these grounds contributed less than 70 percent, and the Nova Scotia about 26 percent. As the fish have become scarcer on George's Bank, fishermen have been forced to make longer trips to the Nova Scotia grounds, increasing operating costs.

The haddock catch has declined greatly since 1929, reflecting a decrease in the abundance of the species. A smaller size of fish is also now being captured.

Studies by the Fish and Wildlife Service, under the direction of William C. Herrington, indicate that the use of larger-meshed otter trawls would greatly reduce the number of immature haddock taken. By protecting the baby scrod haddock (fish less than 1½ pounds) until they have finished the period of most rapid growth, increased abundance and production could be obtained.

In 1953, regulations were passed that required haddock fishermen operating in certain areas to use nets having a mesh of 4½ inches or larger. In 1957 these regulations were extended to codfish in the same area. These regulations, recommended by the International Commission for the Northwest Atlantic Fisheries, were based on research by the U.S. Fish and Wildlife Service in cooperation with research agencies of Canada and several European countries.

A white-meat, firm-flesh fish with a mild and pleasant flavor, haddock is especially suitable for filleting and quick freezing. In addition, it may be smoked or salted, made into fish flakes, or used in fish chowders.

The smoking of haddock originated about the middle of the eighteenth century at Findon, Scotland. The smoked haddock originally cured in Findon were called Findon haddocks. Later, this was shortened to Findon haddies, and finally abbreviated to finnan haddies. About 1850, the industry was introduced into the United States at Rockport, Massachusetts. However, it did not become important here until 1875. By 1919, the industry had grown to such an extent in New England that over 13 million pounds of haddock were smoked that year. Today, some haddock is still smoked and sold canned, as finnan haddie.

8

Good Companions

Companions, good and bad, among the fishes range from true parasites such as the sea lamprey and candirú to food sharers like the remora and pilotfish. There are also the fish cleaners, the goby, butterfly fish, and wrasses, that remove attached parasitic worms and crustaceans from the skin of other fishes. Certain fish associate with invertebrates, such as the damselfish which lives without harm among the toxic tentacles of the sea anemone, the slender fierasfer hiding in the body cavity of sea cucumbers, and the pearlfish which is at home within the shell of pearl oysters.

The Remora—Seagoing Hitchhiker

The ancients knew the remora, the fish that attaches itself to others. Pliny gave it the power of retarding or stopping ships. The legends remind me of one of those surrounding the octopus. Although the story of the remora is an old one, it is among those that stand retelling. Its very novelty seems to give it freshness.

Of the suborder *Discocephali* (from the Greek meaning "disk head"), the remora, also called shark sucker, pilot sucker, and sucking fish, is found in all the warm seas and visits our northeastern coast in the summer. The powerful sucking disk, as indicated by the Greek name, is on top of the head.

Remoras are found attached to swordfish, sharks, rays, sunfish, and porpoises. One species—there are a number—is found on larger

A remora attaching itself to a sea turtle

sharks exclusively. This is the pegador of Cuba, a 2-foot free rider.
Different species vary in length from 1 to 3 feet. The mouth is wide, with
lower jaw protruding. Small, pointed teeth are found in the roof of the
mouth and sometimes on the tongue. The kind that specializes in hoist-
ing a ride on whales is called the whalesucker.

The interesting feature of the remora is, of course, the disk. With
it, the fish is able to attach itself to any surface by raising a series of
transverse plates, or laminae, which resemble the slots of venetian
blinds. When the slots are raised, a row of vacuum chambers is created
between the remora and the object, causing strong adhesion. To remove

a remora, it is necessary to pull the fish forward, lowering the plates. A backward pull only strengthens the attachment because the plates are raised even higher.

In a test of strength, remoras were once placed in pails of water in the New York Aquarium, and each was lifted by the tail. One specimen lifted a pail of 21 pounds. Another had the power to lift 40 pounds.

The disk is a modification of the spiny dorsal fin of other fishes. In the remora the spines are bent outward in opposite directions and divided in two, forming a transverse plate. The transformation of the dorsal fin into the disk is shown in fossil remains that have a very narrow disk behind the head.

Fishermen catching large sharks and rays frequently find one or two remoras attached. However, once out of the water the remoras drop off their hosts. They are not always on the external surface. Sometimes they are inside the mouth or beneath the gill covers of swordfish, tuna, and oceanic sunfish. On occasion they have been found deep inside the mouth of the gigantic manta ray.

There appear to be three reasons for the remora's attachment to a larger fish: (1) the host serves to protect the small remora from its enemies; (2) the remora picks up morsels of food left over from its host's meals; and (3) the remora receives transportation to new feeding grounds. The remora is not a parasite itself.

The normal food of the remora consists principally of other fish, herring, sardines, and small portions of its host's meals. Once it sights suitable prey, it lets go of its host and catches its dinner. When filled up, the remora will look about for another large fish and attach itself. It will then digest its meal in comfort and seclusion. This may be attributable to the remora's occasional parasite-cleaning activities. Curiously, sharks don't seem to object to these companions and messmates. This writer knows of no record of the remains of a remora being found in a shark's stomach.

The remora was the subject of imaginative terror to the Greeks and Romans. Pliny wrote, "Why should our fleets and armadas at sea make such turrets on the walls and forecastles, when one little fish [the remora] is able to arrest and stay our goodly and tall ships?" The common name is derived from the Latin meaning "holding back" and refers to the mythical power of the fish to slow down ships.

The remora is used by people of various tropical countries as a means of capturing fishes. In northeastern Australia, Malaya, China, Zanzibar, and Madagascar it is used by the native populace to capture turtles. The aborigines of the Barrier Reef of Australia fasten a line to the remora by means of a hole made in the base of the tail fin. When a turtle is located, the remora is scrubbed with dry sand to remove the slime and excite the fish. It is then released and immediately attaches itself to a turtle. As long as the line is taut, the remora is unable to let go of anything it clings to. Turtles and fishes up to 100 pounds have been captured in this manner.

One of the first fishes described by the early discoverers of North America was the remora. A graphic description of the way the West Indians used the remora in capturing other fish was described in Ogilby's *America,* published in 1671. The event takes place in the Caribbean.

> Columbus from hence [Cuba] proceeding on farther westward, discovered a fruitful Coast, verging the Mouth of a River, whose Waters runs Boyling into the Sea. Somewhat further he saw very strange Fishes, especially of the Guarican [remora], not unlike an Eel, but with an extraordinary great Head, over which hangs a skin like a Bag. This Fish is the Natives Fisher; for having a Line or handsome Cord fastened about him, so as soon as the Turtel, or any other of his Prey, comes above Water, they give him Line; whereupon the Guarican, like an arrow out of a Bowe, shoots toward the other Fish, and then gathering the Mouth of the Bag on his Head like a Pursenet holds them so fast, that he lets not loose till hal'd up out of the Water.

The color ranges from a light reddish brown to a dark gray. It is a voracious creature and will take a hook eagerly if baited with fresh fish. When hooked, the remora is not easily landed, for as soon as it feels the prick of a fishhook and the pull of a line, it darts to the bottom or the boat's keel and affixes itself with such tenacity that the hook may be torn out of the mouth before it will let go its hold. It is necessary to jerk the remora out of the water into the boat as soon as it is hooked.

The Pilotfish—Travels with Shark or Boat

If you happen to observe a small striped fish, usually 6 to 10 inches long, in the company of sharks following your boat or gliding along under a floating barrel or piece of driftwood, you are probably observing a pilotfish, or rudderfish.

In Atlantic waters, two principal species are given this name. The first of these, the true pilotfish *(Naucrates ductor),* was described by Linnaeus in 1758. It is global in distribution, found chiefly in warmer seas. The second species, which is similar in habits and appearance to

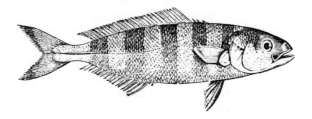

the first, is the banded rudderfish *(Seriola zonata)*, and is found from Halifax, Nova Scotia, to the Gulf of Mexico.

Closely related to skipjacks and amberjacks, pilotfish have elongated bluish bodies with five or six black vertical stripes.

The name pilotfish results from its habit of accompanying ships, boats, and large sea creatures such as sharks, whales, and turtles. Pilotfish have been known to follow an oceangoing vessel for as long as eight days; they will generally leave a ship when it approaches land but have been known to accompany vessels into harbors.

The pilotfish circumvents being eaten by other creatures by accompanying large sharks and living in association with them. Mutual benefit is derived from this association. The pilotfish, like the remora, receives protection and feeds on bits of food left over from the shark's meals, but of course does not attach itself physically to the shark. The shark, in turn, benefits by having some of the parasites that infest it swallowed by the pilotfish. This type of mutual association is known biologically as *symbiosis*.

Sharks and pilotfish appear to get along peaceably in their intimate association, as there has never been a record of a pilotfish being found in the stomach of a shark. In several cases, when a large shark has been hooked and half hauled out of the water, a number of pilotfish have been observed swimming around its tail in an agitated manner.

The pilotfish is common in the southern Atlantic and in the Mediterranean Sea. It was well known to the Greeks and Romans as *pompilus*. According to mythology, Pompilus was an Ionian fisherman who ran off with Ocyroe, a girl friend of Apollo. He angered the gods, and as a result, his boat was changed into a rock and Pompilus into a pilotfish.

It seems somewhat curious, but nearly all classical accounts of the pilotfish refer to its association with dolphins and whales, rather than sharks. Aristotle refers to this fish as the "Dolphin's louse." Oppian recorded the unusual habits of pilotfish in his writings.

Aelian stated that these fishes were kindly disposed toward sailors, and therefore they liked to approach ships and guide them across the seas. Pilotfish were believed to announce the proximity of land by their sudden disappearance.

According to J. R. Norman, spawning of the pilotfish seems to take place in the open ocean during early summer, at which time the young may be encountered in large numbers. They differ from their parents so much in form and coloration that they were long considered a different species. The young are in the habit of swimming around in small groups under large jellyfish, Portuguese men-of-war, sargassum weed, and driftwood.

As a food fish, the pilotfish is of no importance. Its flavor has been described as resembling that of dry mackerel. Some pilotfish grow rather large and are recorded as reaching a length of 3 feet.

Butterfish Wear a Living Umbrella

Although it was used to fertilize the soil for planting during the beginning of the eighteenth century, the butterfish is now considered one of our best table fishes.

Often it is called by various local names such as the dollar fish in Maine, the sheepshead around Cape Cod, the pumpkinseed in Connecticut, and the starfish in Norfolk. Other fishermen sometimes call them harvestfish, skipjack, shiner, and La Fayette.

Scientifically called *Peprilus triacanthus*, the butterfish derives its most common name from the fact that it is covered with a coating of slippery mucus resembling soft butter. Flattened and oval-shaped, it is distinctive by virtue of a short head, small mouth, weak teeth, and long, pointed pectoral fins. Its color is grayish blue on the sides with a silvery belly.

A deep-water fish, it can be caught all the way from the coast of Nova Scotia to Florida, but is most abundant off the New England and the Middle Atlantic states.

Pound nets, floating traps, purse seines, and otter trawls all take large quantities of butterfish in New England. Dragger captains report that they catch several times as many butterfish by night as by day, which leads them to believe that the fish are active enough to dodge the otter trawls in daylight.

Schools of butterfish arrive in the shallow coastal waters of Rhode

Island during the latter part of April and around Woods Hole by the middle of May. Seldom found in large quantities north of Cape Cod before July, they become most numerous during the months of August and September. Often they migrate close to shore in sheltered bays and estuaries where they are frequently captured by pound nets. Catches by traps show that they have a decided preference for sandy bottoms over rocky or muddy ones. During the winter months they are sometimes taken in Nantucket Shoals and George's Bank.

Large butterfish feed on small fishes, squid, copepods, and annelids. In September the smaller ones feed principally on the amphipod beach flea in pursuit of which they venture so close to the breakers along ocean beaches that they are occasionally washed ashore by the surf.

During the beginning of summer the mature butterfish leave shoal water and head a few miles out to sea to spawn. After they are spent they return to inshore waters. The eggs are spherical, transparent, buoyant, and extremely small—ranging from 0.7 to 0.8 millimeter in diameter with a single buoyant oil globule usually present. At 72 degrees F. incubation occupies less than 48 hours. At the time of hatching, larvae are 2 millimeters long and grow very rapidly. After a length of 20 millimeters is reached, the larvae attain the general appearance of the adult form. According to Bigelow and Schroeder, fry hatched earliest in the season grow to a length of 3 to 4 inches by autumn; large numbers of that size are taken in Rhode Island waters during October. Fry hatched late in summer are no more than 2 to 3 inches long at the beginning of winter but are unable to grow much during the cold season; small fish, 3 to 5 inches, are seen again in the spring.

An unusual habit of young butterfish in their first year is that they will often take shelter and live under the umbrella of floating jellyfish. Goode graphically describes young butterfish fry, 2 to 2½ inches long, swimming among the tentacles of the red jellyfish, with sometimes as many as 10 or 15 little fish under a single individual. They have also been seen underneath Portuguese men-of-war. Here, under the float of the jellyfish, they find protection from predators and have a constant supply of food from the copepods and other small food animals that get snared by the dangling tentacles. Although jellyfish tentacles have powerful sting, or lasso, cells, the small butterfish seem to be protected from them by virtue of the thick coating of mucus they have. Occasionally, however, a butterfish will fall victim to the stings of the jellyfish and be devoured by it.

Frequently, many unmarketable butterfish 3 to 5 inches in length are caught in pound nets. As a rule these small fish are not culled from the catch until the pound net boats are en route to or have reached shore, with the result that many thousands of fishes do not reach maturity. Most marketable butterfish are 7 to 9 inches long; those of 10 or 11 inches are not uncommon. A butterfish 6 inches long weighs about 1¾ ounces, while one 8 inches long weighs around 4½ ounces. In prime condition an 11-inch fish will weigh about 16 ounces. The maximum length is 12 inches with maximum weight 1¼ pounds.

Hildebrand and Schroeder give an illustration of the severe mutilations by predators that this fish can sometimes overcome. They mention a specimen about 8 inches long that had met with an accident during its life in which it lost its snout from the nostril forward. This butterfish had not even the rudiments of jaws. The mouth was represented by an oval-shaped opening, and this fish not only survived but at the time of its capture was fatter and apparently in better condition than many normal individuals.

The market for butterfish is fairly steady with a continuous moderate demand. It had long been thought that butterfish would never take a hook. However, anglers have recently discovered that hungry butterfish will sometimes bite a very small hook greedily if it is baited with a small piece of clam or a bit of sea worm.

Fat and delicately flavored, the butterfish is an ideal panfish that fries to a crisp golden brown and literally melts in the mouth.

9

Voracious for Their Fellow Kind

Almost all fishes will eat other fishes, either the eggs, larval fishes, or more mature ones. Great variation occurs in the size and shape of mouths, teeth, and jaws. The anglerfish has a big mouth and large jaws. Sharks possess an abundance of teeth and strong jaws. Gars and barracuda have sharp needlelike teeth. Bluefish and pike terrorize the smaller fish in their territory. Fishermen frequently catch fishes with scars or chunks missing, reflecting the voraciousness of their fellow kind.

The Dogfish—Troublemaker

The dread of most college students who study comparative anatomy is a gray rough-skinned fish with the Latin tag *Squalus acanthias*. Students have to learn the proper name of every organ by dissecting odoriferous specimens preserved in formaldehyde.

Commercial fishermen and anglers know this fish by other names: grayfish, spiny dogfish, cod shark, thornback shark, bone-dog, and skittle-dog. By far the most plentiful member of the shark family on our Atlantic coast, it is one of the smallest members of the shark family, the maximum weight recorded being 20 pounds. Most dogfish average between 7 and 10 pounds; an occasional fat female will reach 15 pounds.

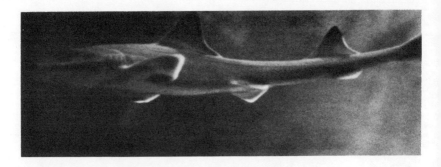

Dogfish may be so plentiful at times that they become a real annoyance to trawl and net fishermen. Frequently a trawl of baited hooks will be completely cleaned by a school of dogfish, and sometimes they will bite the snoods off a set of long lines.

This "spiny" fish differs from other members of the shark family by possessing a sharp-pointed spine in front of each of its two back fins; it has no anal fin; the adults have rounded heads with flattened snouts. Each tooth is smooth-edged and sharply pointed, and the teeth are small and bent toward the outer corners of the mouth, which give it a vicious tearing quality that defies a hook.

Picking up a spiny dogfish with your bare hands can be dangerous. Those sharp spikes before each dorsal fin are capable of inflicting nasty wounds as the fish twists and squirms about. When you grab a dogfish it will bend itself in an arc or bow and then spring violently in the opposite direction, its spine piercing anything in its path. J. R. Norman (1931) states that uniquely for sharks the spine has a mild poison secreted by a venom gland that causes intense pain and discomfort. Fishermen are incapacitated for several days by a wound on the hand. In Europe, where there is a wide market for the fish, the spines are invariably cut off soon after the fish is caught.

This shark's rough skin is usually colored slate gray on the back and light gray or whitish on the belly. Occasionally specimens may be found with light brown coloration, and the young up to 2 feet in length may have small white spots in a line on their sides. These disappear when the fish reach maturity.

It has been known since ancient times that dogfish give birth to living young (ovoviviparous), although usually only large sharks bear live young; smaller sharks are generally egg-producers. The number in a litter of dogfish may range from 2 to 11, depending on conditions.

The young embryos develop in a thin, horn-colored capsule known as a "candle." This capsule deteriorates as the unborn sharks develop in the mother. When they are born, baby dogfish range in size from 6½ to 13 inches, depending on the size of the mother. The gestation period is from 18 to 22 months, the longest period of internal development known in sharks.

Dogfish are fast-swimming, frisky fish; often they tear and snarl the twine in seines and pound nets, causing a great deal of damage. During a year of peak abundance this damage has been estimated to run as high as $400,000 off the Massachusetts coast alone.

They are usually found in schools or packs, although stray members of the clan are sometimes encountered. Exceedingly common off the New England coast, their area of greatest abundance appears to be from Cape Cod to Cape Sable, Nova Scotia. On our Atlantic coast we find them as far south as South Carolina, on rare occasions slightly farther down. This species is also found in European regions of the North Atlantic and on our northern Pacific coast south to California. They also range around Hawaii, Japan, and northern China, completing the circle of the northern oceans.

In New England waters the dogfish is most plentiful during the spring, summer, and fall. Henry W. Fowler, of the Academy of Natural Sciences, wrote in "The Sharks of New Jersey" in *The Yearbook of the Ocean City Fishing Club* for 1920 that "along the New Jersey Coast the spiny dogfish appears in late October or during November and reappears in March and April." It is fortunate that the schools seldom stay in any one place for a great length of time, as they are constantly preying on other fish. And this predator is benthopelagic—that is, it is found and feeds at all depths of the ocean.

With a ravenous appetite, dogfish are voracious feeders. Hildebrand and Schroeder (1928) report finding eight partly digested menhaden in one fish and a 7-inch squeteague in another. When traveling along the coast in schools, dogfish will attack almost any fish they encounter. Fishermen frequently describe groups preying on schools of mackerel, even attacking them in seines by biting through the netting. Adults will attack cod and haddock two or three times their size. Even recently born dogfish have been observed attacking herring larger than themselves. In addition, dogfish are known to feed on squid, lobsters, scup, whiting, pollack, razor clams, crabs, shrimp, and jellyfish.

In Northern Europe and England the spiny dogfish is of considerable value, and large quantities are sold for human food each year. In the

United States it has little value except as a trash fish prepared as animal feed and fertilizer. Occasionally its liver appears in meat markets, as it is known to be rich in vitamin A.

Though not widely marketed, the flesh is excellent food if properly prepared and cooked. Soaked or boiled in vinegar, or any other slightly acid solution, it should be cooked thoroughly with plenty of butter or oil. Captain William Young in his book *Shark! Shark!* says: "Dogfish, similar to other sharkmeat, when properly cooked tastes somewhat like lobster . . . fillets should not be baked, but fried in butter. They make a tasty dish to suit the palate of the most exacting epicure."

The Mysterious Frostfish, or Whiting

On a crisp, moonlit night in fall or winter, when the tide is receding, you might find warmly dressed people with bushel baskets and flashlights walking along the edges of New England's sandy beaches. Ask what they are doing, and the reply will undoubtedly be, "Frostfishing."

If conditions are ideal, groups of *Merluccius bilinearis* will be preying upon schools of herring, mackerel, or alewives in the surf. The whitefish frequently get stranded on the sandy shore in their frenzy to attack schools of smaller fishes. Frostfishermen near the stranded fish quickly scoop them up and put them in the bushel basket.

The American whiting is a typical fish of prey, with its sharp teeth, large mouth, and highly muscular body adapted for rapid locomotion. It commonly inhabits the middle depths of the ocean, but frequently comes to the surface where it chases schooling fishes such as herring, menhaden, and alewives. It feeds on almost all young fishes, including its own kind, and a keen observer can sight whitings chasing schools of small fishes into such shallow water that both pursued and pursuers get stranded in the sand. This is what makes frostfishing a popular sport.

Merluccius bilinearis has many other names, including silver hake, whiting, winter weakfish, New England hake, and winter hake. This species is not to be confused with the Atlantic tomcod, *Microgadus tomcod*, which is also sometimes called a frostfish.

The whiting is found from Newfoundland to Charleston, South Carolina, on the continental shelf. It has been reported from the Grand Banks to the Bahamas, and recorded from the water's edge to depths of

nearly 2000 feet. The areas of greatest abundance exploited by commercial fishermen are located from southern New England to Cape Sable Island off Nova Scotia.

Because of their roving habits, silver hakes do not concentrate in any particular area at spawning time, but shed their eggs at intervals during the summer along the entire coast from southern New England to Grand Mahan. Most of the eggs observed in the Gulf of Maine have been found floating over water less than 300 feet deep. Successful spawning of whitings is unknown in the cold waters of the New Brunswick shore of the Bay of Fundy because these eggs need water as warm as 55 to 60 degrees F. for their normal development.

We do not know how many eggs a female whiting produces, as only part of the eggs mature at one time. When released, the eggs are buoyant and slightly under a millimeter in diameter. Incubation is fairly rapid, being about 2 days at Woods Hole, Massachusetts. During the end of their first summer or autumn, when they are from 1 to 3 inches long, baby whitings take to the bottom. Whitings reach maturity at 2 years of age and a length of about 12 inches.

In the Gulf of Maine, whitings are summer fish, appearing first in the Cape Ann–Massachusetts Bay region in March, and becoming increasingly abundant as the waters warm. Off Long Island, they are common most of the year, being taken offshore by otter trawlers from November through March, and by pound netters from April through July. Otter trawlers, particularly of the Gloucester, Boston, and Provincetown fleets, have taken increasing amounts of whiting during the past decades due to increasing prices and consumer demand. It is still one of the less expensive fish—one reason for its increasing popularity.

Although becoming more available fresh in the states bordering its native waters at about 70 cents a pound, the whiting is one of the best known and most widely used Atlantic fishes in sections of the Midwest. This surprising market exists largely because of this species' popularity in the fried-fish shops of the region. Properly prepared and served with appropriate sauces, whiting is a sort of midwestern fish 'n' chips—and is even called that. New York markets it at a very reasonable price—69 cents a pound. Porgy is 89 cents, croaker 79 to 89 cents.

The whiting is one of the sweetest fish if eaten fresh or slightly salted overnight and eaten for breakfast. However, since whitings soften and lose their firmness quickly, there was hardly any demand for them until the beginning of this century. Today, they are marketed both fresh and frozen.

The U.S. Fish and Wildlife Service is carrying on investigations into the life history and habits of the whiting. Major effort has been made to define stocks of whiting and to determine seasonal movements of this species along the Atlantic coast, principally by tagging. Prior to 1957, returns from tagging experiments were disappointing. During the summer of 1957, a new device was used, and recent returns have been more encouraging. The marker consists of a piece of vinyl plastic tubing, inserted at the base of the second dorsal fin, with a special tag attached at one end. Tagging experiments have been conducted in inshore waters from Massachusetts to New Jersey and offshore on George's Bank. Returns have been as high as 9 percent from one area, but there was no indication of seasonal movement.

In addition, X rays are being taken to examine skeletons of whitings from various localities along the Atlantic coast. Differences in skeletal structure are being used to determine geographical variations among separate stocks of fish.

John Dory Uses Hypnosis

A curious fish occasionally taken by offshore draggers on the New England coast is the John Dory, *Zenopsis ocellata*. Belonging to the family Zeidae, this species is a very close relative of the European dory, *Zeus faber*, which is highly regarded as a food in Britain and on the Continent. The Dory was known to the Greeks, who called it Zeus after their principal deity.

The name John Dory is believed to be either a corruption of the French *jaune dorée*, because of the yellow hue on its sides, or the Italian *janitore*, which means "doorkeeper."

The John Dory is easy to identify by the long, slender filaments on its first dorsal fin's rays. One authority states that the Dory uses its fin elongations to attract prey by partially burying itself in the sand and letting its filaments undulate in the water, resembling worms. As a result, curious smaller fish come within easy reach of its powerful jaws. The jaws of the Dory are actually retractable, and it can push them forward with great rapidity. When a victim comes close to the thin Dory, it keeps its large eyes fixed intently on the approaching fish; some writers suggest that the John Dory actually hypnotizes its prey.

Another distinctive characteristic of the John Dory are the dark and conspicuous spots on its side, which are believed to be a symbol of the mark of St. Peter's thumb when he took a piece of money as tribute from the fish's mouth. (This belief also applies to the haddock because of similar markings.) In Germany, the Dory is called *Peterfisch* because of this belief. Some persons, however, contend that the marks were due not to St. Peter but to St. Christopher. As a result of this latter tradition, the Greeks call this fish *christophoron*.

The John Dory is an exceedingly voracious species, feeding on mollusks, shrimp, and the young of other fishes. Jonathan Couch (1789–1870), author of a *History of British Fishes*, states that from the stomach of a single Dory he had taken 25 flounders, some 2½ inches in length, and 5 beach stones up to 1½ inches long.

In this hemisphere, the John Dory is found along the edge of the continental shelf from Chesapeake Bay to Nova Scotia. Two John Dorys that I examined from off Block Island had a bluish silvery color, with dark black spots. I have observed members of this species ranging in size from 11 to 17 inches in length. Bigelow and Schroeder (1953) mention a 24-inch John Dory weighing 7 pounds that was taken 85 miles off Martha's Vineyard by the dragger *Eugene H.* on May 15, 1950.

Some fishermen call the John Dory roosterfish, but it is not a true roosterfish. The roosterfish, or *papagallo*, is a South American species sometimes found along the coasts of Mexico and southern California, having the scientific name *Nematistius pectoralis*. It is a game fish reaching a weight of 70 pounds.

Bluefish—Glutton of the Sea

Have you ever heard of a fish so bloodthirsty and greedy that after it has filled its belly to capacity, it will throw up the fish it has eaten in order to go out and feast on more fish? This glutton of the sea is *Pomatomus saltatrix*, the bluefish, found along our Atlantic coast at various times of the year from Key West, Florida, to Penobscot Bay, Maine. The bluefish is also cosmopolitan, cruising the waters of Australia, North Africa, Cape of Good Hope, Madagascar, South America, the Azores and West Indies.

Usually traveling in dense schools, the greenish blue bluefish voraciously feeds on almost all small fishes it encounters. A graphic description of bluefish habits was written in a report by Spencer F. Baird of the U.S. Fish Commission back in 1874. It still holds true today. "There is no parallel in point of destructiveness to the bluefish among marine species on our coast."

The bluefish has been compared to an animated chopping machine, the business of which is to cut to pieces and otherwise destroy as many other fishes as possible in the shortest space of time. All writers are unanimous in regard to this demonic activity of the bluefish. In pursuit of fish not much inferior to themselves in size, they move along like a pack of hungry wolves, slashing everything before them. Their trail is marked by fragments of fish and by the stain of blood in the sea; where the fish is too large to be swallowed entire, the hind portion will be bitten off and the anterior part allowed to float away or sink. It is even maintained, with great earnestness, that the bluefish kills many more fishes than it consumes for its own needs. Bluefish have been known to attack swimmers in Florida waters.

The youngest bluefish, as well as the adults, perform this devastation, and although they occasionally devour crabs, worms, and other small creatures, the bulk of their sustenance throughout the greater part of the year is derived from other fish. Nothing is more common than to find a small bluefish of 6 or 8 inches in length under a school of minnows, making continual dashes and captures among them. The stomachs of bluefish are sometimes loaded with 30 or 40 kinds of prey, either entire or in fragments.

The rate of growth of the bluefish is evidence of the amount of food they must consume. The young fish, which first appear along the shores of Martha's Vineyard Sound, Massachusetts, about the middle of August, are about 5 inches in length. By the beginning of September, they have reached 6 or 7 inches, and on their reappearance in the second year they measure 12 to 15 inches. After this they increase in size at a still more rapid rate.

Bluefish are especially fond of menhaden, which they follow along the coast and attack with such ferocity as to drive them onto the shore, where thousands of menhaden sometimes pile up in windrows to the depth of a foot or more.

The numbers of fish bluefish destroy, consumed or not, is almost incredible. It has been estimated that this fish will eat twice its weight in a day, and this is perhaps an understatement. They will generally swallow a fish of a very large size in proportion to their own, sometimes taking it down whole. The peculiar armor of certain fish prevents their being taken entire, and it is not uncommon to find the armored head of a sculpin or other fish whose body has evidently been cut off by the bluefish.

In the summer the young are apt to establish themselves singly in a favorite locality, accompanying the fry of other fishes. They usually play above them, and every now and then dart downward and capture an unlucky individual while the rest dash away in every direction. They go after young mullet, and are very fond of squid, which are frequently detected in their stomachs. In August 1970, at Fire Island, New York, S. I. Smith found bluefish stomachs filled with marine worms, which at that season give up their burrowing habits and swim freely on the surface to carry out reproduction. Like the squid, they are a favorite bait for the bluefish; and bluefish appear to care for little else when these are to be had. This is probably the reason why, at certain seasons, no matter how abundant bluefish may be, they cannot be taken with drail or squid boat.

In general bluefish move northward in spring and southward in

autumn. They are taken during the winter in southern Florida, then off the Carolinas in March and April, off New Jersey and Long Island in April and May, and off the south shore of Massachusetts in late May or early June. By November they appear again in the Carolinas and at the end of November on the east coast of Florida.

Bluefish are unpredictable in their abundance and vary in numbers from year to year. The year 1936 was a fine one for bluefishing, but the following year there were far fewer bluefish along the coast. In the early 1940s bluefish were scarce along the Atlantic; to catch one was a rare occurrence. In 1948 they reappeared dramatically and each succeeding year has brought increased catches to both commercial and sport fishermen.

Commercial fishermen catch bluefish chiefly with traps, pound nets, haul seines, gill nets, trammel nets, and with hand or troll lines. At times bluefish devastate nets and twine with their razor-sharp teeth. They bite at the mesh and push themselves through the holes to freedom. Most commercial fishermen who use hook-and-line methods for bluefish either chum for them or use the heave-and-haul method.

The latter technique is generally used in tide rips and races where the blues are known to congregate, such as at Plum Gut in Long Island Sound and the race off Fishers Island. A tarred line is often used with a heavy lead jig, called a drail, at the end. The heavy drail, weighing about a pound or two, withstands the powerful surge of the tide in these places. The lure and line are thrown over the side, and as soon as the drail reaches the bottom it is rapidly hauled up by hand. The blues usually strike the leaded drail on its way up. Because of the strong tides billowing out the line, occasionally 100 feet of twine are used to reach a 50-foot bottom.

On the offshore ruts and shoals the chumming method is generally employed. A batch of fish, usually menhaden or butterfish, is ground up and slowly thrown into the water off the stern of the boat. If bluefish are around, they are quickly attracted to this foul-smelling oily mess and begin to gorge themselves on the pieces of fish. Then small fragments of the chum are baited on hooks, and the ravenous bluefish are hooked and pulled aboard.

Bluefish average 5 or 6 pounds. A large specimen taken off the U.S. coast for which we have an early record was caught off Nantucket in 1903 and was 3 feet 9 inches long weighing 27 pounds. The world record on rod and reel is a blue weighing 31 pounds 12 ounces taken off Hatteras Inlet, North Carolina, January 30, 1972, by James M. Hussey.

Very little is known about the spawning habits of the bluefish. It is generally agreed among scientists that they spawn offshore in the early summer. A few ripe fishes have been captured in June, but spawning fishes have not yet been observed by divers.

The bluefish is one of our most popular food fish. Many people are of the opinion that the bluefish is comparable in taste to the pompano or Spanish mackerel. However, in order to have a tasty bluefish, it should be cleaned as soon as possible after capture. It is good practice to cut the blue's throat so as to remove most of the blood and then split the belly as far back as the vent to remove the entrails. It is not necessary to scale a bluefish, and the quicker it is put on ice after it is caught, the firmer and tastier the meat will be. Bluefish can be baked whole or filleted.

10

Protective Devices

Most, but not all, fish have hard scales as a protective shield. Many fish, such as the flounder, can change colors rapidly as a form of camouflage. Sharp spines on triggerfish, filefish, and sculpins retard enemies. Electric eels, torpedos, mormyrids, electric catfish, and stargazers shock their enemies with electricity. Some venomous fishes use their spines to cause a wound into which they inject poison. Others, like some catfish, stingrays, weeverfish, scorpionfish, and toadfish inject toxic venoms in different ways. No specific antidotes have been developed for fish venoms. Some fish, like the blowfish, protect themselves by inflation; others merely bury themselves in mud or sand to escape predators. The majority simply outmaneuver those chasing them. A great variety of protective mechanisms have developed among the world of fishes.

The Big Puffer

Among the puffers, the sea squab or blowfish is best known, but he is not the only one of his kind. Witness the unusual smooth puffer, *Lagocephalus laevigatus*, locally called rabbitfish. The generic name of this species is from the Greek *lagos*, meaning "rabbit," and *cephalus*, meaning "head"; the specific name means "smooth." The smooth puffer occurs from Cape Cod to Brazil and is also found on the coasts of Southern Europe. Its usual habitat is southern regions, but it is an occasional straggler into northern waters.

Called smooth puffer because of its lack of elongated spines, it is also referred to as bottlefish or jugfish because of its resemblance to a container. Fishermen have a few other choice names for this troublesome species when it turns up in their nets.

From the photograph, it is easy to see why this species is also called rabbitfish. Its two broad incisor teeth closely resemble those of a rabbit, and its eyes look like those of a hare.

This is the largest and most distinctive American member of the puffer family. It inflates when alarmed, reaching a length of 3 feet. In 1957, I obtained two specimens of the smooth puffer. One, 16 inches long, was taken in an otter trawl net by Captain Sterling Eyer on the dragger *Theresa* off Block Island during November; the second specimen, 14 inches long, was taken off the Point Judith Breakwater by Captain Willis Clark in his fish traps during July.

This particular species is easy to identify from its general body shape and the gray-purple color on its back surface, silvery sides and white belly. Very small, three-rooted spines are found on the belly, but it is distinct from all other puffers by the smooth, shiny skin on its sides, its large dorsal and anal fins, and its concave tail fin.

Goode (1884) mentions that rabbitfish are found only occasionally in New England waters, but they are quite abundant in the Gulf of Mexico, where they are occasionally taken with disappointment by the fishermen along the red snapper banks. According to Stearns, it breeds near Pensacola, Florida, in June and July.

Although this fish is of no economic importance to American fishermen, it is sometimes used for food in Cuba. There it reaches a length of 3 feet and can weigh 5 or 6 pounds.

The Striped Burrfish—It Poisons and Punctures

An interesting Atlantic coast fish that doesn't have to worry too much about being molested by its associates is the striped burrfish, or spiny boxfish, *Chilomycterus schoepfi*. Found in tropical waters and from Florida to Maine, this unusual fish is a member of the Diodontidae, comprising 14 species of porcupine fishes.

Studded with rows of sharp spines that resemble the thorns of a rose bush, it is capable of inflicting painful wounds, so caution should be used in handling it with bare hands. Instead of possessing common

scales, the burrfish has only thorny spines in the epidermal layer. Fixed in a permanent erect position, the spines taper slightly to the rear.

During the summer, it is a visitor to inshore waters of New England and may stray to Maine. Bigelow and Schroeder in their *Fishes of the Gulf of Maine* mention a burrfish captured in a trap at West Point, Maine, on August 5, 1949. Frequently it is observed and chased by free divers, being slow enough to be caught by a good swimmer.

A relative of the swellfish, or puffer, the burrfish can inflate by gulping air. The young can blow themselves up easily, but as they grow older they can inflate only slightly. The burrfish is sometimes regarded as a degenerate fish because it lacks many desirable characteristics. It is less active, less competent, and more restricted in its abilities. At the same time, it is specialized in its means of protection. Its projections serve a defensive purpose, preventing it from being easily swallowed by its adversaries. The roots of the strong, stout spines are in contact with one another and provide a more or less continuous coat of armor. Its short fins are also defensive, as they cannot be bitten off easily by other fish. The teeth in both jaws are fused, somewhat blunt-edged, and contracted. The diet is chiefly slow-moving crabs and snails.

According to Jordan, even the flesh of the burrfish, thin and dry as it is, seems fitted for its protection. Whatever eats one burrfish will be unable to feed on others. Its flesh contains an alkaloid substance similar to strychnine, poisonous to fish, beast, or man.

Sharks, which feed on almost any creature in the seas, do not handle this one successfully. Charles Darwin tells of an inflated burrfish found floating alive in the stomach of a large shark. He also mentions another shark killed by a burrfish it had swallowed.

In tropical waters, some species reach a length of 2 or 3 feet, and may be as large as a basketball when inflated. The dried skins are sometimes made into grotesque lanterns by being illuminated with colored lights placed inside the belly. South Sea Island warriors cut holes in these inflated dried fish and use them as protective helmets.

The spiny burrfish is one of the smaller members of the family. It reaches a length of 10 inches. Its eyes are large and bulging. Wavy dark lines are found running along its back and sides. Usually the belly is light orange or yellowish, and the sides and back are olive-brown or tan. This species is known in some localities as cucumber fish, spotted balloon fish, and rabbitfish.

Aquarium enthusiasts find that young burrfish make excellent specimens. If tickled gently they will swell. They usually eat all kinds of fish food, but show a preference for clams and shrimp.

Aside from their value as aquarium specimens and as dried-out ornaments in curio shops, these fish are of no economic importance.

Sea Raven Eggs in Sponges

Frequently occurring in the catch of trawlers off our northeastern coast is a most unusual fish, the sea raven, *Hemitripterus americanus.* With fleshy tabs projecting from its head and a body covered with harlequinlike markings and warty spots, the raven ranks high among grotesque fishes.

Described by Gmelin in 1788 from reports about a *Diable en crapano de l'Amerique* ("American devil frog") by de Moureau, its scientific description first appeared in the 14th edition of *Systema Naturae.*

Ranging from Nova Scotia to the Chesapeake Bay region, the sea raven is known by a great variety of local names including red sculpin, rock toadfish, raven, King o' Norway, and sally growler.

Common off the northeastern coast of North America, sea ravens

have been reported from Anticosti on the northern side of the Gulf of St. Lawrence, Sable Island Bank, Banquereau Bank, Cape Breton, the Grand Banks, and George's Bank south to Chesapeake Bay. They have been caught in waters from a few fathoms depth down to 105 fathoms. Usually they are found in waters less than 50 fathoms deep.

Sea ravens range in color from a brilliant crimson to a reddish violet, grayish brown, and yellowish brown. They are generally speckled with spots of a lighter or darker color. There is no mistaking the raven due to the 4 to 8 fleshy flabs coming down from its chin and its very warty appearance. Amateur fishermen are usually alarmed and repelled if they bring one up. The sight is unbelievable.

When dumped on the deck of a fishing vessel from the cod end of an otter trawl net, sea ravens generally appear in a very bloated condition because they can inflate their belly with water much as the blowfish or puffer can. If thrown back into the sea, they will sometimes float helplessly, tail waving, until the water is expelled and equilibrium regained.

Sea ravens have larger teeth than sculpins and will occasionally snap at any object that comes near them while they are lying on the deck. Sometimes they will bite the hand that is throwing them back into the sea. In the water they are voracious. Fish such as the tautog, cunner, herring, launce, and sculpin have been found in ravens' stomachs. They also feed on squid, crustaceans, sea urchins, clams, and snails, as well as on the eggs of their own species and of sculpins.

Usually ravens move into inshore waters in the fall and winter and migrate offshore into deeper waters in the summer. Considerable investigation into the spawning habits, eggs and larvae of sea ravens was carried out by Herbert Warfel and Daniel Merriman of the Bingham Oceanographic Laboratory of Yale University during the early 1940s. The studies were made in cooperation with Captain Ellery Thompson on his dragger *Eleanor* in Connecticut and Rhode Island waters.

Drs. Warfel and Merriman found that the eggs of the sea raven were deposited in compact clusters at the base of the fingerlike branches of the finger sponge *Chalina* and less frequently on the smaller sponge *Halichondria panicea*. This association of sea raven eggs and sponges was definitely established by careful examination of many trawl hauls. In their spawning season, from October to January, it is believed that the females deposit many clusters, each of which contains an average of 242 eggs.

The sponge provides the large eggs (4 millimeters in diameter) with an ideal hiding place from predators. Their coloration is almost exactly the same as the sponge, a pale yellow, amber, or light orange.

On January 23, 1944, three clusters of raven eggs were collected by Drs. Warfel and Merriman on the *Eleanor* and immersed immediately in seawater. On the trip back to the laboratory, three eggs hatched. At the Yale University laboratory one cluster was placed in cold, aerated seawater; the eggs hatched a few at a time on and after January 28.

Another cluster was placed in a jar with its open end covered with gauze and attached to a floating buoy in Long Island Sound on January 25. These latter eggs hatched slowly until March 12. When first hatched from the eggs, the larvae were 12 millimeters long but did not live longer than a few days in captivity.

Like their close relatives, the sculpins, sea ravens are very tasty fish but are seldom eaten. When captured by trawlers or draggers they are generally placed in with the trash or industrial fish to be rendered into fishmeal. Sometimes they are saved for lobstermen who occasionally use them as bait in lobster traps.

11

Most Popular in Streams and Lakes

Gliding over a pebbled stream bed, trout are the universal quarry of anglers. In a lake, with its vegetation and cycle of nutrients that provide a stable abode for its finned inhabitants, the musky stands out as supreme predator in its dominion.

Brook and Rainbow Trout—They Went West

In cool, clean streams and lakes, one of the finest of native freshwater game fish is the speckled brook trout, *Salvelinus fontinalis*. Known by a dozen common names—brookie, square tail, mud trout, speckled trout, eastern brook trout in the Rocky Mountains—the brook trout is a favorite of stream and lake anglers. In state and national hatcheries of the United States and Canada, millions of brook trout for stocking cool streams and rivers are raised by artificial propagation. In this way the native eastern brook trout was transplanted to the West, especially in swift running brooks and mountain "rivers" that might be only 300 or so feet wide, in the wilds of the national parks.

A member of the group of fishes known as chars, the brook trout is

Brook trout

universally sought after by anglers for its fighting qualities and wonderful flavor. Unlike the brown trout, which was transplanted to American waters from abroad, the brook trout is native to our streams. It was sought after by the Indians and early colonists in the clear and cool streams of North America. The brook trout cannot tolerate pollution and is found only in clean, running waters that hold its preferred food of insects and insect larvae. Caddis fly larvae, mayflies, and nymphs along with small fishes and worms provide its favorite fare.

Adult brook trout are somewhat variable in color. The color of the back may be olive greenish to dark brown or almost black. From the back, heavy dark wavy lines extend on to the dorsal and caudal fins. Its sides have small, well-defined red spots bordered by a bluish halo. When males are breeding, they become particularly colorful with a strong orange to reddish tint along the lower portions of their body.

Brook trout generally run from ½ to 2 pounds with an occasional larger specimen. One record brook trout was a 14½-pound, 31½-inch specimen taken in the Nipigon River, Ontario, in July 1916 by W. J. Cook.

From September to late November, mature male and female brook trout migrate leisurely to spawn in the upper reaches of streams and rivers, in some of the most colorful wild canyons of the Rockies. The most knowledgeable sport fishermen say that high Rocky Mountain boulder-strewn streams are so swift they fall 5 miles in 20 and provide the greatest fishing grounds in the world. They seek out shallow gravel-bottomed clear rapid water where the female clears out small beds of pebbles and gravel by the active fanning of her tail. Both adults assist in the hollowing out of an oval depression, called a *redd*, in the stream bed.

After the nest, or redd, is constructed, the female moves to a position close to the bottom. The male moves to her side and arches his body over her while she releases her eggs. The male then discharges his cloudy milt over the eggs. Sometimes a second male may join the pair. Shortly after spawning, the male leaves the female. The eggs are sticky and adhere to pebbles in the bottom of the redd, usually in calmer backwaters of the fierce mountain streams. The female trout pushes loose pebbles into the depression of the redd and covers the eggs with sand and gravel. She may spawn several times, and if large, may release as many as 5000 eggs. Small females produce only from 90 to 500 eggs. Spawning of the brook trout usually occurs during daylight hours. The eggs remain in the redd until the waters warm in the following spring. It may take as long as 140 days for the young trout to hatch. Sometimes natural hazards sweep away most of the eggs. With the rush waters of the spring, large numbers of eggs may be swept out of the protective redd by strong new currents. Other fish, including trout themselves, may dislodge the pebbles of the redd and feed on the loose eggs. Suckers and freshwater sculpins like the flavor of trout eggs. Those eggs on the surface of the redd are frequently destroyed by a fungus. If the eggs are covered with sand particles, they usually receive enough protection and camouflage to allow them to hatch successfully.

The orange eggs are round and hatch in 40 to 140 days, depending on water temperature. No parental care is given to the newly hatched young trout. During their first few days they live on nutrients absorbed from the yolk sac. After the yolk is absorbed, they begin to feed on microscopic phytoplankton and zooplankton. According to V. D. Vladykov, each female brook trout from fingerling to adult carries eggs in her two ovaries at all times. In spring and summer the eggs are very small, from $1/15$ inch to $1/12$ inch in diameter. In the fall during spawning time the eggs reach the size of a small pea.

Some brook trout head downstream to the tidal estuary after spawning where they remain in brackish and salt water for several years. These sea-run brook trout are called salters.

Because they usually hide under rocks, logs, and overhanging banks, brook trout are not easy fish to catch. These trout have keen eyesight and are very wary of humans. A good angler will keep low and out of the line of vision of the fish as much as possible. Brook trout seem to be most active at sunrise and sunset and will take both wet and dry flies at dawn and twilight. They also like earthworms and can be taken on a worm-baited hook.

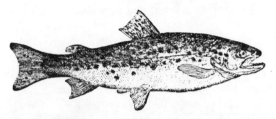

In the past few decades, a vigorous strain of brook trout has been developed in hatcheries by crossing lake trout with brook trout. The desirable fast-growing hybrid product of this union is called splake. Splake grow faster than either parent and are sought after by anglers for their game fighting qualities and great flavor.

Brook trout have many natural enemies including pickerel, bass, and snapping turtles. Mink and otters also relish brook trout when they can catch them. Man, however, is the brookie's most dangerous predator, especially when he is a fly fisherman with a colorful "Royal Coachman" or "Parmechene Bell" at the end of a fly line.

Native to North American streams of the Pacific coast from Alaska to California, the rainbow trout is a favorite of freshwater anglers around the world because it has been transplanted to many foreign nations. Fertile rainbow trout eggs can be shipped long distances with the result that strains of this species have been successfully transplanted to Australia, New Zealand, India, Europe, South America, and Japan.

Often called steelhead, kamloops, and silver trout, the rainbow trout, *Salmo gairdneri*, can survive in warm-water streams that reach temperatures as high as 85 degrees F. These waters would prove lethal to brook trout and brown trout. Rainbows have spring spawning runs, while many other trout species spawn in the fall.

The rainbow trout is easy to recognize as it is silvery with a blue-green back and a scarlet red streak running down the sides in mature fish. It has small black spots on the sides, back, and fins. This species is called rainbow trout because of the vivid red or reddish purple broad band that runs from behind its eye and extends to the tail fin in adult fish.

The spawning habits of the rainbow trout are similar to those of the brook trout except that spawning usually occurs in April or May. As the spawning season approaches, the mature males develop a hook, or kype, on the lower jaw. Adult males and females head upstream in early spring to the clear, rapid water of the headwaters where a redd is scooped out of the clean sand and gravel. From 400 to 3000 eggs may be laid in the nest, depending on the size of the female. After spawning, the spent adults move downstream to resume habitation in their native lake or water body. The eggs hatch in about 50 days, depending on the temperature of the stream. When they are 2 to 3 years old, the young rainbows leave the stream in which they were hatched and migrate to lakes or reservoirs until they reach maturity.

During the summer months, silvery rainbow trout are caught by anglers. Sometimes they are wrongly identified as salmon. It is when the rainbows are in their silvery phase that they are often called steelheads.

The so-called Kamloops strain of rainbow from the state of Washington is a distinct popular variety of rainbow, sometimes reaching the enormous weight of 50 pounds. The Kamloops, developed through careful breeding experiments, can live in waters of higher temperatures than most other rainbows. It is also somewhat less migratory than other varieties of rainbow trout.

With regard to size, generally large rainbows are found in large bodies of water and small rainbows in small brooks and streams. Giant rainbow trout often reach weights of 40 pounds, and a 52½-pound rainbow has been recorded from British Columbia.

Many fishermen regard the rainbow as their favorite trout species. When hooked on a fly, spinner, spoon, or live bait, the rainbow puts up a terrific fight to test the angler's skill. Frequently a rainbow will break water and jump six or seven times in rapid succession. Many a prize rainbow has fought his way off the hook and gained freedom.

Rainbow trout

Brown Trout and Lake Trout—Immigrant and Native

The brown trout, *Salmo trutta*, is native to Old World streams from the Mediterranean Sea eastward to the Black Sea and Siberia, north to northern Norway and west to Spain and Great Britain.

American anglers owe a debt to Frank Mather, U.S. representative to the International Fisheries Exposition of 1880 in Berlin, Germany, who arranged for shipment of brown trout to American waters. Mather, a New York State angler and fish culturist, noted the desirable characteristics of the brown trout while fishing in European streams. He arranged with a German fishery scientist in Berlin, F. Von Behr, to ship fertile brown trout eggs to America. On February 24, 1883, the German ship *Werra* arrived in New York City with 80,000 fertile brown trout eggs. These were taken by Mather to the New York State Hatchery at Cold Spring Harbor, Long Island, where they were raised and stocked in northeastern streams. The following year additional brown trout eggs were brought over from Scotland. For many years, most of these trout were known as German trout. Brown trout originating from the British Isles were frequently called Loch Leven or Scottish brown trout.

Although native to the Northern Hemisphere, the brown trout has become a cosmopolitan species. It provides exciting fishing in Argentina, Chile, Australia, Tasmania, and New Zealand. The wide-ranging distribution of brown trout is due to the fact that the fertile trout eggs can be kept viable for a month or so under controlled temperatures during shipment.

Brown trout

It is fortunate that the brown trout were introduced to North American waters and elsewhere around the world because of their ability to thrive in waters several degrees warmer than native brook trout. They thrive in many streams where native trout populations have died out. It appears evident that southern New England, New York, New Jersey, Pennsylvania, and Maryland depend on brown trout as the mainstay of their trout sport fishery, tolerating as they do limited amounts of water pollution that would prove lethal to other trout species.

Brown trout exhibit wide color variation. Usually they are olive brown or greenish shading to golden yellow or yellowish white on the abdomen. Their sides are speckled with numerous dark brown or black spots. Along the lateral line and below are red and orange spots with pale margins. The bottom pelvic and anal fins have a light yellowish edge on the lower margins. Brown trout in lakes and those that carry on sea runs usually are quite silvery. When male brown trout are in their spawning run, they develop brightly colored reddish sides and form a hook, or kype, at the end of their lower jaw.

Sexual maturity of the brown trout occurs between 2 and 3 years of age. Their spawning habits are similar to those of the brook. A female brown trout will release from 450 to 3000 eggs, depending on its size.

Young brown trout feed on small aquatic insects and zooplankton. As they grow they become more voracious in their appetites, turning to crayfish, moths, clams, snails, frogs, other fish, and even their own kind.

Brown trout reach a size close to 40 pounds. The all-time world record "brownie" was taken over a hundred years ago in 1866 by W. Muir in Loch Awe, Scotland, and weighed 39 pounds 8 ounces. North American record brown trout include a 26-pound 2-ounce specimen taken by George Langston below the Dale Hollow Dam in Tennessee and a 29-pound 9-ounce brown taken in 1970 near Bayfield, Wisconsin.

Although they are not considered as delicately flavored as brook trout, browns provide great sport to anglers by rising readily to both wet and dry flies. They provide a sporting fight when hooked and will take a wide variety of live baits including worms, minnows, and crayfish. Brown trout seem most active during twilight or dawn and on cloudy, rainy days. These periods generally prove most productive for anglers.

In many locations the brown trout population is naturally self-sustaining by successful spawning in local streams. However, with brown trout there are extensive put-and-take stocking programs in

North America that are maintained through extensive hatchery-produced stocks. In 1973, U.S. federal and state hatcheries produced over 1.9 million pounds of brown trout which consisted of 7.5 million fishes. These trout were raised to a catchable size of 7 to 9 inches in hatcheries and then released into public fresh waters for anglers. In addition, during 1973, 6.8 million immature brown trout fingerlings were released in suitable American waters.

The largest trout is the lake trout, *Salvelinus namaycush*. This species is found throughout northern North America from New England, across Canada, in the Great Lakes, Columbia River, and Alaskan waters.

Lake trout

Lakers are native to deep, cold lakes. They are cold-water fish preferring water temperatures less than 65 degrees F. Their lakes should have water depths of 100 feet or more. In Lake Superior they have been found at depths of 600 feet during summer months.

The lake trout has always been a popular game fish and in some localities a commercial species. It is referred to by many popular names, depending on locality. In the western United States, lake trout are sometimes called Mackinaw trout. In Maine it is called togue, and elsewhere it is called gray trout, mountain trout, and salmon trout.

The lake trout ranges in color from gray to black with a whitish belly. Small lakes seem to harbor dark fish; larger lakes contain lighter-hued specimens. Lake trout have big heads and deeply forked tails. Well-developed teeth occur on the jaws of the large mouth.

Lake trout reach a huge size when favorable conditions exist. A 63-pounder was caught in Lake Superior in 1952. In August 1961 a 102-pound giant was caught in commercial fishing gill nets in Lake Athabaska, Saskatchewan. This huge trout was 50 inches long and had a girth of 44 inches.

During the early 1940s the lake trout, which was the foundation of the fishing industry in the Great Lakes, suddenly began to diminish. The lake trout catch in Lake Huron dropped from over 5 million pounds annually before 1940 to about 300,000 pounds in 1953. In Lake Michigan the lake trout catch dropped from over 6 million pounds in 1946 to 402 pounds in 1953. This sharp decline was a direct result of predation by the parasitic sea lamprey, which almost destroyed the entire lake trout population of the Great Lakes. Fortunately, fishery research led to successful methods of eradicating the lamprey by chemical means.

Lake trout thrive only in deep lakes that have a large volume of cool, well-oxygenated water into which the fish can become established during the warm summer months. In the fall, during late September, October, and November, the lakers move into shallower water to spawn at depths ranging from 1 foot to over 260 feet. The ideal water temperature for spawning seems to be around 40 degrees F. In many northern lakes, spawning occurs just before ice forms. A female lake trout usually releases about 750 eggs per pound of body weight. Gravid females usually release about 6000 eggs. After spawning, the spent fish leave the eggs and retire to deeper water for the winter. Lake trout eggs usually hatch in 16 to 20 weeks, depending on the water temperature.

Newly hatched trout feed on zooplankton. As they become fingerlings and get larger, they feed on mysis shrimp, small smelts, alewives, ciscoes, perch, and whitefish.

One of the more common methods of angling for lake trout is trolling a silver spoon with a heavy sinker to bring the lure down to 50, 75, or several hundred feet. The fishing depth depends on the lake and time of year. In Lake Superior, some fishermen prefer still-fishing with minnows at a depth of 70 feet. A lake trout will strike a lure or bait hard and put up a game fight, but if brought up suddenly from great depths, it will lose much of its strength.

The flesh of the lake trout is very flavorful and ranges in color from almost white to pink and light red. In the larger lakes of Canada, commercial fishing is carried on for lakers, using large mesh gill nets running thousands of feet in length.

As a large trout of northern lakes, the laker is esteemed by both sport and commercial fishermen.

How Many Names Has the "Musky"?

The "musky," or muskellunge *(Esox masquinongy)*, is the largest and most sought after member of the pike family by freshwater anglers in the United States and Canada. In the Great Lakes region, musky is a magical word to many a growing child who is taken on a first camping trip to the northern Great Lakes. It is as though he has become a part of legend, especially when he has caught one in the far reaches of Lake Superior and Canadian lakes.

The muskellunge is one of the largest North American freshwater fish, exceeded only by the white sturgeon *(Acipenser transmontanus),* which reaches 360 pounds, and the alligator gar *(Lepisosteus spatula),* at 279 pounds. Most authorities, including Jordan and Evermann, record that the muskellunge reaches a length of 8 feet and is a magnificent fish weighing 100 pounds or more.

Although the average size of most muskies caught by anglers ranges from 5 to 10 pounds, fish over 20 pounds are frequently caught, and hardly a year passes when a muskellunge weighing more than 40 pounds is landed by an angler. In the 1800s large muskies were captured by spearing the fish, using fish traps and hand seines. Today they are mainly the quarry of the angler, with the world-record fish taken by hook-and-line fishermen being a 69-pound 15-ounce muskellunge caught in the New York waters of the St. Lawrence River on September 22, 1957, by Arthur Lawton. Lawton's fish was 5 feet 4½ inches long and just managed to replace the previous record fish, which weighed 69 pounds 12 ounces and was caught in Chippewa Flowage, Wisconsin.

Some years ago, a commercial fisherman by the name of Gauthier, operating in the vicinity of the Bustard Islands in Georgian Bay, Ontario, caught a 125-pound muskellunge in his net. For many years the head of this fish was nailed up on the side of one of his fish houses.

Anglers find that the musky is a cunning fighter that lurks in the shadows and the shallows as it stalks its prey.

The usual way to fish for muskies involves either live bait such as a sucker minnow or with an artificial lure such as a spoon, spinner bucktail, or pike minnow. These can be used in either casting, trolling, or still fishing. Catching a big musky is something akin to hauling in a swordfish, but without oceangoing equipment.

As a predator the musky resembles the saltwater barracuda. They both make fierce rushes and have powerful mouths filled with sharp voracious teeth.

Native to North America the muskellunge appears in the upper Mississippi River and its tributaries, as well as the lakes of Minnesota and Wisconsin, the Great Lakes, the St. Lawrence River, the Ottawa River, and numerous Canadian lakes and streams.

The official name in Canada is moskinonge. In the statutes of Canada, moskinonge is the only name used in reference to this species. A careful search of the literature reveals over 24 different ways in which muskellunge has been spelled. In his 1815 edition of *The Fishes of New York*, S. L. Mitchill used the name "masquinongy." C. A. LeSueur in his *Observations on Esoces* in 1821 refers to the fish as "maskallonge." In 1836, John Richardson, in his *Fauna Boreali Americana* calls it "maskinonge." James DeKay in his *Natural History of New York* published in 1842 names the fish "muskellunge." In the 1850 edition of *Fishes of Ohio*, J. P. Kirtland uses the name "muskallonge" for the pikelike fish.

The name *masquallonge* was evidently given by the early French settlers of Canada to pike and pickerel in general. In French *masque* means "face" and *allonge* "lengthened"—thus its name "long face." Yet some writers are of the opinion that the fish's name derived from the tongue of the Ojibwa tribe of Indians where *mash* means "strong" and *kinoje* means "pike." James A. Henshall, writing in 1892, mentions "maskinonje" as being of Chippewa Indian derivation.

According to the 1901 edition of the *Century Dictionary* we find the name of this fish given with the following variations: maskalonge, mascalonge, maskalunge, maskallonge, masquallonge, masq'allonge, mascallonge, muscalonge, muskalinge, muskellunge, modkalonge, moscononge, maskinonge, maskanonge, maskenonge, maskenozha, maskinoje, and masquelongue to which we can add "lunge" and "longe." It's a record series of names for a fish. For scientific purposes, in 1975 the American Fisheries Society (Special Publication #6) gives the preferred common name as muskellunge and the scientific name as *Esox masquinongy* (Mitchill).

Three varieties, races or subspecies of muskellunge are recognized by some fishery scientists. These are *Esox masquinongy immaculatus* (Girard), which occurs in Minnesota and Wisconsin, including Lake of the Woods and the Rainy River. The subspecies *Esox masquinongy masquinongy* (Mitchill) is found in the Great Lakes drainage, and the Ohio muskellunge *Esox masquinongy ohioensis* (Kirtland) is found in the drainage of the Ohio River. Geographical isolation and distribution are the major factors for the development of the three subspecies.

The form of the muskellunge is quite similar to that of its related species, the northern pike, and many large northern pike have been incorrectly called muskellunge. There is also a close resemblance to the pickerel. All three species have a similar placement and number of

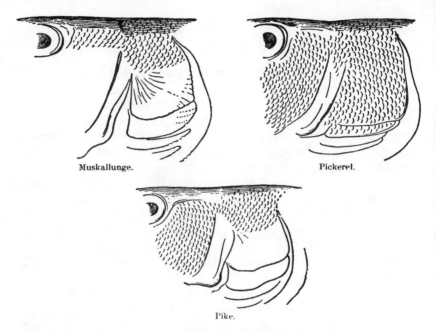

Muskallunge.

Pickerel.

Pike.

fins. The simplest and easiest way to distinguish between these three fish cousins is by the scales on the cheeks and gill covers. With the musky there is only a narrow strip of scales on the top of the cheek-gill cover. With the pike the entire cheek and upper half of the gill covers have scales. On the pickerel all the cheek-gill cover is covered with scales. These differences are important for anyone interested in this important game fish.

The so-called tiger musky of Minnesota and northwestern Ontario has broad and irregular bars along the side of its body and head. It appears from scientific investigations that this variety is a hybrid fish resulting from natural crossbreeding between the muskellunge and northern pike.

Experiments carried out at the University of Minnesota in the late 1930s and early 1940s showed that large numbers of muskellunge eggs could be successfully fertilized with pike milt. In addition, pike eggs were successfully raised after being mixed with musky milt. Some of the resulting young fry were reared in large aquariums and ponds until they were four years old. The hybrid fish had greater vitality and a lower death rate than the pure pike or musky. In addition, the hybrids had a much faster growth rate than either the normal muskellunge or pike. The experiment revealed that muskellunge hybridize readily with northern pike in the same bodies of water. However, the Fisheries Research Board of Canada found that muskellunge-pike hybrids appear to be sterile or infertile.

Depending on the locality, muskellunge will reach sexual maturity in 3 to 6 years. Maturity occurs in 3 years in Tennessee streams and from 4 to 6 years in Wisconsin. Spawning occurs in the spring when the water temperature ranges between 49 and 60 degrees F. The spawning location is usually a shallow water marshy area 1 to 3 feet deep. As with almost all fish species, the number of eggs produced depends on the size of the female. A 2-foot musky will release about 22,000 eggs, while a 40-pounder has been recorded as expelling 225,000 eggs. The eggs are cast out at random in the shallows along the shoreline. Fertile eggs will hatch in 1 to 2 weeks, depending on water temperature.

Musky fry are preyed upon by many organisms including dragonfly nymphs, water beetles, minnows, pike, and their own kind. The young survivors feed on small zooplankton, fish eggs, water fleas, and rotifers. From the fingerling stage onward they become voraciously carnivorous, feeding on fish fry, tadpoles, frogs, salamanders, rats, mice, chipmunks, muskrats, ducks, coots, grebes, and shorebirds. Mainly piscivorous, the larger the muskellunge, the larger the fish it will eat. Yellow perch and white suckers form a large part of its diet, but many other species are its prey: sunfish, rock bass, and catfish. Cannibalism is frequent among fingerlings and common in adulthood. A 28-inch muskellunge was caught with a 16-inch musky in its stomach. They will usually seize the fish they plan to eat in the middle, wait a short time until it stops struggling, and then swallow it head first.

Fishermen note that there is frequently a reluctance on the part of pike and musky to take a bait or lure during late summer, usually August. Some fishing experts maintain that during the middle of August, usually for two or three weeks, the musky is in teething season. During August 1932 a fishing party including the scientist C. A. Porter of the Harvard Dental School visited several muskellunge lakes in Ontario during this so-called teething season. They found looseness of the teeth in all specimens captured, and the fish were preserved and sent back to Harvard Dental School for analysis. The looseness of the teeth was found to be a normal condition. The teeth develop in the floor of the mouth, becoming hinged teeth attached to the jawbone. The teeth are used for offensive purposes, not mastication. When teething, the front teeth are shed and then replaced by a new set from below.

12

Strange and Curious: Odd or Unique

Extreme diversity is exemplified among all varieties of water life. Possessing hues in every conceivable shade, fishes occur in an incredible variety of sizes and shapes from the streamline to the grotesque. Strange habits governed by instinct create remarkable reproductive behavior, with forms of courtship and reproduction unlike anything on land—from clever depositing of eggs to constructing nests to merely casting roe into the waters by the millions and covering them with milt. Anatomical variation is typified by the elongated pipefish and sea horse, flattened eye-traveling flounder, and triangular-winged sea robin.

The Fascinating Courtship of the Cunner

Over the past three decades, observations by marine biologists and naturalists equipped with Aqualungs have resulted in totally unexpected findings about the habits of the cunner, *Tautogolabrus adspersus*. J. M. Green and M. Farwell, scuba diving in Canadian waters, found that cunners remain torpid and inactive under rocks in the winter months when water temperatures fall below 5 degrees C. Underwater observations by John Clark and R. Stone showed that the cunner was the most abundant species of fish on an artificial reef constructed in 1962 off Fire Island Inlet, New York. R. I. Wickland saw the unusual group-mating behavior of cunners in their natural habitat at Shrewsbury Rocks, New Jersey, in June and July 1963. He noted,

> Prespawning behavior took place within small aggregations of three to fifteen cunners which became more active than usual, milling and darting about. Chasing ensued, one fish pursued by several others, moving in small circular paths in and out of rock crevices and over rises on the bottom. The spawning act took from two to three seconds. In each instance, the group of fish made a quick turn upward to converge at a point one or two meters above the bottom, where the fish either contacted or merely touched each other. Then they immediately swam down and glided in a curving path toward the bottom away from a white cloud, presumably milt and eggs which they had discharged at the apex of the upward spawning movement. . . .

If it were larger, the cunner would make a more common food fish, but cunners are usually only 4 to 7 inches long.

The cunner is one of the most familiar saltwater species to marine anglers. The favorite dwelling places of this fish are in the vicinity of shipwrecks, dock spiles, jetties, breakwaters, submerged boulders, and seaweed beds to a depth of 35 fathoms. From the coast of Newfoundland to Chesapeake Bay, hardly anybody wants to catch cunners, but almost everybody in the northeastern and mid-Atlantic region gets them when bottom fishing for cod, sea bass, tautog, and flounder.

Having prominent lips like its close relative, the tautog, the cunner nibbles on barnacles, blue mussels, snails, small crabs, and seaweed attached to rocks and dock piles. The top of its mouth and its pharynx have conical knoblike teeth that crush and grind the hard-shelled mollusks and crustaceans on which it frequently feeds. Hook-and-line fishermen call these fish nibblers, bait stealers, and various unprintable names, as this small finned creature has the habit of rapidly cleaning a hook of its bait before a flounder or cod can get to it.

Cunners also feed on small fishes such as sticklebacks, silversides, and pipefish, along with fish eggs, for which they have special equipment. They feed on dead animal refuse and are scavengers of entrails when they are thrown overboard after fish are cleaned. Lobster fishermen frequently find cunners in their lobster traps feeding on dead bait intended for the crustaceans.

Cunners are found from low-tide levels along the seashore to a distance of about 30 miles out to sea. They are also very abundant around beds of eel grass *(Zostera)*, Irish moss *(Chondrus)*, and rockweed *(Fucus)*.

A wide range of colors appears on cunners allowing them to blend in to their particular habitat. Those living among kelp and rockweed have a brownish hue, and red appears in specimens that dwell among Irish moss and other red algae. Sandy-bottom dwellers have various shades of tan and a speckled hue. Cunners, like other color changers, have pigment cells, or chromatophores, in their skin that provide continual protective camouflage. The color changes are stimulated by vision and a neurological stimulation of specialized skin pigment cells called melanophores. A proper neurochemical stimulation results in an aggregation of pigment with blanching of the skin color.

The eggs of the cunner are transparent and buoyant and lack an oil globule. They range in size from .75 to .85 millimeters in diameter. (About 26 eggs end to end equal 1 inch.) Spawning occurs generally from May through August, with water temperature playing a key role in the incubation period. It usually takes about 5 days for hatching to occur when the water temperature is about 56 degrees F. In 70-degree water incubation will take only about 40 hours. Cunner larvae are about 2 millimeters long, and cunners resemble their adult form when they reach a length of 15 millimeters. Cunners grow relatively rapidly, reaching their normal length of 6 to 7 inches when 3 to 4 years old. Female cunners tend to run larger in size than males of the same age.

According to A. L. Leim and L. R. Day, the largest recorded cunner was a 17¼-inch male specimen weighing 3¼ pounds caught September 9, 1953, off Head Harbour, Campobello, New Brunswick, Canada. I have seen 15- and 16-inch cunners taken in otter trawl nets by fishing draggers off Block Island, Rhode Island.

Occasionally black spots or conspicuous cysts invade and appear on the fins and scales of the cunner. The cysts are an early stage (cercariae) of the trematode worm, *Cryptocotyle lingua,* which is one of the many varieties of parasites that occur on cunners. These parasites will not infect humans as they are usually removed in preparing the fish for cooking. The heat of cooking the fish will also kill the parasites.

The cunner has numerous local names. In southern New England it is sometimes called chogset, or choggy, a name of Indian origin derived from the Mohegan dialect. In the Canadian provinces and most of New England the name cunner is in widespread use. This originated with the English colonists who found that the fish resembled a species *(Crenilabrus melops)* they knew back on the coasts of Sussex and Hampshire as "connor." Along the Long Island shoreline and New Jersey coast the fish is called bergall after a European species, *bergylt*.

Cunners were important as food fish as far back as 1616 when Captain John Smith observed in his *Generall Historie of Virginis, New England:* "And in the harbors we frequented, a little boye may take of cunners . . . at the ship's sterne, more than sixe or tenne (men) can eate in a daie."

In the eighteenth and nineteenth centuries the cunner was a favorite panfish along the North Atlantic coast. During the 1870s over 300,000 pounds of cunner were taken each year by small boats fishing along the New England coast. In 1879 the market could dispose of considerably more than the quantity landed, but for some unknown reason the catch began to decrease at that time; only 160,500 pounds of cunner were taken by Massachusetts fishermen. In 1902 the Boston cunner fishery was carried on near islands in Boston Harbor by nine fishermen with three boats. The catch for that year was taken with hoop nets, or fyke nets, and amounted to 57,600 pounds valued at $3840. The boats made two fishing trips a week to the Boston harbor islands, averaging 2400 cunners per trip during eight months of the year. The fish tended to be of small size, weighing about ⅛ pound each, and sold for an average of 10 cents a dozen.

On some of the islands off Bristol, Maine, cunners replaced flounder as lobster bait, according to G. B. Goode (1887). For securing cunners, a box-shaped lath pot, about 2 feet high and 18 inches square and open above was used. It was ballasted, baited with herring, and lowered to the bottom. It was usually hauled up every five minutes, and by drawing it up quickly the cunners that had been attracted to it by the sight of the bait were prevented from escaping. By this method of fishing, sufficient lobster-pot bait was obtained in a comparatively short time.

Today, most fishermen throw away or feed to the sea gulls any cunners they catch. But knowledgeable fishermen know that cunners are delicious broiled, baked, or fried and are an excellent ingredient in fish chowder. Although the cunner is not regarded as a sport fish, it provides millions of youngsters and tourists to our northeastern Atlantic coast the easy recreational opportunity to catch an edible fish with a hook and line.

Hakes Live in Scallop Shells

Did you ever hear of a fish that spends its immature stages inside the shell cavity of the giant sea scallop and, as an adult, locates food by feeling it with the sensitive tips of fins projecting from its underside? You are probably familiar with this common New England fish but are unaware of its unusual characteristics.

Belonging to the cod family, the squirrel hake, *Urophycis chuss*, is also called red hake and ling. The squirrel hake, caught from the Gulf of St. Lawrence to the Virginia capes and North Carolina, is exclusively an American fish, living only on the western side of the Atlantic. It is typically a cold-water inhabitant found at depths of 300 fathoms in the summer and around the tide line in winter. During late fall and winter

squirrel hakes have been known to enter harbors along the northeastern coast of the Gulf of Maine, and on occasion may even run up some of the rivers.

Offshore, larger hakes prefer deeper waters with soft muddy bottoms. Usually they are found in the deep valleys between the banks as well as on the sloping sides of the banks. Those hakes that are caught on George's Bank are taken pretty well down on the slopes, with an abundance of them at depths greater than 60 and 70 fathoms all along the southern slope of George's Bank.

One recent summer, the Chesapeake Biological Laboratory at Solomons, Maryland, was deluged with fish brought in for identification by sport fishermen, who caught them in Chesapeake Bay and the lower estuaries. In almost every case the strange fish turned out to be small hakes. All hakes examined by the laboratory were less than 10 inches long, indicating that they were members of a dominant-year class that had migrated to the rich feeding grounds of the bay. They were believed to have come from the ocean in the spring as fingerlings and had grown large enough to be caught on the hook by fishermen. Hakes had been recorded previously in Chesapeake Bay, but this time they were far more abundant than usual and so uniform as to seem a "foreign" species.

The unusual habit of the squirrel hake is the use of its ventral fins in feeding. It swims close to the bottom and with the sensitive tips of its fins drags over the mud feeling for shrimp, crabs, amphipods, and small lobsters. Many years ago the investigations of Francis Herrick at the former Bureau of Fisheries Laboratory at Woods Hole proved that the squirrel hake depended chiefly on its delicate sense of touch rather than on its sight for food. This is not surprising since the adult hake lives in murky regions and does most of its feeding at night.

Way back in 1616, John Smith wrote: "Hake you may have when the cod fails in summer, if you will fish in the night." It is fairly common knowledge that hakes bite best after dark since they are out foraging. A hake will readily take a bait on a hook. In fact, most hakes taken on long line are caught with pieces of herring. They are also caught frequently with hunks of clam on the hook. Commercially, however, roughly one-eighth of the landings are taken on long line; the large majority of the yearly catch, about two-thirds of it, are taken by otter trawl; and approximately one-fifth of the hake are caught by gill nets.

The most unusual characteristic of the squirrel hake was described by William Welsh after an oceanographic cruise of the U.S. Bureau of Fisheries schooner *Grampus* during the summer of 1913. He noticed that numerous sea scallops dredged within the 20-fathom curve of southern New England, New York, and New Jersey had small hakes, 1 to 2½ inches long, living inside the mantle of the scallops' shells. Hakes do not feed on the scallops but use them for hiding places. Welsh recorded as many as 27 hakes taken from 59 scallops in another haul. Nichols and Breder also record young hakes as rather common in the mantle cavities of sea scallops during November, in about 20 fathoms of water off New York.

Baby hakes begin life in the summer on the surface of the sea, emerging from spherical transparent eggs about ¾ millimeter in diameter. Hake fry have been observed darting about on the sea surface, probably chasing minute zooplankton. Gradually the young ones follow their instinct and move down to the bottom, with some of them taking up residence inside the shells of living sea scallops for protection. It's believed that hakes 2 to 3 inches long are in their first year, those 6 to 7 inches long at the end of their second year, and those 7 to 14 inches long in their third year.

Paternal Pipefish—A Special Lifestyle

Examining the catch of a minnow trap set in 4 feet of water in Little Narragansett Bay, Rhode Island, I discovered I had made an unusual catch. It was about 8 inches of elongated fish, which was whipping its tail from side to side and swimming rapidly among the silversides, sticklebacks, and mummichogs that had also been ensnared. At first glance I thought it was a small eel, but when the creature slowed down a little I could see that it was too slender to be an eel. I gently picked up the fish, and its elongated snout told me that it was a pipefish.

In my palm the fish's eyes, moving in short, continuous jerks and setting somewhat out from the head, looked straight at me. This was the first pipefish I had ever encountered in my minnow trap, so I put him into a 5-gallon glass tank used for marine specimens. The pipefish lived in the tank for almost two weeks before he succumbed.

Found along the eastern coast of North America from the southern side of the Gulf of St. Lawrence and outer Nova Scotia to South Carolina, the northern pipefish, *Syngnathus fuscus*, generally lurks among seaweed and eel grass in salt and brackish water. Pipefish, when closely examined, cannot be confused with any other species, for their characteristics and peculiarities are piscatorially distinctive. The pipefish is a long, slim, bony creature with a small, toothless mouth at the end of the tubelike snout. It does not appear to have scales but, instead, an armor of segmented bony plates similar to those of the ganoid sturgeon. Its fins are somewhat oddly shaped, with a delicate, rectangular, soft-rayed dorsal fin on the back and a triangular, somewhat fan-shaped caudal fin at the end of its tail. This is important to the fish's manner of locomotion.

Pipefish vary in color from individual to individual, depending on their habitat. They range from a muddy green to a reddish brown, corresponding to the hue of the seaweed among which they may be found. Pipefish differ from most other bony fishes in the structure of their gills, which form tufts of small, rounded lobes instead of the usual gill filaments.

Another peculiarity of this fish is its ability to swim in either vertical or horizontal position. In vertical position the pipefish performs like its close relative, the sea horse, by using its dorsal fin, located back of the gills, for equilibrium and to maintain itself upright. When alarmed, or when wishing to go from one place to another in great haste, it thrusts into a horizontal position and glides rapidly by making sinuous

right and left whiplike movements of its tail, reminiscent of the propelling motions of snakes and eels.

Still another interesting habit of these fishes is their method of feeding. Their food consists mostly of small crustaceans such as amphipods and copepods, fish eggs, and small fish fry. When the pipefish feeds, a curious snapping noise is made as it moves its head with a birdlike pecking motion. The pipefish gathers food into its small oral cavity by expelling water from the narrow snout and pharynx with a muscular action of its cheeks, causing a slight vacuum to form in its mouth. It then thrusts its head at the food particles, sucking them in by suddenly opening its mouth, creating the clicking sound. Although its snout and mouth appear to be rather small, the pipefish can swallow larger prey than one would expect because these parts are flexible and stretch a great deal. In the act of catching its prey the pipefish is also greatly aided by the mobility of its eyes, which are able to work independently of one another. The eyes are similar to those of a chameleon.

By far the most unusual characteristic of the pipefish is its method of reproduction. The female of the species shirks her maternal duties and deposits the eggs in a sort of marsupial pouch in the male, again like the sea horse. The father takes care of all the baby pipefishes needs until they are able to manage for themselves.

Apparently the earliest mention of the pipefish was in the third century B.C. by the Greek philosopher Aristotle. Pliny repeats Aristotle's observations in A.D. 1, and then for nearly 1500 years there is no further mention of the pipefish. In 1554 Rondelet published his *De Piscibus Marinis* wherein he described the pouch in which the pipefish eggs are placed. He said the pipefish casts the eggs into the pouch of the female. Rondelet studied fishes alive in the water, and his observations are quite accurate except for his mistake on the sex of the pouch-bearing fish. This error persisted for nearly 300 years. In 1831 the Swedish naturalist Eckstroem wrote that only the male possesses the pouch. His statement caused a 40-year controversy among zoologists, until it was definitely determined that only the male pipefish has a pouch for holding fertilized eggs.

In the summer of 1903 E. W. Gudger made a study of the life history of the pipefish at Beaufort, North Carolina. According to Dr. Gudger, a female pipefish ready to give up her eggs can be recognized by her much-enlarged abdomen. The act of transferring the eggs from the female to the male is preceded by a curious ritual.

The two fishes swim around with their bodies in nearly vertical positions, the head and shoulder regions bent sharply forward. They then swim slowly past each other, their bodies touching and the male perhaps the more demonstrative of the pair. Just before the actual transfer, the male becomes violently excited, shakes his head and anterior body parts in a corkscrew fashion, and with his snout nuzzles the female on the belly. The female responds to this but does not become as excited as the male pipefish. This act is repeated several times, the fishes becoming more excited whenever they touch each other. Presently, quick as a flash, the female pipefish transfers the eggs to the male's pouch and the fishes separate, only to begin again in a few minutes.

In the embrace the fishes intertwine their bodies like two capital *S*'s, one interlocked with the other and coming face to face. They thus hold their bodies together while the eggs pass from the oviduct to the pouch. About twelve eggs are transferred at a time and are presumably fertilized at the moment of transference from one parent to the other.

The dozen eggs, each about a millimeter in diameter, are now in the top portion of the male's brood pouch. Before the male can receive any more eggs he must move the eggs to the lower part of his pouch. In order to accomplish this the male performs some curious movements. He stands nearly vertical, and resting on the back part of his tail, he bends backward and forward, twisting his body spirally from above downward. This activity is performed until the dozen eggs settle to the bottom of the pouch, and then the father is ready to receive more. As many as 570 eggs have been found within the pouch of a single male.

The eggs become embedded in the lining of the pouch. Here they receive nourishment. Incubation takes about 10 days, and the baby pipefish are held in the brood pouch of the father until the yolk sac has been absorbed, when they are about 8 or 9 millimeters long. Then the young are ready to go out into the water world. According to Mrs. C. J. Fish, who studied pipefish at Woods Hole, Massachusetts, unlike the sea horse, once the young pipefish leave their father's pouch, they never return to it.

Baby pipefish that have been kept in aquariums have been observed to grow about 2 inches in the first 2 months after hatching. At the end of their first year they are believed to be mature.

Because they are bony, hard, and almost fleshless, pipefish are seldom preyed upon by other fish. The only enemy of the pipefish of which I can find mention is the Portuguese man-of-war. On numerous occasions the pipefish has been observed hopelessly entwined in the many tentacles of this jellyfish.

The rigidity of the bony-plated skeleton of the pipefish makes these fish easy to preserve as curiosities. You simply let them dry out in the sun. On top of my desk as I write this is the dried-out specimen of a pipefish I captured last summer.

Eight different species of pipefish are found in the offshore waters of our Pacific coast, and 12 species live on our Gulf and Atlantic coasts from Texas to Maine.

Fishes closely related to the pipefish include the sea horse, trumpet fish, cornet fish, and snipe fish.

Father Becomes Mother—The Sea Horse

One of the most unusual marine fishes more closely resembles a miniature Chinese dragon or a knight on a chessboard than a finned creature of the sea. Having a head like a horse and a tail like a curled-up worm, one can easily see how the Latin name *Hippocampus*, which means "bent horse," was chosen for this species in 1758 by Carolus Linnaeus.

Numerous species of sea horses are scattered around the world in tropic and temperate waters. They range in size on the Atlantic coast from the 1-inch dwarf sea horse, *Hippocampus zosterae*, of Florida and the Gulf to the northern sea horse, *Hippocampus erectus*, found from South Carolina to Cape Cod and straying to Nova Scotia, that reaches 7¼ inches. In the Pacific Ocean off the western coast of Mexico a large species of sea horse, *Hippocampus ingens*, reaches a length of nearly 12 inches. In Chinese and Australian waters a giant genus of sea horse, *Solenognathus*, occurs that reaches lengths of nearly 2 feet. Also in Australian waters is a species that is an excellent example of protective camouflage, *Phyllopteryx* (which means "leaf wing"). The ragged skin growing all over its body resembles the fronds of algae and gives it a very bizarre appearance. When this species sits still its shreds of ragged skin look so much like seaweed that it is very difficult to tell where the seaweed ends and the sea horse begins.

The sea horse has several distinctive characteristics. It has a neck. There is only one small propelling fin, the short dorsal, and no caudal or tail fin at the posterior end.

The sea horse resembles South American monkeys in that it is able to support itself by its prehensile tail. It can move one eye independently of the other, like a chameleon. The male of the species has a protective pouch for the young, very similar to the pouches found in kangaroos and other marsupials. The body of the sea horse is covered with a banded bony outer shell like that of the armadillo. One can readily see why the early students of nature were in doubt as to whether this was truly a fish or some other aquatic animal.

To ichthyologists there is no doubt that *Hippocampus* is a fish. It possesses platelike bony scales, fins, and lobelike gills. Having chromatophore cells in its skin, like most other fishes, the sea horse is able to change color to camouflage itself in its surroundings. It can transform its color into hues of red, yellow, brown, and white.

Unlike all other fishes, which usually swim in a horizontal plane parallel to the bottom, the sea horse generally swims in an upright position slightly coiled, using its tail to grasp eel grass and other seaweed.

The tail is restricted for grasping and does not serve as a fin. The anal fin is greatly reduced and has lost its function. The two delicate pectoral fins are just behind the gills and are used to keep the vertical position and maintain equilibrium. The major source of locomotive power is the dorsal fin, which can oscillate at the rate of 10 flaps per second, propelling the sea horse at a fairly slow gait.

Usually the sea horse does not swim much if it can help it. It can drift along supported by its buoyant air bladder or hook itself to kelp and eel grass where it will await a choice morsel of zooplankton drifting by.

Having an elongated snout that opens and closes with a rapid jerk, the sea horse makes a faint smacking or clicking sound as each food particle is sucked in. Its food consists chiefly of minute copepods, shrimp larvae, and fish eggs swallowed whole without being chewed, going down to the gullet alive.

Even more curious are the reproductive habits of the sea horse, which are similar to those of the closely related pipefish. When the time for mating approaches, the adult male and female sea horse approach each other with rhythmic gyrations that approach a primitive dance.

The male possesses a pocket, or pouch, in its middle abdominal region under the pelvic bone. At the conclusion of the rhythmic undulations the female inserts her cloacal appendix into the male pouch and expels 200 to 800 eggs into the convenient pocket. It is thought that the eggs are fertilized in transit. The transfer of eggs takes from 24 to 48 hours. This event constitutes the end of the responsibility of motherhood for the female as the male takes over the job of nurturing the young.

While the fertilized eggs are in the male's pouch, the connective tissue in the chamber's wall expands through capillary action and engulfs many of the developing eggs, providing a sort of pseudo placenta. The male's belly becomes very expanded from the developing young, and he resembles a pregnant female. Usually 40 to 50 days are required for the eggs to develop.

When the period of development of the young is completed, the male begins the arduous task of expelling the living babies. He can be seen writhing on the sandy bottom or rubbing his body against pebbles or hard projections. Finally, with considerable effort, the male spurts his burden of tiny sea horses out in a billowing cloud along with the residue of eggs and gas bubbles. The male's pouch does not empty all at once. Several expellations extend over several days. The newly released sea horses are about ¼ inch long and closely resemble the adult form.

Sea horses are a favorite species among saltwater aquarium enthusiasts because of their unique qualities. Many fishermen in southern Florida add to their income by capturing thousands of live sea horses in dip nets for fish enthusiasts.

There is also considerable demand for dried sea horses as souvenirs. The rigidity of the bony skin makes it easy to preserve dead specimens. They are mummified by exposure to air and sunshine.

Flounder—The Doormat

Angered at his rudeness, rose the mighty Whale;
"Thwack!" upon the Flounder smote that dreadful tail,
Made him as a pancake, deep upon his face,
Like a butter pattern, stamped that weird grimace!
That's the way it happened; that's the reason, Honey,
Why the poor, flat Flounder looks so awful funny!
—Arthur Guiterman

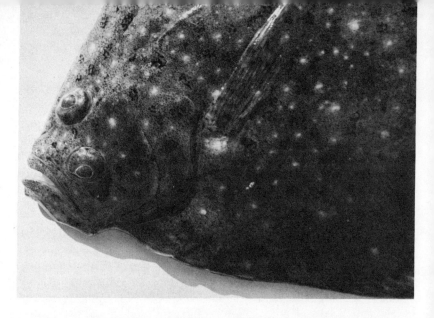

The common flatfish, or flounder, has three pecularities: (1) the two eyes are on one side of the body in the adult form; (2) the upper or eyed side is colored and the lower side white; and (3) the dorsal fin extends forward as far as or beyond the eyes along the edge of the head, not between the eyes as in most fishes.

Toward the end of May, into the shoal water along the sandy beaches and bays of the Middle Atlantic and southern New England swims the summer flounder, *Paralichthys dentatus*, commonly known as fluke. They are present all through the summer, then gradually decline in inshore waters at the beginning of October and almost completely disappear by the end of the month.

The summer flounder, or fluke, is sometimes confused by novice fishermen with the winter, or blackback, flounder. If one were to place the two types side by side, it would be obvious that the fluke is "left handed"—its eyes are found on the left side—while the blackback is "right handed," with eyes on the right side. In addition, the summer flounder possesses a large mouth with prominent teeth as compared to the tiny mouth of the winter flounder. If there is still any doubt as to the flatfish's identity, you can count its dorsal fin rays. Summer flounder have from 85 to 94 rays; the winter flounder have from 60 to 76 rays.

The first record we have of flukes were specimens sent by a Dr. Garden of South Carolina to the Swedish biologist Carolus Linnaeus during the eighteenth century. In South Carolina at this time the fish were called plaice, after a similar species found in Europe.

This species receives the name summer flounder because it is the most prevalent species of flounder in inshore coastal waters during the summer months. Most of the larger members of this species are believed to spend the summer in waters off northern New Jersey, New York, and southern New England; smaller members of the species are generally found from southern New Jersey to the Virginia capes. Evidence from tagging experiments indicates that older flukes return to the same locality year after year.

The name of fluke for this species of flounder may have developed because of this species' large size. They sometimes reach a weight of 20 pounds. Summer flounder that weigh 10 pounds or more are affectionately called doormats. A few doormats between 15 and 20 pounds are taken each summer by lucky anglers. Nichols and Breder (1927) mention a 30-pound fluke taken off Fishers Island, New York, about 1915. Goode (1887) mentions a 26-pound fluke that was an estimated 46 inches in length taken in June at Noank, Connecticut. In 1895, Fred Foster, fishing on the banks off New York, landed a 19-pound summer flounder with rod and reel. The current world-record fluke taken on rod and reel, as recognized by the International Game Fish Association, is a 20-pounder caught at Oak Beach, New York, September 7, 1948 by F. H. Kessel.

The summer flounder is generally found from Maine to South Carolina and is most abundant south of Cape Cod. Research over the past twenty years has determined that flukes spend the winter months on the edge of the continental shelf from off Rhode Island to North Carolina, at a depth of 30 to 80 fathoms. In recent years New England fishing draggers have gone "fluking" in this area during the winter months and have come up with sizable catches of summer flounder in their otter trawls.

Very little is known of the spawning habits of flukes except that ripe females were taken off Nantucket, Massachusetts, in 70 fathoms of water by the fishing dragger *Eugene H.* on April 15, 1951. Ripe summer flounder have also been recorded in Chesapeake Bay during October.

During the early life history of the flounder a very unusual transformation takes place. Young flounder begin life with an eye on each side of the head and swim upright like other fishes. Usually at the age of 5 to 7 weeks the flatfish tend to swim on one side or the other, eventually dwelling on or near the bottom and resting on one side. The upper side develops protective coloration to blend with the environment, and the underside loses its color. The eye on the lower side slowly migrates to the upper side of the head, its optic nerve still intact. This remarkable transformation is an excellent illustration of structural adaptation to the environment.

Another strange characteristic of the fluke is its chameleonlike ability to change color. It can assume a wide range of color patterns from checkerboard and spotted arrangements to various shades of gray, blue-green, brown, pink, orange and almost black. This ability to camouflage itself is attributed to specialized pigmented cells in its skin called chromatophores. These chromatophores are regulated by nerve and hormonal stimulus influenced by what the flounder sees.

The fluke's diet is made up of a wide variety of marine organisms including squid, small clams, crabs, shrimp, sand dollars, and young fish. In inshore waters around docks and breakwaters the favorite food of the summer flounder is the saltwater minnow, or mummy. The fluke usually lies on the sandy bottom, covered with sand except for its eyes. When it sees a choice item of food passing by, it rushes from the sand and captures it.

Spearfishermen stirring up the sandy bottom find the flounder

X-ray of a flounder

fluttering off to another hiding spot as soon as it is disturbed. The wide and flat outline of the fish offers a big target for spearmen.

Some fishermen get a good haul of flukes at night by the method known as gigging. With a bright flashlight shining into the water from the bow of the rowboat, they drift over tidal flats armed with a 10- or 12-foot pole with a 2- or 3-pronged spear attached on the end. When the light is reflected by the gleaming fluke's eyes, its outline is visible, and the flatfish is easily speared. Under ideal conditions, a bushel of flukes can be speared in a relatively short time.

Beach seiners sometimes set their long nets for flounder along sandy shorelines, and fishing draggers frequently get large quantities of flatfish in their otter trawl nets. Summer flounder are a favorite with the sinker bouncers, and these line fishermen get quite a few drifting with minnows or squid on the long-shanked flounder hook.

Summer flounder and another flatfish, halibut, are the highest-priced flatfish on the market. Their firm white flavorsome flesh makes them a favorite with the housewife. Flukes are sometimes sold as chicken halibut because of their close resemblance to young halibut.

In restaurants flukes generally appear on the menu as fillet of sole. Flukes are served in a great variety of ways including *Fillet de sole calypso*, which is a slice of fluke rolled up with finely ground lobster, or *Fillets de sole amandine*, which is flounder fillet cooked with butter and almonds.

The Noisy Searobin

Although it presents a rather gruesome appearance, the searobin is one of the most tasty morsels that can be placed before an epicure. The flesh is firm, snow white, and similar to that of a kingfish or whiting.

In the United States, only a few commercial fishermen and even fewer consumers seem aware of the appetizing appeal of the searobin, or striped gurnard. In Europe it is much appreciated.

Searobins belong to the genus *Prionotus*, and we have two species prevalent off our North Atlantic coast: the common searobin, or Carolina searobin *(Prionotus carolinus)*, and the striped, or red-winged, searobin *(Prionotus evolans)*.

Found from the Bay of Fundy to South Carolina, the two species of searobin are generally located on the sea bottom. They occur in inshore shallow regions during spring, summer, and fall, and move offshore in the winter. Robins prefer a sandy bottom. I have often observed them while skin diving; only the top of the head and the eyes are visible, the rest of the body being buried in the sand. This trait is also common among flounder and sand dabs.

The searobin resembles the sculpin with its large spiny head and tapering body. However, searobins can easily be distinguished from sculpins because robins possess three fleshy feelers originating from the lower pectoral fins. Robins also have smaller mouths than sculpins, the entire head is encased in bony plates, and they have a bright red color.

As searobins move along the bottom, they frequently appear to

crawl by moving their fleshy feelers as though they were fingers. Some observers have reported the robins using their feelers to stir up the weeds and sand to rout out the small animals on which they feed.

Their diet consists chiefly of small crustaceans such as mysis shrimp, crabs, clams, squid, and small fishes. Saltwater anglers are frequently annoyed by searobins that take bait intended for flounder, cod, and mackerel.

Searobins make grunting noises when they are disturbed or taken out of water. Marie Fish, who made a scientific study of fish sounds, considered the two species of searobin the noisiest fish along the North Atlantic coast during most of the year. Fish, who carried out most of her investigations at the Narragansett Marine Laboratory of the University of Rhode Island, said the noise made by searobins had a drumlike quality similar to that made by drawing a wet finger across the surface of an inflated rubber balloon. The rhythmic outbursts of the two common species suggests the cackling and clucking of barnyard fowl. The average frequency of the sound produced by the robins decreased as the length of the noisemakers increased. Fish continued:

> The common searobin responded with sound to every type of stimulation attempted. Specimens began grumbling when they were first captured and continued sporadically after they appeared to be fully acclimated to captivity. Captive specimens soon tamed, would lie quietly on the bottom clucking softly during gentle stroking by experimenters; if this manual stimulation were applied too long or too heavily, the fish would break away in seeming annoyance and emit a louder burst. Electric stimulation brought forth clucks that were followed by bursts of higher pitched cackling. Routine listening over common searobin grounds in Narragansett Bay picked up typical sounds, and the hauling of trawls in such areas was accompanied by a pandemonium of squawking.

The production of sound by the searobins appears to result from gas released under pressure through the muscular, balloonlike air-bladder lobes.

Spawning of the sea robin occurs during the summer from June to August, after the inshore migration has taken place. The eggs are slightly yellowish when released and about a millimeter in diameter. At a temperature of 72 degrees F., they will hatch in about 60 hours. By November the young robins have grown to a length of from 2 to 5 inches.

The common searobin is usually about 12 inches long, reaching a maximum of 15 to 16 inches and a weight of 1¾ pounds. The striped searobin is slightly larger, reaching a maximum length of 18 inches. In the waters around Great Britain, a close relative of the searobin in the gurnard family, *Trigla hirundo*, can weigh 11 pounds and have a total length of over 2 feet.

13

The Unpopular and Pug Ugly

"Old blubberlips" is a name given to ocean pout by some commercial fishermen. Slow-moving, large-mouthed toadfish, they are beady-eyed, belligerent, and quick to bite. Warty tubercules and mounds, along with the sucking disk on the lumpfish's belly, complete the queer shape. During the mating season the grotesque male lumpfish has a red belly, and the female has a yellow belly.

Ocean Pout Eat Sand Dollars

Macrozoarces americanus is known to fishermen by many names: eelpout, congo eel, muttonfish, ling, blenny, yowler, snakefish, and rock eel. This great diversity of names led to confusion with other species. On February 1, 1943, the U.S. Fish and Wildlife Service's Marketing Service decided that the prevailing name, eelpout, was misleading because this species is not related to eels. Dealers found it difficult to market any fish with "eel" in its name because of public antipathy to eels, so the Service decided to adopt the name ocean pout for this species. Some commercial fishermen call this species blubberlips.

One of the earliest American descriptions of ocean pout was by W. D. Peck (1804):

> It is sometimes called conger eel. In the consistence of the muscles it is like the eel, and deprived of its head and skin, it is sometimes sold as such; but it is preferable to the eel, as it feeds on living food; whereas the eel feeds on carcasses.

Ezekiel Holmes (1862), in his report "The Fishes of Maine," stated:

> Early in the spring and first of summer the fishermen sometimes take, in company with cod, this fish to which from its general resemblance to the conger eel they frequently give the name Conger eel and Ling. It is also caught at other seasons of the year but not so often. It is much prized by some people as a savory fish. Its common length is from one foot and a half to two feet. Occasionally one is caught from three to four feet long but those of that size are rare.

A bottom-dwelling fish, the ocean pout is elongated, eel-like, with small scales and slimy skin. It can readily be identified by its mottled reddish brown, yellowish salmon color and eyes located high on the head. The upper jaw projects slightly beyond the lower jaw, and it has thick, fleshy lips. In its upper and lower jaws it possesses blunt, irregular, conical-shaped teeth.

Y. H. Olsen and Daniel Merriman (1946), who examined the stomach contents of over 850 ocean pout, found that this species feeds chiefly on sand dollars, crabs, isopods, scallops and other mollusks, and longhorn sculpin eggs.

In southern New England, Deep Hole east of Block Island is one of the best sources of pout. Spawning of this species takes place in the fall when the fish withdraw from trawlable areas and head to rocky locations to release their eggs. According to Bigelow and Schroeder (1953), the ocean pout lays large yellowish eggs about 6 or 7 millimeters in diameter in clumps on the bottom in protected areas. A 21½-inch fish contained 1306 eggs; one of 34½ inches had 4161 eggs.

In late winter and early spring, there is one inshore migration of this species. Pout have been found from shallow inshore waters to depths of 105 fathoms. A 12-inch pout is estimated to be 3 years old, 2-foot specimens from 6 to 7 years old, and 3-foot specimens from 12 to 16 years old.

Commonly found from the Gulf of St. Lawrence to Delaware, the ocean pout was never highly regarded as a food species until the food shortages of World War II, when pout was marketed filleted. During 1943 and 1944 over 10 million pounds of this species was marketed, the majority of it taken by draggers in 15 to 25 fathoms off southern New England. Today the fishery has dropped to less than 200,000 pounds sent to market each year. How did this decline come about?

During World War II, prices on all foodstuffs were carefully regulated by the Office of Price Administration. In the spring of 1943 the OPA attempted to place a price ceiling of 15 to 17 cents per pound on frozen fillet of ocean pout, but because of confusion in this species' name, the price limit was placed on conger eel, a different species. As a result, ocean pout had no price ceiling. From December 1943 to February 1944 ocean pout was marketed at prices ranging from a penny to $2.50 per pound. During this period, it was common practice for buyers to bid fantastic prices for species not under price regulation in order to obtain the boatload of regulated fish. In one instance a wholesaler paid $500 for one skate in order to obtain a boat's catch of price-fixed fish.

On March 23, 1944, the U.S. Fish and Wildlife Marketing Service reported prices as high as $3 per pound for ocean pout; then an OPA regulation set a ceiling of 5 cents per pound, or the current market price, on species without previous limits.

The fishery for ocean pout was short-lived. As pout were filleted and packed, it became apparent that large quantities of this species were unfit for marketing because of large boils, sores, and tumors found in the flesh. There were rumors that illness could result from eating pout, but no factual evidence supported these assumptions. Many shipments of ocean pout were declared unfit for human consumption by municipal and federal public health officials. In the spring of 1943 R. F. Nigrelli determined that the sores in ocean pout were chiefly the result of a protozoan parasite, *Plistophora macrozoarcidis*, which infects the fish. There was no evidence that this parasite could infect human beings, but a slight possibility existed of mild food poisoning from eating infested fillets.

Some fishermen and their families had been eating ocean pout for generations with no apparent ill effects. However, the vast amount of irregular blotches in the flesh of this species has greatly curtailed its economic value. In 1954 the total U.S. landing for ocean pout was less than 200,000 pounds, with a value of about $3000. In 1944, 4,449,600 pounds of ocean pout were landed in Massachusetts ports, but because of publicity about the parasitized fillets, the Massachusetts catch dropped to 6100 pounds by 1948. Today the majority of the ocean pout caught is placed with trash fish for reduction to fishmeal.

The Tramp of the Sea—The Toadfish

One of the noisiest and ugliest fishes along the Atlantic coast is the toadfish, *Opsanus tau*. Its mottled gray and brown scaleless skin, along with its grotesque wrinkled shape, account for its common name. Even the young of this species are tadpolelike in appearance.

Around the head of the toadfish one sees conspicuous projections of skin; there are fleshy fringes around the underside of the mouth about the eye sockets. These flaps probably serve as camouflage; they bear a striking resemblance to rockweed, especially brown algae.

Toadfish are variable in color depending upon the color of the bottom in which they are found. They are sometimes muddy green, reddish brown, and various shades of gray.

The species is very common along our Atlantic coast from Maine to Florida. It was first recorded in the 1700s by Dr. Garden of South Carolina, who sent a specimen to Linnaeus in Sweden who named it *Gadus tau*. M. E. Bloch's *Atlas of Fishes*, published around 1782, has a plate of a toadfish.

The first American to describe the toadfish was S. L. Mitchill in 1815. He placed it with anglerfish because of its large head, skinny tentacles, and huge mouth. C. S. Rafinesque in 1818 described a toadfish from the south shore of Long Island and gave it the name *Opsanus cerapalus*. He noted that this fish is found spawning along the shore during summer but is not seen in winter. C. A. LeSueur, writing in 1824, remarked on the resemblance of this fish to a frog and added that they are known as toadfish to the inhabitants of Massachusetts, Rhode Island, Egg Harbor, and also Carolina. In 1842 DeKay described the young of toadfish, which were frequently found in oysters. He also mentioned a shower of toadfish that fell in the streets of New York in 1824.

Toadfish have many unusual habits. Their large eggs are deposited in nests that may be found in discarded tin cans, bottles, rotting logs, stones, and empty shells. Cornelia Clapp, writing in 1899, says that the toadfish retreat in pairs to large stones, especially near the low-water mark, and scooping out a cavity beneath, remain there for days. She further writes that the toadfish of Eel Pond, near the laboratory at Woods Hole, seem to prefer the debris of civilization to the excavation beneath the rock—for example, tin cans, old boots, broken jugs.

Ryder (1886) found that the adult toadfish burrows a hole under one side of a submerged boulder, and to the solid rock of this cavity the female attaches her ova in a single layer. The eggs are very adhesive and quite large, measuring about ¹/₅ inch in diameter. Like the male catfish, the male toadfish assumes charge of the eggs and remains by them until they are hatched. The eggs are dirty yellow, almost amber-colored, and are spread out in an area about as large as one's hand, numbering about 200. Gudger records as few as 22 eggs in one nest and as many as 723 eggs in another.

Like certain mammals such as seals and walruses, toadfish are polygamous. One male may watch over the eggs of several different females in his nest.

After the eggs have been laid, the male seldom leaves them. He may snap up unwary minnows and crabs that happen to pass close by the nest, but he does not eat regularly. Males captured guarding nests are much thinner than free-swimming males the same age.

Goode (1884) writes that the father toadfish takes considerable interest in his young. When the young have been hatched, the older fish seems to guard them and teach them the devices of securing food, in much the same manner as a hen does her chickens.

A toadfish seems to secure its food by strategy and stealth rather than by swiftness of motion. Hiding under or between rocks and weeds, it observes its victims until they are close by and then from ambush captures a meal of crabs or small fishes.

With a large mouth, powerful jaws, and blunt conical teeth, the toadfish is a formidable adversary to any crustacean or small fish. Toadfish that have been teased snap viciously at anything near them. Gudger tells of a 9-inch fish that was prodded with an oyster shell that clinched its teeth so tightly to the shell that the fish was lifted out of the water and placed in a pail still grasping the shell.

Usually toadfish never hold on to what they bite but just snap and let go. They move exceedingly fast when they snap or bite. One toadfish will sometimes swallow a smaller member of its own species if it is hungry enough.

Toadfish are very hardy and can remain alive as long as 24 hours out of water. During the winter months in northern waters they seem to bury themselves in the mud in a state of hibernation.

Although many fishermen discard toadfish because they do not believe them palatable, toadfish are very edible. Storer (1855) writes that the flesh is delicate and good. . . . Baird states that the flesh is very sweet and palatable. Gudger writes that toadfish taste as good, if not better, than any bottom-dwelling fish he has eaten.

Toadfish average lengths of 7 to 10 inches, but may reach 15 inches. Anglers sometimes catch toadfish, and to their dismay and disgust, they find that the fish has not only swallowed the baited hook but the sinker as well.

Study of the toadfish life history has been of considerable interest to U.S. Navy researchers because the fish is one of the loudest and most distinctive noisemakers in the sea. Its foghornlike sounds have been recorded by sonar operators on numerous occasions. Tavolga has written that under water at a distance of 2 feet, the sound output of a single toadfish can reach an intensity of over 100 decibels, which is as loud as a riveting machine or a subway train.

Two kinds of sounds can be detected from these fishes. There are powerful, foghornlike "oonks" and short grunts or growls. All sounds come from the heart-shaped air bladder. Broad muscles seem to set the air bladder in motion, causing the sound, but the precise mechanism of sound production is yet to be determined. Some sounds are believed to be associated with mating, and others are produced when the fish is irritated. Why and how these sounds are produced is under scientific investigation at several U.S. marine laboratories.

My Bout with the Lumpfish

On the first day of spring in 1953 I took a walk along the docks at Stonington, Connecticut, to see what the fishing boats were catching. At Longo's Dock, four draggers were waiting to unload their haul, and I saw a fish lying helpless on the hatch cover of the 80-foot dragger *Jane Dore*.

It was a bluish gray fish, almost as wide as it was long. The slightly grotesque creature was vaguely familiar, but its name slipped my mind. On its back were two lumps, a big hard one and a small one, and its skin was completely covered with dark specks and blotches. On its sides were more lumps, in three rows. It had a large white suction apparatus on the undersurface. The fish was about 2 feet long.

I asked the boat's skipper, Captain Silva, where he had found such a strange fish, and he said it came up in the nets about 3 miles from Watch Hill, Rhode Island. "I catch a few of these every spring," he said, "but the rest of the year they don't seem to be around."

I asked if I could take the fish to the University of Rhode Island Marine Laboratory, where it might have some scientific value.

"Sure," he said, "help yourself. We've got a good load of 'junk' today."

He was bringing in trash fish, the kind that are rendered and processed for fertilizer and meal. I later found out that the draggers were getting only 80 cents a hundred pounds.

"Better take some ice with it," warned the captain, "or you won't be able to stand the odor in the car."

I put the slimy fish into a wooden box with some ice on top. That evening I went through Breder's *Field Book of Marine Fishes of the Atlantic Coast.* I found the odd fish to be a lumpfish, *Cyclopterus lumpus.* The next morning, I took it to the University at Kingston. Most of the ice had melted, and the fish was beginning to make its presence known.

Robert A. DeWolf saw me coming with it and said, "That's a pretty big lumpfish, Gordon. I don't believe I've seen one quite that big."

I told DeWolf that I had brought the creature in to study its anatomy. He seemed a bit surprised but replied: "I've got a box of tools on the shelf. Do you want to start in on the dissection?"

"Okay," I said nonchalantly, "but I want to take its weight and measurements first."

The lumpfish weighed 21 pounds 4 ounces, and its length was 23½ inches. I carefully checked all the books on fishes in the college library and found that my specimen of *Cyclopterus lumpus* was larger than any other previously reported in North America.

I began to dissect the largest North American lumpfish in captivity. I found it to be a female with its body bulging with pink eggs. I carefully removed the egg masses, getting them all, since I thought I would want to count them to see just how prolific this "lump" was.

The eggs and ovaries weighed 5 pounds 4 ounces, or approximately a quarter of a lumpfish's total weight. Nichols and Breder, in their book on New England fishes, state that lumpfish eggs are pink when first laid, so I assumed that this female had been about to issue her eggs.

It was impossible for me to count the eggs right away, because mid-semester exams were coming up. So DeWolf suggested that I put them in a glass container with a little formaldehyde until I could take a lumpfish egg census. I did this, and in the formalin solution the eggs shortly changed from pink to yellowish orange.

A week after exams were over, I began the tedious task of counting the multitude of eggs. Breder mentions in his book that large lumpfish females up to 18 inches produce as many as 136,000 eggs. My female lumpfish was 23½ inches long. When I started to count the eggs, I found to my dismay that the formaldehyde had for some reason not produced the desired effect. The eggs had assumed the fragrance of a dead fish that had lain in a dark, damp corner for months.

So, holding my nose with one hand and the fish eggs with the other, I began to count them, at first singly, then by unit of weight. The faculty members of the Zoology Department took a deep breath and closed the door of the laboratory I was in. All the windows on the second floor of Ranger Hall were open that day, but it was a tossup whether I should burn my clothes when I got through or take a chance with the cleaners. However, my efforts were rewarded. After the odorous escapade, I

Lumpfish eggs being weighed before being processed into caviar

totaled my figures and found that this "lump" contained 279,620 eggs. Perhaps you can imagine my pride in having bettered the celebrated Breder (no pun intended) by 143,620 eggs!

Donald Zinn had seen quite a few lumpfish, but they had always averaged between 3 and 5 pounds—less than the egg mass alone from my fish. I photographed the fish, but by now it had become somewhat notorious, and the university's publicity bureau sent over a photographer to photograph Dr. Zinn, the lumpfish, and me. This picture appeared in the Providence *Evening Bulletin*.

I did a bit of research into the life history of lumpfish and found that they have some unusual habits. The male "lump," like the stickleback, guards the eggs until they hatch. Throughout the period of guardianship, the male remains unfed but continually fans the egg mass, thus keeping it free of silt and bathing it in flowing water. He never leaves the eggs except to drive off intruders. To protect them, he has been known to attack and kill such a fearsome creature as the wolf fish. By the time his vigil has ended and the eggs are hatched, he is thin and exhausted. The females, on the other hand, take no part in guarding the eggs and are said to move into deeper water as soon as they have finished spawning.

Yearling "lumps" average a little over 2 inches in length, and the fish are said to attain maturity in the third year. They become about 10 inches long in their fifth year. I guess my "lump" was pretty well along in years.

Large lumpfish are usually found hiding in rockweed or holding fast by the sucker to stones or other objects. In Massachusetts Bay they occasionally attach to lobster pots, and in Maine and Scottish waters they have been found clinging to the posts of a trap or weir. There is a record of one "lump" stuck to a mackerel. Since they are weak swimmers, lumpfish can be easily preyed upon, and are said to be a favorite food of seals.

The lumpfish is never eaten in the United States, but it is an important fish in Greenland, Iceland, and Northern Europe. One may also see the eggs sold as "lumpfish caviar" in New York City and elsewhere.

14

Sometimes Hard to Catch —For Different Reasons

Soft lips, weak jaws, and giant size make catching certain fishes difficult. A large basking shark can weigh over 4 tons and reach a length of 45 feet. An Australian species of grouper reaches a length of 10 feet and is known to stalk divers. Oceanic sunfish feed on drifting jellyfish and sometimes weigh over a ton. Blackfish or tautog sometimes wedge themselves between rocks when hooked and are almost impossible to pull out. Many fishes, such as the menhaden, feed almost entirely on small plankton and will almost never take a fishhook.

Grouper and Giant Sea Bass—The Sluggish Fighters

One of the remarkable characteristics of the smaller species of groupers is their ability to change color instantaneously. Some years ago, C. H. Townsend, director of the New York Aquarium, noted eight radical color changes in the Nassau grouper, the result of skin pigment cells called chromatophores that change hue to enable the fish to blend in with its surroundings to avoid detection.

In his observations on the Nassau grouper, which ranges from North Carolina south to Brazil, Townsend reported the following color phases in groupers. In one phase the fish is uniformly dark, in another creamy white; in a third it is dark above with white underparts. A fourth phase shows dark bands, the whole fish taking on a light brown coloration. In a fifth phase the fish is pale, with all dark markings tending to disappear. The sixth phase shows a light-colored fish with the whole body sharply banded and mottled with black. The last common phase provides the grouper with a dusky hue above and white below, with a black band in the middle region from head to tail. William Beebe described a blue grouper with three broad vertical bands of brown that swam into a clump of coral, emerging a few minutes later clad in brilliant yellow and thickly covered with black polka dots!

Groupers are perchlike members of the large and varied bass family Serranidae that has representatives in almost all tropical and temperate seas. Fossil remains date back to the Eocene period.

Over a hundred species of groupers and their close relatives are known from tropical and subtropical seas. The name grouper is a corruption of the Portuguese *garoupa*, a name for another fish. All groupers are voracious and carnivorous, feeding on other fish, shrimp, crabs, shellfish, and cuttlefish.

The large spotted grouper is sometimes found with hard, irregular blackfish lumps lying free in the body cavity or bound by tissue to the viscera. On examination, one of these lumps was found to contain the mummified body of a sharp-tailed eel. The eel must have been swallowed by the grouper and in its death paroxysms inserted its sharp tail through the wall of the stomach or some other portion of the grouper's alimentary canal. It was then able to squeeze into the body cavity where it became transformed into a mummified fish. Similar cases of penetration of the food tract by eels have been recorded among large perchlike fishes from Ceylon. Large cod also have been noted with mummified butterfish and blennies dried and shriveled in their body cavities. One would expect a fish cutting its way out of the food canal of its swallower to cause a hemorrhage or the death of the predator, but the intruder causes no harm to its consumer.

Groupers are edible and fairly tasty. Their pale flesh is sought after by both commercial and sport fishermen.

Some groupers and their close relatives, the giant sea bass, are sometimes called jewfish. They attain immense size, growing to lengths of 5 to 7 feet and weights of 600 to 800 pounds. These giant black bass live on the bottom in the tropical Atlantic, along the California coast, and in the Indo-Pacific region. The Queensland grouper of the Great Barrier Reef off eastern Australia is reported to reach a weight of 1000 pounds and a length of 12 feet.

The California giant bass, *Stereolepis gigas*, has been recorded as weighing 800 pounds. These huge, clumsy fish are sluggish in their movements among the rocks on the sea floor. Charles Frederick Holder, author of *The Log of a Sea Angler* and other books on fishes, describes his first giant California black sea bass:

> What a wonderful creature it was! The experience of the moment, the sensations, could not have been purchased. It was worth going a long way to accomplish. Imagine, you casters of the black bass fly, a small-mouthed black bass lengthened out to six feet, bulky in proportion, a giant black bass—one that you would dream about after a good day's fishing. . . ! Imagine this and you have the jewfish, black sea bass or *Stereolepis gigas*, of the Pacific coast—a noble fish, a gamy fellow, especially adapted to the man who desires animated dumbbells, or who, sedentary in his habits, requires violent exercise combined with much excitement.

The giant black bass can be fished year-round and is taken by anglers with live bait. Holder tells us it is

> fished for on the edge of the kelp in 30 or 40 feet of water. The strike comes as a nibble, but when hooked the fish is away with a rush that has been known to demoralize experienced anglers. . . . I have seen a 200 pound fish snap the largest shark-line like a thread, and large specimens straighten out an iron shark-hook; yet the skilled wielders of the rod catch these giants of the tribe with a line that is not larger than some eye-glass cords.

In fishing for groupers and giant sea bass the angler must keep them with taut line to prevent their getting into holes and crevices in the rocks. If they wedge themselves between rocks, they are almost impossible to dislodge. They should be brought to the surface as soon as possible after hooking and kept near the surface until they can be gaffed or netted.

The appellation jewfish appears in the writings of the English buccaneer William Dampier (1652–1715). Dampier wrote: "The Jew-fish is a very good Fish, and I judge so called by the English, because it hath scales and Fins, therefore a clean Fish according to Levitical law."

According to the list of accepted standard names prepared by the Committee on Names of Fishes of the American Fisheries Society (1970), jewfish should be used only when referring to members of the grouper genus *Epinephelus* belonging to the species *itajara* usually found in the tropical Atlantic. The preferred common name for the giant California bass variety, *Stereolepis gigas*, is giant sea bass.

The largest member of this group of fishes appears to be the half-ton Queensland grouper. This species has been known to stalk pearl divers and shell divers the way a cat stalks a mouse and has been recorded as rushing a diver in an apparent attack. It is the basis for stories of skin divers being swallowed by giant groupers.

"Sea Serpent"—The Basking Shark

Of the hundreds of species of fishes that inhabit our North Atlantic coast, the distinction of being the largest falls on a member of the shark family, *Cetorhinus maximus*, the basking shark, known also in some localities as the elephant shark and the bone shark. This fish reaches a maximum length of 50 feet and is second in size only to the whale shark of tropical waters, the largest of all fishes.

A giant 293-pound grouper

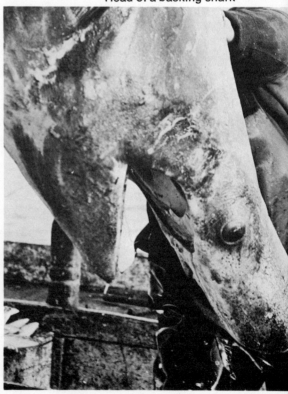

Head of a basking shark

The basking shark derives its name from its habit of lolling lazily at the ocean's surface, its dorsal fin and portions of its back showing above water. On various occasions this fish has been observed with its white belly exposed to the warm sun's rays. It's a sluggish fish and not too wary of boats; there have been quite a few reports of small boats coming alongside basking sharks, and sailors stepping onto the little "island."

This shark is easy to recognize because its numerous teeth are extremely small (about ⅛ inch long). It has an elongated proboscis that is frequently red, and its gill openings are unusually large, extending around the neck.

Norman and Fraser (1949) tell of two large basking sharks swimming one behind the other in tandem fashion, giving rise to the rumor of a "sea serpent." One can easily visualize sailors' getting such an impression, especially if the lead shark is swimming with its mouth open and above the surface.

The basking shark has been reported off North America from the outer coasts of Nova Scotia and Maine to North Carolina. During the first half of the eighteenth century these sharks were very plentiful off New England and were widely pursued for their livers. Basking shark liver is about 60 percent oil and was frequently used for illumination purposes. Whenever they encountered these sharks, whalers would harpoon them. Since the flesh of the basking shark is soft and flabby, it is not for human consumption like the meat of firm-fleshed sharks. However, basking shark flesh is sometimes used for fishmeal.

Today, the basking shark is still pursued commercially by harpoon off the west coast of Ireland. Here the shark is found in large numbers and taken for its liver oil. These sharks have a liver of tremendous size—for example, the weight of a liver from a 30-foot basking shark reported by MacGinitie was 1800 pounds. Patterson tells of a basking shark 28 feet 10 inches long taken off the Irish coast that yielded 102 gallons of oil. Some vivid scenes of basking-shark hunts appeared in the film *Man of Aran*, made on the west coast of Ireland during the 1930s.

Another very graphic account of capturing basking sharks was given by a Mr. Couch in 1877:

> The boat approaches the fish with a man in the bow ready to harpoon it; the line attached to the harpoon is 200 fathoms long, and is coiled up in the bow; a man stands by with a hatchet, ready to cut it, should it get entangled or foul of anything in running out. When a fish is struck, he will

at first dart and carry out from 70 to 150 or 200 fathoms of line; he makes this rush to the bottom, where he rolls himself, and rubs his wound against the ground to free himself from the harpoon.

Fishermen generally allow the shark to tire itself before they begin to haul up on the harpoon line; they coil the slack again, ready for it to make another rush, and play it in this way, sometimes for eight or nine hours, before they can get it to the surface. When it does surface they are ready to strike it with two or three more harpoons; when these are fixed, the men pull the shark alongside the vessel with the harpoon lines. They stretch the shark fore and aft along the vessel's side, getting a jowl rope around its head and the bight of a hawser around its tail.

The basking shark is then given two deep hatchet cuts, one on each side of the tail, and in its agony and its efforts to get free, it works its tail so hard that it snaps the bone across which the cuts were made. The fishermen then cut flesh holes on both sides of the body of the fish and reeve ropes through the holes. By hauling taut on the side of the fish next to the vessel, they cant it over on its back. Then they split down the stomach, take out the liver, which is the only part they use, and discard the rest of the fish.

Basking sharks are incredibly powerful in the water and if harpooned in the shoulder are very difficult to kill, often carrying off the whole harpoon line. Experienced harpooners strike them in the body, near the dorsal fin, rather low down, either into the intestines or near the vertebrae toward the tail. A shark must be struck with great caution, as it will stave in the boat with one blow of its tail if it is at all within reach.

On several occasions when the carcass of a basking shark has washed ashore, first reports classified the remains as a "sea monster." As basking shark remains rot and deteriorate, the fins, jaws, and skin are washed away, leaving an oblong cranium and a long, ridged backbone. During January 1937, a would-be sea serpent washed ashore near Provincetown, Massachusetts, on the outer coast of Cape Cod. This denizen was given widespread publicity on the radio and in newspapers, but it turned out that the monster was nothing more than the skeleton of a 25-foot-long basking shark.

In several recorded cases of "serpents," the basking shark involved happened to be a male. Remains of the claspers and pectoral fins still attached to the body gave the appearance of feet and caused the mistaken identification.

One such monster was found beached at Stronsay in the Orkney Islands at the beginning of the nineteenth century. This specimen was actually described in a leading scientific journal as an unknown animal species and given the imposing name *Halsydrus pontappidiani*. In the case of this newfound species of "sea serpent," remains of the backbone were preserved. Later investigation showed the vertebrae to be identical to those of a basking shark.

The basking shark is sometimes referred to as a bone shark by fishermen because of the close resemblances of its gill rakes and gill arches to the baleen plates of the whalebone whale. The gill rakers of this shark and the whalebone plates of the whale perform the function of filtering food (minute plant and animal life) from seawater. This is an example of parallel development of a similar functional apparatus in two widely different groups of animals.

The way in which the basking shark satiates its appetite is an extreme example of laziness. With its gaping mouth wide open, the immense fish swims slowly among the myriad plankton, swallowing into its gill cavity large quantities of water and thousands of minute creatures of the sea. As the gulped-in water is forced out through the gill slits, plankton is filtered out by the fine gill rakes, leaving the next meal on the interior of the gill arches where it can be swallowed at leisure. An interesting sidelight is that as the food-filled water passes through the gills, oxygen is removed and taken into the bloodstream; thus it can be said that the basking shark eats and breathes with the same mouthful.

During the summer of 1956, basking sharks were present off the Rhode Island coast. Four medium-size ones, averaging between 15 and 20 feet in length, were captured at intervals in the fish traps off Point Judith. These fishes were taken out of the traps and released, as they have very little market value for fishermen and are difficult to get aboard a vessel.

Nimble Pollack

Each spring, off Provincetown, Block Island, and Montauk Point, countless sea gulls dive in at the approach of ravenous schools of migratory pollack. At such time, the fish school at the surface, breaking water like porpoises; they chase small fish, squid, and shrimp in all

directions. These agile fish gather in the strong tide rips, constantly searching for food carried along by the tide.

Their most widespread name derives from the old English vernacular name for this species, polog. Sometimes they are called coalfish, or green cod, as well as Boston bluefish on the Massachusetts coast. Scientifically, they are classified as *Pollachius virens*. Found on both sides of the Atlantic Ocean, pollack have been recorded from Hudson and Davis straits to Cape Lookout, North Carolina, most plentifully from the southwestern tip of Cape Cod to Cape Brenton.

The pollack, like its close relatives the cod and the haddock, has three dorsal fins and two anal fins. It differs from the haddock by possessing a pale or white lateral line, and can be distinguished from the cod by its lack of spots and blotches. The pollack's chief difference from its close relatives is the shape of its head, with its pointed snout and projecting lower jaw. Its skin is a greenish color on the topsides, blending into a silvery gray on the lower surface. Usually young pollack are a darker brownish green than their elders.

Pollack also differ from cod and haddock by being a much more active species. They are benthopelagic fish, being found in both surface and bottom waters at various times. Frequently they are encountered on the surface, like mackerel; at other times, they may be present at mid-depths. Again, otter trawlers may pick up considerable quantities of them as their nets travel along the bottom.

The largest pollack on record was taken on May 26, 1975 by John T. Holton off Brielle, New Jersey, weighing 46 pounds 7 ounces according to the International Game Fish Association.

Using their keen sight to search out food, pollack feed mostly on small fish such as herring, butterfish, and weakfish, along with immature cod, haddock, whitings, and porgies. They also prey upon squid, shrimp, and copepods. H. M. Smith reports that one 9-inch pollack kept under constant observation ate 77 herring up to 2½ inches long at one meal. H. B. Bigelow states that young pollack that infest the harbors are the worst enemies of young cod and that a single young pollack 7 or 8 inches long is so fierce it will scatter a school comprised of hundreds of cod fry, causing the little fish to hide among weeds and between stones and sheltering rocks.

The pollack generally is a late autumn or early winter spawner in waters that usually range from 15 to 50 fathoms. It is also a cold-water fish, preferring temperatures between 40 and 50 degrees F.

Pollack almost rival cod in egg production. According to Earll, a pollack 23½ pounds contained 4,029,200 eggs.

The eggs are buoyant and drift near the surface, generally hatching in from 7 to 10 days. Young pollack are usually 5 to 7 inches long at the end of their first year; about 12 inches long at 2 years of age; and 17 to 18 inches at 3 years of age.

According to Bigelow and Schroeder (1953), small pollack 8 to 10 inches long and weighing less than ½ pound swarm inshore after early April in the Gulf of Maine; they report thousands of pollack taken at this time from traps at Gloucester and Magnolia. In the southern part of Massachusetts Bay, the harbor pollack, as they are called locally, move out in June to avoid rising temperatures and return again in autumn. Larger pollack tend to keep farther offshore than smaller ones. However, a large fish may appear inshore in pursuit of small schools of fish. During their spawning season, large pollack are sometimes taken in great numbers in gill nets in Massachusetts Bay, and from Cape Ann to the Isles of Shoals. In southern New England, numbers of small pollack appear inshore during September and October, providing great sport for youngsters fishing off piers with small hooks and squid or clams for bait.

As a food fish, the pollack is highly regarded by many, and some prefer it to cod when it is salted. It is a white-meat, firm-bodied fish of pleasing flavor suitable for filleting. Considerable quantities of pollack are frozen and packaged as "deep-sea fillets." At the fish market, pollack generally bring a slightly lower price than haddock or cod.

All along the Middle Atlantic and New England coasts pollack are highly regarded by rod-and-reel fishermen. At the time of their spring and fall migrations, great numbers are caught by anglers trolling from slow-moving boats, using jigs or feathers. Pollack are very voracious, taking the hook readily just before or after the turn of the tide. At some places on the Maine coast, pollack are referred to as Quoddy salmon because of their game qualities when taken on a hook.

Sunfish—Giant Pancakes of the Deep Sea

A gray saucer-shaped mass, about 5 feet in diameter, floated placidly on the surface of the sea 4 miles southeast of Block Island. Occasionally there would be gentle undulations from the flabby rear rim of the creature, which caused little swirls in the water as we approached. This was a unique member of the world of fishes—the ocean sunfish, *Mola mola*. The rounded eye located near the front and center portion of the flabby mass glared at us, but the colossal fish did not move.

Resembling a giant pancake, the mola is somewhat of an oddity among fishes. It is rounded and rather compressed; the tail appears to have been cut off behind the long dorsal and anal fins. Because of the lack of a distinct tail, this creature is sometimes called the headfish by fishermen and seafarers.

The dorsal and anal fins cannot be laid back, as in most fishes; and they propel the sunfish by going from side to side, somewhat like the sculling of a boat. The mola has a degenerate, flabby skeleton; the spinal cord of a 9-foot sunfish is about ½ inch long. In addition to its other peculiarities, this species lacks a swim bladder.

Belonging to the order of fishes called the Plectognathi, the ocean sunfish is closely related to the filefish, puffers, and porcupine fish. The scientific name *Mola* is from the Latin meaning "millstone" and refers to the fish's general shape.

All members of the giant sunfish family are oceanic. There are two

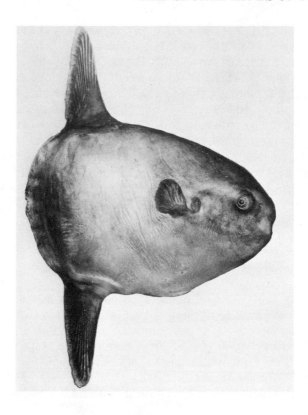

major species: the common, or round-tailed *(Mola mola);* and the
pointed-tailed, or sharp-tailed *(Mola lanceolata),* which has the hind
end of its body pointed in the middle. The ocean sunfish is more frequently encountered. It belongs among the giant fishes, weighing a ton
or more in the adult stage. Van Campen Heilner in *Adventures in
Angling* described a specimen 10 feet 11 inches long taken off Avalon,
California. David Starr Jordan and Barton Warren Evermann recorded
another Californian fish, 8 feet 2 inches long and weighing 1800 pounds.
Each year a few giants are reported off the Middle Atlantic and New
England coasts.

The largest mola on record is an Australian specimen reported by
David G. Stead in *Giants and Pigmies of the Deep.* On September 18,
1908, a little after 1:00 P.M., the S.S. *Fiona,* off the coast of New South
Wales, about 40 miles from Sydney, suddenly shook from stem to stern,

and her port engine stopped dead. A boat was lowered, and it was noted that a large sea creature had collided with the vessel. It was impossible to dislodge it. The *Fiona* limped into port taking the jammed sea monster with her. In port, while a curious crowd of onlookers watched, the jammed fish was removed with a huge iron hook specially forged for the purpose. The creature turned out to be the largest mola ever recorded, measuring 13 feet 4 inches from the tip of its dorsal to the tip of its anal fin. It weighed over two tons—4400 pounds!

The ocean sunfish is a lethargic creature, usually showing no alarm at approaching boats. Would-be sunfishermen find that, although the mola is an easy target for a harpoon, it is extremely difficult to capture because its leatherlike hide and the tough, gristly material just below the skin form a protective shield.

The following extract from *The Voyage of the Scotia* (1906) provides an interesting account of the capture of a mola off Montevideo:

> The catch consisted of a large sunfish weighing about three-quarters of a ton. Some half-dozen of these huge fish were seen during the day basking at the surface, the largest being the size of a small haystack. The one we captured was really quite tiny, but it was all we could do to haul it on board. Its stupidity was amazing; unable to swim faster than the boat could row, all it had to do to escape was to sink . . . and this they can do quite well . . . but, although hit by harpoon a dozen times before one held, it made no attempt to escape. Davidson, an expert harpooner, managed to insert a harpoon into the gill cleft; then the beast allowed itself to be towed to the ship, apparently dying of disgust.

Another account tells of a big sunfish that was harpooned and proceeded to sink slowly but steadily as the rope was played out. When the end of the rope was reached, however, the fish continued to sink with such determination that the bow of the launch was pulled down; finally, to the great relief of the aspiring sunfishermen, the rope parted under the strain, and the prize catch disappeared.

On another occasion, a harpooned sunfish acted more vigorously. Its physical protest was so vehement that it nearly wrecked the launch. Another boat was dispatched and a second harpoon sunk into the mola. Still it fought on, splashing and beating the surface of the sea into a maelstrom. Only after a continuous struggle of three hours' duration did it succumb.

When captured, the mola has been described as uttering sounds that are comparable to the grunting of pigs. One writer reports an oceanic sunfish making "hideous groans" when it was dragged ashore on a beach in Dorset, England. The creaking sound is produced by grating the upper and lower pharyngeal teeth.

The huge sunfish has a relatively small mouth lined with beaklike fused teeth. It feeds chiefly on jellyfish, ctenophores, and other small invertebrates. G. E. and Nettie MacGinitie's *Natural History of Marine Animals* gives the following firsthand description of ocean sunfish feeding in Monterey Bay, California:

> The Mola slowly swims to a jellyfish and begins a sort of nibbling, sucking performance around the edge of the bell. By beating with its dorsal and ventral fins as it nibbles away, the fish makes from three to five revolutions around the jellyfish before the latter is consumed. The eating activities of the fish have a tendency to push the jellyfish to the surface, and the sucking noise that the Mola makes as it bites off pieces of the jellyfish can be heard for some distance. When the Mola has finished with one jellyfish it swims to another and the performance is repeated. How long a Mola continued to feed on a school of jellyfish is not known, but judging from the size to which Molas grow, and the fact that their food consists chiefly of coelenterates which are 96 percent water, they have to spend considerable amounts of time feeding.

Ocean sunfish live in the open sea, and although sometimes seen singly or in pairs, they are gregarious at certain seasons, banding together in small schools consisting of upward of a dozen individuals.

The mola provides an ideal habitat for parasites. Its flesh and alimentary tract are frequently infested by numerous nematode worms, and barnacles and large copepods attach themselves to its leathery hide. Even little suckerfish *(Remora)* set up housekeeping in the mola's gill cavities.

Practically nothing is known of the breeding habits of this fish, but it has been established that the species is extremely prolific. According to J. R. Norman, author of *Giant Fishes, Whales and Dolphins,* the ovary of an oceanic sunfish has been found to contain no less than 300 million unripe eggs. The eggs are about $1/20$ inch in diameter when released into the open sea, and an extremely small percentage survive to reach maturity. The minute size of the eggs and larvae of the mola caused one scientist to make the following comparison: "The larval sunfish is to its mother as a 150-pound rowboat is to 60 *Queen Marys!*"

The larva when hatched is about $1/10$ inch in length and resembles other bony fish larvae. However, it soon loses its tail and caudal fin and is modified into its distinguishing pancake appearance.

The flesh of the sunfish is generally regarded as worthless because the fish is a close relative of the globefish and puffer, which are highly poisonous to humans. People rarely eat mola fillets; even though the fish seems harmless, it is tough and tasteless. A portion of mola was once sent as a present to a gentleman whose cook made it into soup. The gentleman described it as the best turtle soup he had tasted in a long time.

Actually, the oceanic sunfish has no commercial value except among the Japanese, who relish its liver.

Why Weakfish Are Good Sport Fishing

"Got any chickret on board?" shouted the old-timer standing on the wharf at Galilee, Rhode Island. A small fishing dragger had pulled into the dock and was tying up. The captain took a couple of small speckled fish from the wire basket and handed them to the man.

The chickret, as it is sometimes called, is probably known by a greater variety of names than any other fish on our Atlantic coast. Chickret is a corruption of an old Narragansett Indian name for this fish, *succoteague*, or *squeteague*. Local variations of this name include squil, squintee, and squit. Along the rest of the coast most fishermen know this fish as sea trout, gray trout, drummer, and weakfish.

The designation weakfish seems to have originated from the jargon of the early Dutch colonists of America, who referred to this species of fish as *weekvis*. Some authorities say the fish was once called wheatfish because this species used to appear at harvest time. Weakfish is a name easily attributed to this species because the fish offers feeble resistance by not pulling very hard when hooked. There is also the old wives' tale that this fish is supposed to be weakening to those who eat it habitually. Lastly, the fish has soft, tender flesh about the mouth, which allows a hook to rip out easily if the fish is not played properly.

The weakfish is a member of the generic tribe of *Cynoscion* of which there are three species on our Atlantic coast. The northern weakfish, or squeteague *(Cynoscion regalis)*, is found from Maine to Florida. The southern weakfish, or spotted sea trout *(Cynoscion nebulosus)*, occurs from New York to Texas. The third and least known of this group is *Cynoscion nothus*, the silver sea trout, which is found in

the Gulf of Mexico and occasionally encountered on the Atlantic coast of Florida.

The northern weakfish is subject to periodic fluctuations in abundance. This species may be plentiful for a few years and then disappear almost entirely, only to appear again in large quantities a number of years later.

The weakfish is a coastal fish that prefers sandy shores and shallow waters. The weakfish swim either near the bottom or at the surface in schools.

Mute testimony to the schooling habits and periodic abundance of weakfish can be found in an item by Barnet Phillips that appeared in the *New York Times* in July 1881:

> A great catch of weakfish was made yesterday about two miles off Rockaway Beach, by the steam smacks *E. T. DeBlois*, Capt. J. A. Keene; *Leonard Brightman*, Capt. Elijah Powers and *J. W. Hawkins*, Capt. J. W. Hawkins. These smacks are engaged in the menhaden or "mossbunker" fishery for the oil-rendering and fish-scrap works on Barren Island and were cruising off Rockaway yesterday in search of schools. About noon a vast school of what the fishermen supposed at first to be menhaden was discovered stretching along the coast for miles. To borrow their language, "The water was red with fish, but they didn't break the surface as menhaden always do." The boats were lowered, the seines spread, and then it was discovered that the school was of weakfish and not menhaden. "I have been in the business for twenty years," said the mate of the *Brightman*, "and I never saw anything like it before." The fish varied in length from one and a half to three feet, and in weight from three to seven pounds. The *DeBlois* took over 200 barrels, and *Hawkins* 150 barrels, and the *Brightman* 350 barrels. The entire catch was estimated at something over 200,000 pounds, which, at the ordinary market price for weakfish—seven cents a pound—would amount to $14,000. But, of course, the market price could not be maintained in the presence of such a catch as this, and it was said yesterday afternoon that a strong effort was being made by the wholesale fish dealers of Fulton Market to prevent the greater part of the fish from being put on sale. . . . Fish-dealers say that there will be no difficulty in selling all the fish this morning at from one to three cents per pound.

In recent years weakfish have been rather scarce along the New England and Middle Atlantic coasts, but fishermen are hoping for an increase in this species' abundance.

The weakfish can be recognized by its silvery color, somewhat greenish on the upper part of the body. It has numerous small irregular dark blotches on the sides, which form undulating lines running downward and forward. The fish takes on a green metallic hue when it is drying, and the green becomes more intense after the fish is dead.

Sometimes weakfish are called by the name of drummer because of a croaking, drumming noise made by the male of the species. The female, usually larger than the male, is the silent partner and is unable to make a sound. The sex of weakfish can be determined by feeling the belly wall of the fish. The male has a very thick abdominal wall that covers the croaking muscles. Females have a very thin belly wall. The air bladder, which is also used in making the sounds, is present in both sexes. The process whereby the male croaks and drums by virtue of his special muscle has been described in part by Smith (1907): "The muscle, with the aponeurosis (thick connective tissue) is in close relation with the large air bladder and by its rapid contraction produces a drumming sound with the aid of the tense air bladder which acts as a resonator." The exact purpose of the sound apparatus of the male has yet to be determined.

Weakfish have been recorded up to a maximum size of 30 pounds, but specimens over 10 pounds are very rare. The record for rod-and-reel fishermen is a "squet" taken off Trinidad in the West Indies on April 13, 1962 by Dennis B. Hall. This fish weighed 19 pounds 8 ounces.

The food of weakfish consists mostly of small fishes such as silversides, mummichogs, and small menhaden. They also feed on squid, clams, shrimp, and crabs. This species is also cannibalistic; the stomachs from weakfish of about 4 pounds have been known to contain several baby "weaks" about 6 inches long.

A few weakfish appear in New England waters by the end of May, but it is usually mid-June before they arrive in quantity. Anglers anxiously await the arrival of the "weaks" as they provide fine sport for their size. Some fishermen chum for them with shrimp, while others drift for them with clam worms and shedder crabs for bait. They are also caught with squid and mummichogs.

On occasion, surf casters fishing for striped bass will encounter a school of weakfish, and the "squet" will hit a small plug or jig as furiously as a striper. Weakfish will occasionally run up tidal rivers and canals, but they seem to prefer bays and the mouths of rivers.

Weakfish spawn in the Middle Atlantic and in New England bays from May to September with June the month with the greatest reproductive activity. Spawning usually takes place near the bottom in 3 to 5 fathoms. The eggs float up and drift at the surface for the short time it takes them to hatch, which is about 1½ days according to Breder. Weakfish fry grow rapidly, about 4 to 6 inches during the first 6 months. As far as is known, both male and female "weaks" mature at 2 to 3 years of age when they are about 10 to 13 inches long.

It has often been suggested by fishing biologists that weakfish are scarce when bluefish are plentiful, and vice versa. This occurrence is understandable, because "blues" and "weaks" prefer the same food, especially menhaden. Since the bluefish is the more voracious feeder and swifter swimmer, it would disrupt the squeteague's food supply when present in abundance.

The Elusive Blackfish (Tautog)

When chestnut leaves are as big as thumb-nails
Then bite blackfish without fail,
But when chestnut leaves are as a span,
Then catch blackfish if you can.

This little rhyme is from a publication printed in 1814 called *The Fishes of New York*, by S. L. Mitchill. Blackfish, or tautogs, as they were called by the Narragansett Indians, are a familiar species to all commercial and sport fishermen along our North Atlantic coast.

The first mention we find of the tautog was back in 1643 in Roger Williams' *Key to the American Language* where the fish was described as one of the edible species of southern New England. Today the names blackfish and tautog are synonymous; in addition, this species is also known by various local names including oysterfish in North Carolina, Moll or Will-George on the eastern shore of Virginia, saltwater chub at the mouth of the Chesapeake, and whitechin off the New Jersey coast.

Belonging to the wrasse and hogfish family Labridae, of which there are numerous species scattered around the world, the blackfish, *Tautoga onitis*, is limited in its general range from the outer coast of Nova Scotia to South Carolina. It is an inshore coastal fish with almost the entire population living within a mile or so of the shoreline. It is most plentiful in the region between Cape Cod and the Delaware capes.

Blackfish are a mottled chocolate brown that varies between light and dark depending upon the fish's age and sex. Young blackfish are a very light brown with blotches of dark brown, while older fishes are a uniform dark brown or blackish. The male of the species is usually darker than the female. Many large tautogs have a light white patch under the chin, hence the origin of the name whitechin.

Most blackfish usually range from 1 to 6 pounds, but blacks from 7 to 12 pounds are captured occasionally. The largest blackfish on record was captured near New York in July 1876. Its length was 36½ inches and its weight 22½ pounds. This specimen was mounted and is now on exhibition at the U.S. National Museum in Washington, D.C.

A rocky shoreline is the favorite habitat of the blackfish. They are almost always plentiful around jetties, breakwaters, bridge abutments, dock pilings, and shipwrecks. The tautog has large, stout, conical teeth in the front of its mouth, which it uses to chomp up the mussels and crabs that abound in its rocky haunts. In the back of its mouth are small rough teeth for grinding food. Blackfish are also said to eat large barnacles attached to rocks and pilings. Young tautogs eat seaweed, small crustaceans, mollusks, and worms.

Blackfish are present in New England all year round; however, during the cold months of winter they migrate to somewhat deeper waters where they are believed to hibernate under large stones and in crevices in the rocks.

During October and November there is usually a heavy run of blackfish to their wintering grounds. On rare occasions during the winter when there is a very severe cold spell during a time of low tides, great fatalities are known to occur among the tautog population. The records show that in February 1857, after a period of very low temperatures, hundreds of tons of dead blackfish drifted onto the beach at Block Island and along the shores of Massachusetts and Rhode Island. Similar occurrences were observed in 1841, 1875, and 1901.

Blackfish are sometimes caught on hook and line as late as December by cod fishermen, but they usually become sluggish and begin hibernation at the end of November. If the temperature is mild, many tautogs remain active and do not enter a state of lethargy. At the southern limit of their range they are taken year-round.

During April and May there are large inshore runs as the blacks head into shallow waters to spawn. Blackfish generally spawn in May and June inshore along patches of eel grass and pebbly bottoms. The eggs hatch about 2 days after being released. By the end of their first summer the young blacks are about 2½ inches long.

Because of the stubborn fight they put up when hooked, blackfish are a favorite species with sport fishermen. As tautogs are bottom dwellers, a sinker heavy enough to keep the line on the bottom is needed to reach them.

Large submerged rocks and boulders are favorite haunts of tautogs. Blackfish usually stay within a few feet of an exact spot and do not venture from it. A person fishing 30 or 40 feet from the hangout of the tautog will be out of luck. Sometimes it takes years of experience to learn the exact spots for good tautog fishing. If one is successful in catching blackfish on an outing, it is a good idea to take observations on shore landmarks and line up ranges with other objects so the productive spot can be found again. At some locations blackfish bite best at flood-tide; at others, at ebb. It is a good idea to study local conditions and check with old-time fishermen.

Some fishermen chum for blackfish by throwing broken clams, crabs, and mussels over the side to attract the tautog; this method often provides an excellent catch.

Favorite baits for the tautog are green crabs hooked whole if small, split in half if large. Rock crabs and hermit crabs are also good when available. Sea clams, small softshell clams, and sandworms also are excellent bait, but they usually are nibbled off the hook by cunners and other small fishes before the blackfish can get to them. Because of their hard coarse mouths, tautogs are sometimes difficult to hook, and it is advisable to give your line a good hard jerk when you think you have a blackfish on it. When extracting the hook from the blackfish's mouth, care must be taken not to get your finger bitten by the fish. Because of his powerful jaws and sharp incisor teeth, a bite on the finger by a large tautog will not be quickly forgotten.

Fried or baked, the firm, white meat of the tautog makes a fine dish. During the springtime, female blacks have large sacs of spawn in them, which are very tasty fried. Some people prefer blackfish eggs to shad roe.

When cleaning a blackfish, after first removing the entrails, the simplest method is to make two long incisions on each side of the dorsal fin. Then, holding the fish with a gloved hand or cloth, pull the thick heavy skin off with a pair of pliers. The fish may be left whole to be baked or filleted for broiling. Blackfish are also good in a chowder.

Although there is not an intensive commercial fishery for blackfish, many are taken in pound nets set near breakwaters and occasionally caught in otter trawls.

Garfish Taken with Spider Web

It was on May 9 several years ago that I noticed two long, thin, silvery fish lying on the deck of the trap boat *Wilmar* at Point Judith, Rhode Island. Captain Clark was unloading butterfish and scup, and these silvery fish, 18 inches long, stood out like a sore thumb. On closer examination, their long beaks made it evident that they were garfish.

Spring and summer visitors to New England waters, the silver gar *(Tylosurus marinus)* and the ribbon gar, or flat needlefish, *(Ablennes hians)* look more like silver pipes than fish. These species have been recorded from the Gulf of Maine to Brazil.

About 50 different species of garfish or needlefish belonging to the family Belonidae are known around the globe. This family is named after Pierre Belon, French naturalist and ichthyologist, who lived from 1517 to 1564. Coincidentally, *belone* is also the Greek word for "needle".

Most garfish occur in warm seas but a few are found in northern waters and rivers and lakes. Some southern species reach lengths of 5 or 6 feet.

The gars are an ancient group of fishes with fossil forms recorded from the Eocene period that are 58 million years old. In this group of fishes both jaws are drawn out to form a long beak. A band of small sharp teeth, as well as a row of long needlelike teeth, are found in each jaw. There are special platelike bones in the throat, also armed with teeth. The coloration is generally silvery white on the bottom and silvery blue or green on top.

Bigelow and Schroeder, in their *Fishes of the Gulf of Maine*, state:

> The silver gar is common enough along the southern shores of New England, e.g., in Rhode Island waters and at Woods Hole, where quite a few are found from June to October. Like many other southern fishes, however, it seldom journeys eastward past Cape Cod, the only definite records of it in the Gulf of Maine being of several collected by Dr. William C. Kendall at Monomoy Island, at Wolfs Neck, Freeport, and Casco Bay, and of one found by Crane in the stomach of a tuna that she examined at Portland, Maine, in July 1936.

Off the coast of England the common garfish *(Belone belone)* appears to accompany schools of mackerel, for it is often taken with them in drift nets in the Channel and North Sea.

Saltwater gars are known by a wide variety of local names, among them long nose, needlefish, green bone, mackerel guide, billfish, and sea pike.

Garfish are extremely predacious creatures. They spend most of the time at the surface of the water or close to the top, usually swimming with undulating wavelike motions of their long bodies. But when startled they can skim along the surface very rapidly.

They generally occur in groups of two or three but sometimes appear in large schools. Gars tend to migrate to inshore waters during the warm summer months and offshore in the winter. When chased by tuna or sharks they will sometimes skim along the surface with the major part of their body out of the water. When chasing smaller fishes they have the appearance of springing over the waves after prey. Needlefish have been observed jumping over driftwood and floating objects, landing in the water tail first.

Gunther writes that while skimming along the surface of the water, garfish seize small fishes with their long jaws, as a bird would seize them with its beak, but their gullet is so narrow they can swallow small fishes only.

A large garfish may be a danger to man when it is skimming the water. One was known to have pierced the naked abdomen of a native fisherman during its headlong flight.

A newspaper account from Georgia in July 1879 tells of a John F. Simmons who had a narrow escape from a garfish on the Flint River. Simmons was fishing in the river and decided to swim across it to get a bateau from the other side. Just as he made a plunge a tremendous gar struck him, catching his thigh in its mouth and leaving an ugly and painful wound. A battle lasting for several minutes took place between man and fish.

Simmons called lustily for help and finally made it back up the river bank. According to the report he had several painful wounds, but none was serious. This large fish was probably an alligator gar, or garpike, which are close relatives of sturgeon.

Samuel de Champlain found the garpike in the lake which today bears his name. Writing in 1609, he mentioned the garpike, saying: "The indians gave me a head of it, which they prize highly, saying that when they have a headache, they let blood with the teeth of this fish at the seat of the pain, which immediately goes away."

Garfish are considered by people around the world to be good food fish, and many are sold in foreign fish markets. A very odd feature of these fishes is the bright green color of the bones, which remains even after cooking. Some people object to eating gars on this account, but such fears are groundless. According to Norman, the flesh is wholesome and well-flavored. When first captured, garfish sometimes emit a strong and peculiar smell, but this vanishes soon after the fish dies.

In the South Pacific in Indonesia and Melanesia one of the strangest fishing methods known is utilized by natives to capture saltwater garfish. They use a kite with a snare or loop to foul the gars when they leap out of the water. In Buka, N.W. Solomon Islands, the natives use their kites with a unique lure—a spider's web.

Attached to a loose string running down from the kite is a tassel of tangled spider's web 3 or 4 inches long and ½ inch thick. The garfish takes the tassel, and its many sharp teeth become so tangled in the mass of fine threads that it is unable to free itself. It is then hauled alongside the native's canoe and dipped out with a landing net.

15

From the Sea to River and Lake

Dromous means "running." Some varieties of fishes run upstream to spawn, i.e., they are anadromous. Others migrate downstream to spawn, i.e., they are catadromous.

Instinct governs the mechanism by which mature fish make their spawning migrations upstream from the ocean estuary. Typical anadromous fish that follow this pattern are shad, salmon, smelt, and alewives. Some movements upriver may cover a journey of 1000 miles or more, as in the Columbia River in Washington and Oregon with the chinook salmon. In Alaska the chinook may travel 2000 miles upriver to reach their spawning grounds.

Rapids, waterfalls, and hydroelectric dams prove obstacles to the migrating varieties, but they persevere to propagate their species. Some anadromous species, such as alewives and sockeye salmon *(Oncorhynchus nerka)* ascend streams to reach the lakes and ponds in which they spawn.

Catadromous fish feed and grow in fresh water but return to the sea to spawn. The best-known example is the common eel of the North Atlantic. Other varieties of this type occur in the rivers of the southern part of South America, Cape of Good Hope, South Australia, and New Zealand. These relatives of salmon and trout, called galaxiids, spend most of their life cycle in rivers but return to the ocean to reproduce. The mullet on occasion acts as a catadromous fish.

Shad with Roe—Harbinger of Spring

A harbinger of spring to hundreds of fishermen along our North Atlantic coastal rivers is the appearance of a fat, silvery fish heavily laden with a delectable roe. Old-timers know that as spring moves north and small white blossoms appear on a shrubby tree known as the serviceberry, or shadbush, the shad are coming up the rivers. At the same time a small gnat appears, which everyone calls the shad fly.

The shad is the largest member of the American herring family. Like the salmon and the alewife, it ascends rivers to spawn. Often shad may be caught by the fisherman-farmer at his doorstep, dozens of miles from the seacoast. Shad can be recognized by their large scales, which loosen very easily, their forked tails, and a deep, oval-shaped body. Young shad have small teeth. But when a shad reaches 12 inches in length, the teeth fall out and never grow back. The shad is bluish green on the back and bright silver on the backside and belly. Coloring and oval shape make it easy to recognize.

The shad is one of the few fish found along the entire Atlantic coast of the United States. Spring spawning runs of this fish have been known

to occur in every suitable river from the St. Johns in Florida to the St. Lawrence in Canada. A rare visitor to the Atlantic coast of Nova Scotia, the shad occurs frequently in the Gulf of St. Lawrence where it travels up some rivers as far north as the Miramichi. There is no record of shad in the Bay of Chaleur, Canada. A shad was taken in 1953 in Bull's Bay near St. Johns, Newfoundland, which seems to be the most northerly record.

Over the past hundred years the abundance of shad has been greatly affected by industrialization. In the early 1800s shad used to travel up most of our Atlantic coastal rivers until they met with impassable falls or reached the headwaters of a stream. Today, hydroelectric and mill dams, along with pollution from manufacturing plants and sewage from cities, have cut down the abundance of the fish to a small fraction of former years. In many rivers, such as the Thames, Blackstone, Saco, and Merrimac, shad have almost disappeared. However, with measures taken to eliminate pollution and the contruction of fishways around dams, the shad are gradually returning to their ancient haunts.

The history of shad fishing in the Connecticut River is an interesting one. The Connecticut originates in Lake Connecticut in the extreme northern part of New Hampshire, then flows south to the boundary line between New Hampshire and Vermont, crosses Massachusetts and Connecticut, and empties into Long Island Sound. In the early 1700s large runs of shad and salmon occurred along the length of the river, and Indians would gather from all over New England to harvest the bountiful fish. When the English settlers came, they readily caught salmon for food but disliked shad, considering it an inferior bony fish, with its streaks of distasteful brown flesh, and left it for food for the Indians. G. B. Goode (1887) wrote with regard to Connecticut River shad in colonial times: "The shad, which were very numerous, were despised and rejected by a large portion of the English colonists for nearly 100 years in the old towns of Connecticut, and for about 75 years in New Hampshire and Massachusetts towns. It was reputable for those who had a competency to eat shad."

A story was told in Hadley, Massachusetts, of a colonial family who were about to dine on shad when, hearing a knock on the door, the platter of shad was put under the bed.

In 1733, John Hawley of Northampton, Massachusetts, recorded in his account book 30 shad that he bought for a penny apiece. Ebenezer

Hunt gave 1½ pence for shad in 1736. There is also a record of Connecticut shad in barrels being advertised in Boston in 1736.

Field's 1819 book on Middlesex County, Connecticut, stated: "Shad-eating became reputable 30 years before the Revolution. Thousands of barrels of Connecticut River shad were put up (in brine) for American troops during the Revolutionary War from 1778 to 1781." By that time, they must have appreciated the roe, and learned how to carve fillets without the infamous bones.

The falls at South Hadley were one of the best places on the Connecticut River for taking fish. Goode gives the following account of shad fishing at the falls: "The best fishing was in May. Shad were caught in seines below the falls, and in scoop-nets on the falls. Boats were drawn to places on the rocky falls, fastened and then filled with shad by scoop-nets. . . . A man in this manner could take from 2000 to 3000 shad in a day and sometimes more with the aid of a boatman. These movements required men of some dexterity. . . . In 1801 . . . sometimes 1200 fish were taken at one haul." Many people arrived on horseback from various sections of New England with bags to carry shad home.

With the building of the dam in 1849 above Hadley Falls at Holyoke, shad fishing slumped; the fish were unable to reach their ancestral spawning grounds in the mid-portion of the Connecticut River. More than a hundred years later, some efforts were undertaken to get the shad over the barrier.

Because of numerous protests by fishing interests, the Holyoke Power Company built several fishways around the dam, one at a cost of $27,000 and another at a cost of $11,000. Both attempts failed to get the shad over the dam. In 1946, an engineer, Alston Nugnier, joined the Holyoke Power Company, and with the aid of U.S. Fish and Wildlife technicians created a revolutionary type of fishway with a fish trap and elevator system. In the spring of 1955, when this new invention was put into action, 4902 shad were lifted above the dam. This was the first time in 107 years that shad were able to travel above the dam to spawn. In recognition of its achievement, the Holyoke Power Company was given an award by the Fish and Wildlife Service.

Shad appear on the New England coast from about early April to May to ascend the rivers. The exact date of their first appearance varies from year to year, depending on weather conditions and water temperature.

Fishery scientists formerly thought that the shad's spawning migration originated from the ocean south of Florida, where the fish were believed to have wintered. As the huge body of shad moved northward along the coast, local groups would split off to return to the streams of their birth. This theory of shad migration is no longer accepted. Today the generally accepted theory is that in the winter the shad move offshore more or less adjacent to their native streams. Then they return in the spring to spawn in their place of origin.

There appear to be several cycles of shad runs spaced at intervals of a few days on most rivers. The first spring runs consist of mostly male "buck" shad while the females, or "roe shad," arrive in later groups. Female shad are larger than their mates, weighing 2 to 3 pounds more than the males.

The shad swim up the rivers until they find the ideal location for spawning. Favorite spawning grounds, or "shad wallows," as they are called by some fishermen, are on pebbly and sandy flats that border streams and the sandbars found at intervals higher up the river. When the fish have reached the area and are ready to expel their eggs, they move to the flats in pairs. This movement takes place between sunset and midnight. In the act of releasing eggs, they swim close together near the surface, their back fins projecting above the water. The vigorous, rapid, fluttering movements that accompany this operation produce a splashing in the water that can be clearly heard from the shore. These sounds and movements are termed "washing" by fishermen.

Adult shad usually average 4 pounds in weight. Large males reach weights of 6 pounds, and big females 8 pounds. The maximum weight attained by shad on the Atlantic coast is about 12 pounds. Along the Pacific coast they are reported to average about a pound heavier. A shad weighing 14 pounds has been recorded from the West Coast.

The average roe shad deposits about 28,000 eggs held in a pair of membranes; very large females have been recorded as having as many as 156,000 eggs. The pale pink eggs are released to the river bottom where they roll around with the current until hatching, 3 to 14 days later, depending on the temperature of the water. At 60 degrees F., they usually hatch in a week.

The baby shad grow rapidly during the summer months, feeding on plankton. They remain in fresh water until the coming of colder weather and then migrate downstream to the sea. By the end of the summer they have reached a length of 3 to 5 inches. The adult shad returns to the sea soon after spawning.

Shad are believed to reach maturity in 3 or 4 years. The males begin their reproductive function when they are a little longer than alewives. In most bays and in the mouths of rivers during the summer months is found a population of small, fat, immature shad with undeveloped reproductive organs. The fishermen call them sea shad and consider them quite distinct from river shad or spring shad. These young are frequently observed jumping and breaking water in river mouths. They are common shad about a year old. Sea shad never go up the rivers as far as the spawning shad and usually stay within brackish water.

Like most members of the herring family, the shad feeds mainly on small plankton, chiefly *Calanus*. They are also known to consume small shrimp, insects, fish eggs, and small fishes. In recent years anglers have been able to catch a few shad in the Connecticut and Thames rivers on artificial flies and live minnows while the fish are on their spawning run.

Each spring an intensive shad fishery is carried out on the Hudson River in the shadow of the George Washington Bridge. New York and New Jersey fishermen trap thousands of pounds of migrating shad in gill nets attached to 60-foot hickory poles driven into the river bed with the nets stretched between. In 1954 the total Hudson River shad catch amounted to 1,249,300 pounds, but the market dropped as the mighty Hudson became drastically polluted. Only recently has the cleanup brought the shad back to the river in numbers, but the occurrence of polychlorinated biphenyls (PCB) has resulted in a 1976 ban on commercial fishing in the Hudson River. Gill nets are the chief method of capturing shad; seines, pound nets, and fyke nets are also used in many locations.

Although containing in the neighborhood of 860 bones, shad is considered an extremely delicious fish when properly filleted and prepared. It is a good idea to remove the backbone of the fish with scissors and a sharp knife. Tweezers can prove helpful in taking out the smaller bones.

Planked shad is a favorite method of cooking the fish. The boned shad is nailed to an inch-thick oak board with strips of bacon to baste it. The plank is then placed near an open charcoal fire and broiled for close to an hour. Care should be taken to change the position of the board every few minutes to ensure a uniform cooking of the fillet. The shad's scientific name is *Alosa sapidissima*, which means "most delicious." Shad roe is considered a great delicacy in many locations, and the roe usually brings a much higher price on the market than boned shad.

Sidewise Swimmer—The River Herring, or Alewife

The anadromous alewife spends most of its life in the sea, ascending into freshwater streams to spawn like the shad, smelt, and salmon. The alewife heads for small streams, brooks, and tributary ponds with quiet waters, which are suitable for the spawning process. Sometimes they go only a short way, using man-made dikes and ditches, to freshwater ponds near barrier beaches behind the dunes. Probably one of the most lengthy alewife migrations is the 200-mile trip from the ocean to the east branch of the Penobscot River. They usually spawn much nearer to the sea.

Josselyn's *An Account of Two Voyages to New England* (London, 1674) states:

> The Alewife is like a Herrin, but has a bigger bellie; therefore called an Alewife; They come in the end of April into fresh Rivers and Ponds; there hath been taken in two hour's time by two men without any Weyre at all, saving a few stones to stop the passage of the River, above ten thousand.

Found from northern Nova Scotia and the Gulf of St. Lawrence to North Carolina, alewives have been of economic importance since colonial times.

Today they are landlocked in New York's Lake Cayuga, Seneca Lake, and Lake Ontario, and in Cobbett Pond, New Hampshire, but alewives enter the coastal rivers of southern Rhode Island in late March. The run reaches the streams of Massachusetts Bay in early April and the Maine rivers in late April and early May.

In Rhode Island alewives still occur in the Pawtucket, Nonquit, Narrow, and Sakonnet rivers. In Massachusetts they are found in the Merrimac, Parker, Saugus, and Wier rivers and in Herring and Stony brooks, among others. In New Hampshire they are found in the Piscataqua River system. In Maine they frequent the St. Croix, Dennys, Machias, Orland, Penobscott, Kennebec, and a few other rivers.

When traveling up the streams the alewives are reported to move chiefly by day, dropping back slightly with the current at nightfall. They seem to prefer warm, bright, sunny days for their migratory journey. They will make their way through rapids of considerable velocity, and according to C. G. Atkins of the U.S. Fish Commission, they will turn on their sides and push themselves up a steeply inclined plane against a sheet of water not half as thick as their bodies.

Early alewife trap

In New England streams and ponds alewives are taken chiefly with dip nets and seines during their spawning migration. Pools are sometimes constructed about the mouths and in the lower part of the streams. The fish are then led into them by nets and stone diversions and are easily captured by dipping them out of the enclosure. Most of the Chesapeake Bay alewife catch is taken by pound nets.

The alewife is a good example of a fishery resource that has declined sharply through careless management. Although the decline occurred throughout the entire range of the alewife, its diminishing volume has been most apparent in New England, where a lack of fishways to pass the fish over dams, pollution, and excessive fishing are responsible.

In New England the size of alewife runs is limited by the extent of the lake area available for the nurturing of the young. The largest runs occur where the destination is a lake of fair size. In order to maintain the largest run that the lake area will support, sufficient adults must be allowed to escape the fishery to cast their spawn. This means adequate fishways providing safe passage of both upstream and downstream migrants, fishways that must be inspected periodically to keep them serviceable.

During the last century, when small dams began crowding into the coastal rivers obstructing the passage of migratory fishes, some citizens went to work to help fish such as the alewife over dams with dip nets and fish ladders. At Damariscotta, Maine, a series of 25 to 30 artificial pools were built of loose stones to allow the alewives to ascend a 50-foot ledge of rock over which Damariscotta Pond spilled its waters to a tidal stream below. The pond was stocked about 1816; in a few years a large run of alewives had developed in this area. In most places fishways were not provided for or were allowed to fall into disrepair.

When running upstream the female's eggs are unripe, but they ripen when the freshwater pond is reached and water temperature reaches 55 to 60 degrees F. The female alewife is larger than the male and is usually escorted by several males on the journey upstream. The female releases anywhere from 60,000 to 100,000 eggs .05 inch in diameter. The eggs are sticky and clumped in masses that sling to sticks, roots, stones, and gravel; the males immediately cover the eggs with milt, thrashing and scattering it with their tails. As soon as the adults have released their eggs and sperm, they return to the sea. Since alewives eat no food during their spawning migration, the return journey is made in a very emaciated condition. They begin to feed as soon as the brackish tidal estuaries are reached. Adult alewives subsist on small crustaceans such as shrimp, small fishes, and insects.

The fertile eggs hatch into transparent wriggling larvae. The young are very active, feeding on mosquito larvae, minute crustaceans, and insects.

Young alewives spend their first summer in the fresh water, growing to a length of 2 to 4 inches by fall. In autumn, the water temperature begins to drop, and the young fish move downstream and into the warmer salt water. After 3 or 4 years the fish reach maturity and head back to their point of origin to perpetuate the species.

Temperature plays a very important part in the growth rate of alewife populations. Rounsefell and Stringer showed that alewives in the Taunton River, which enters the Atlantic Ocean south of Cape Cod, mature at 3 years of age, while alewives running up the Damariscotta and Orland rivers in Maine mature at 4 years of age.

Little is known of the movements of young and adult alewives in the ocean. Like mackerel, menhaden, and sea herring, they form schools comprised of members all about the same size. Sometimes they are taken in large quantities by pound nets and seines along the shore. During the winter months a few appear in the otter trawl nets of fishing draggers on the offshore fishing grounds of George's Bank and South Channel.

As for their economic importance, alewives have been trapped and netted during their spawning migration from salt water to inland lakes and ponds since colonial times. They were salted and dried, eaten locally or sent out as a ship's larder. Salted alewives exchanged for West Indian molasses, sugar, and rum comprised a considerable colonial trade that has existed up to the present century. Today there are still a few alewife smokehouses in New England. Small alewives and alewife roe are also canned. Large surpluses of alewives in bygone years were used to fertilize the fields. Some lobstermen still use alewives as bait for their lobster traps.

Alewives are smoked by being washed in vats and scaled with a knife as soon as practicable after their removal from water. They are next immersed overnight in strong brine containing 12 to 14 pounds of salt to every 100 pounds of fish. The following morning, the round, uncut fishes are strung on smokesticks that pierce the left gill opening and go out the mouth. The strings of fish are then rinsed off in fresh

water and suspended 5 to 6 feet above a fire made from equal quantities of oak and hickory wood. From time to time the fire is sprinkled with sawdust and water to produce a suitable vapor. Only oak or hickory should be used as fuel; other materials do not produce the proper flavor. The fishes are suspended 1 to 3 days above the smoldering fire, the time depending on the intensity of the smoke, and are then ready to be eaten. Smoked alewives can be kept for many months provided they are in a cool, dry place.

The river herring, or alewife *(Alosa pseudoharengus)*, is known by a great variety of local names including spring herring, branch herring, bit-eyed herring, ellwife, ellwhip, goggle-eye, sawbelly, grayback, and buckeye. In Canadian waters they are sometimes referred to as gasperot, gaspereau, or kyauk. The name sawbelly results from the sawlike ridges found along the abdominal region.

The alewife can be distinguished at a glance from the sea herring by its fat belly, more silvery color, and larger scales. Alewives differ from young shad by having smaller mouths and shorter upper jaws. The lack of teeth on the roof of the mouth is a major difference between the alewife and its close relatives the hickory shad, *Alosa mediocris*, and the sea herring, *Clupea harengus*.

Although there is slight variation in alewife color, they are usually a metallic grayish green above with silvery sides and belly. They possess a dark spot on the shoulder just behind the edge of the gill cover. The fins are slightly greenish or yellowish in life. Alewives grow to a total length of 15 inches.

Atlantic or Pacific—Salmon Come Home

"The river salmon surpasseth all the fishes of the sea" wrote the Roman naturalist Pliny. One of the world's most important food fishes is the salmon. Canned salmon can be found in almost every supermarket and grocery store around the globe. Highly nutritious, a pound of salmon contains over 700 food calories; by contrast, a pound of cod contains about 166 calories.

In North America there are two distinct groups of salmon, the six species of the northern Pacific Ocean and the one Atlantic salmon species. The Atlantic species, *Salmo salar*, differs from the Pacific in that it does not die right after spawning. In addition, several species of landlocked salmon do not travel to the sea.

Opposite: Freshly smoked alewives

Found in European and American waters, the Atlantic salmon has been dubbed the "king of fish" because it is so highly prized. Belonging to the family Salmonidae, of which there are some 38 species in North American waters, the Atlantic salmon has typical salmonid features such as soft fin rays and a fleshy, adipose dorsal fin.

Atlantic salmon have declined greatly over the past three centuries. In colonial times they were abundant in almost every eastern stream as far south as the Delaware peninsula. Today they occur with regularity in only a few rivers of Maine and those farther north in Canada and the Maritime Provinces.

The ancient Romans prized the salmon in their Gaelic and British provinces. Normans relished the salmon. Germans called this fish *der lachs,* or *der salm;* Danes called it *lax;* Norwegians, *laexing;* Swedes, *hafslax;* Dutch, *de zalm;* and French, *le saumon.*

Atlantic salmon

Smoked salmon (called lox), so popular with Americans today, was an important item of trade as early as 1273 when Scotch merchants exported it to England and the Continent. In England in 1376 the House of Commons petitioned Edward III that no salmon be caught in the Thames between Gravesend and Henley in "kipper time," between May 3 and January 6.

Izaak Walton in his *Compleat Angler* (1653) writes of the salmon: "He is ever bred in the fresh rivers and never grows big but in the sea. He has (like some persons of honour and riches which have both their summer and winter houses) this fresh water for summer and the salt water for winter to spend his life in."

North American Indians had mastered the art of spearing salmon in the rivers long before the white man came to the New World. In 1497, when John Cabot discovered Newfoundland, he described salmon in

Fishermen taking salmon by nets in the Connecticut River

local waters. Henry Hudson reported a great store of salmon in 1608 when he sailed in the river that bears his name.

During colonial times, Atlantic salmon were prevalent in almost all the coastal rivers of New England. Atkins lists 28 rivers of the eastern United States in which salmon were once common. By 1874 they were to be found with regularity in only eight rivers: the St. Johns, St. Croix, Dennys, Little Falls, East Machias, Wescongus, Penobscot, and Kennebec. In the eighteenth century salmon were also found in the Housatonic, Quinnipaic, Hammonasset, Connecticut, Thames, and Pawcatuck rivers of Connecticut.

The Connecticut River was one of the best salmon rivers in New England. Salmon nets began to appear in the Connecticut in 1700, and a considerable amount of the salmon catch was put up in salt casks. According to colonial records, about the year 1700, salmon was so plentiful in the Connecticut River that it was sold in Hartford for less than a penny per pound. In 1797 a 16-foot-high dam was built by the Upper Locke and Canal Company about 100 miles from the mouth of the river. For two or three years after the dam was built, salmon were seen in great abundance below it. But they disappeared rapidly during the next few years because they could no longer reach their ancestral spawning grounds in the upper reaches of the stream. In 1872 a salmon was caught at Saybrook, and the fishermen did not know what kind of fish it was.

In 1866 Connecticut, Massachusetts, New Hampshire, and Vermont began making joint efforts to restore salmon to the Connecticut River. At first, small lots of salmon fry were placed in the river, but not until 1873 was any planting done on an extensive scale. At that time a large number of fry were planted by Connecticut in the lower branches of the river. According to Fred Mather's report, the stocked salmon returned to the river to spawn in 1886. Within five years after the stocking, "Connecticut River Salmon" received a regular quotation on the New York fish market. However, salmon in the Connecticut River declined greatly in the next few years; it was believed that all the spawning fish were captured near the mouth of the river before they had a chance to reproduce. Merriman reports that the first Atlantic salmon to appear in over half a century in the Connecticut River was taken on June 11, 1948, near Portland, Connecticut. It was taken with a haul seine by William Bennett and John Frazier. The salmon was a female weighing 7 pounds 14 ounces and 2 feet 4 inches long.

A large commercial fishery for Atlantic salmon existed in Maine during the nineteenth century. In 1888, 205,149 pounds of salmon were taken in the waters of Maine. In 1960 less than 500 pounds of salmon were taken by commercial fishermen in Maine. Today Maine Atlantic salmon fishing is closely regulated with a closed season from July 16 to March 31. Angling by rod and line for Atlantic salmon can take place between July 16 and September 15. There is an exception in the St. Croix River; weirs can take salmon in certain areas of the river from May 15 to August 31.

In Canada the 1961 catch of Atlantic salmon (21,000 metric tons according to FAO figures, valued at over a million dollars) shows the annual catch getting steadily smaller during the past quarter century.

At least half the Atlantic salmon's life span is spent in the ocean. Most spawning Atlantic salmon enter western streams of the North Atlantic in April, May, and June with a few stragglers arriving as late as October and November. Good Atlantic salmon rivers have deep, cool pools with a sufficient oxygen content to sustain the fish. About 90 percent of the salmon run in our northeastern streams are "maiden fish" spawning for the first time. Smaller salmon, from 1 to 5 pounds, sometimes return upstream to spawn after only a year in the sea; they are called "grilse." Although grilse are smaller than most of the usual spawning fish, they are sexually mature.

Spawning generally occurs in the headwaters of the rivers in October and November in Maine and Canada. The egg-laden female seeks out a gravelly area that has a continuous flow of water. With her fins and tail she hollows egg pits and piles pebbles, forming a redd on which she deposits her eggs and the male releases his milt to fall nearby and fertilize them.

As salmon enter fresh water to spawn, they gradually stop feeding. The long migratory journey upstream utilizes energy stored as fat in the tissues. When salmon leave the sea they are plump, silvery, and bright; as they progress upstream they become rusty brown or nearly black. The males develop the characteristic hooked lower jaw, known as a kype.

On their way upstream salmon have been known to leap over small falls and other obstacles. According to J. Gray, a salmon is capable of leaping 6 feet up and 12 feet forward in the air. In order to accomplish this, it has to leave the water with a velocity of 14 miles per hour.

According to D. L. Belding, the average Atlantic salmon deposits over 9000 eggs; a very large fish may have 21,000 eggs. After spawning the spent fish are known as "kelts." These drift slowly downstream and sometimes are forced to overwinter in the river because of ice blocking their path. The eggs begin to hatch in late winter through March and April, depending on water temperature and latitude. The larval salmon is slightly less than an inch in length after hatching and possesses a large yolk sac that is absorbed in 40 days. After absorbing its yolk sac the salmon begins feeding on minute phytoplankton and insect larvae. It grows very rapidly and is next known as a "fingerling" and "parr." As it grows larger, dark vertical hairs develop on its sides; these are the parr marks. After spending 2 to 6 years in the streams and rivers and growing from 2 to 7 inches long, the parr heads downstream to the ocean. While going downriver the parr markings develop a bright silvery sheen; the fish is then known as a "smolt."

Smolts, which are 6 to 8 inches long, remain briefly at the river mouth adjusting to the increased salinity and then disappear into the sea. Atlantic salmon remain at sea from 2 to 5 years, feeding on small fishes and crustaceans, experiencing rapid growth. Not much is known about the habits and migrations of salmon in the ocean; this stage of their life cycle is now under investigation by fishery biologists.

It is believed by some fishery biologists that salmon at sea in northern waters occur in small schools in mid-water or up near the surface feeding on euphausids, shrimplike crustaceans, and small fishes. Some of the red coloration of salmon tissue is believed to result from the red pigment of crustaceans. Balmain and Shearer (1956) list 108 salmon taken at sea; of these, 23 were found in the stomachs of sharks.

Tagged salmon from Scotland have been caught in Norwegian waters, and Norwegian tagged salmon have been taken in Scotland. One of the longest salmon migrations on record was a salmon tagged at Loch na Croich on the Blackwater River in Scotland in November 1955 and recaptured in October 1956 in Eqaluq Fjord on the southwest coast of Greenland, a journey of over 1700 miles, according to the April 13, 1957 issue of *Nature*.

On October 10, 1960, an Atlantic salmon 28 inches long was caught off Quassinsaq, Greenland. It had the Fishery Research Board of Canada tag number 1616. A check of records showed that this Atlantic salmon was tagged when 6.9 inches long, on May 22, 1959, in the estuary of Miramichi River near Chatham, New Brunswick. This recapture, about 1500 miles from its place of origin, is the longest migratory record for Canadian Atlantic salmon and gives support to the belief that salmon from both European and North American waters share common fishing grounds around Greenland. Much more research remains to be conducted on the migratory habits and habitats of Atlantic salmon.

The largest Atlantic salmon are caught in European waters. A 79-pound 2-ounce salmon was taken by Henrik Henriksen in the Tana River, Norway, in 1928. There is a report of a 103-pound salmon from Scottish waters. Western Atlantic salmon are rarely above 50 pounds.

About 1600 tons of salmon valued at about 1,250,000 pounds sterling are taken each year by Scottish fishermen. These fish are taken by seines and traps.

Each year large quantities of salmon are taken in the Eastern Baltic sea by fishing fleets from Denmark, Sweden, Finland, Poland, and West Germany. From July 1961 to June 1962 the fleets caught about 2350 metric tons of salmon in the Baltic with long lines and drift nets.

Of the Pacific coast salmon, the chinook, *Oncorhynchus tshawytscha*, is the largest. It averages about 20 pounds but can reach weights over 100 pounds. With a flesh color from deep red to white, it is one of the world's most valuable fish species. Sometimes called king salmon and Columbia River salmon, it is found from Monterey to Oregon, Alaska, and northern China.

Pacific sockeye salmon is a favorite with cooks and housewives because of its flavor and deep orange-red color. Scientifically called *Oncorhynchus nerka*, it is also known as blueback, red, quinalt, and nerka salmon. This species averages 6½ pounds in weight; almost the entire catch is canned. Most of the commercial catch of sockeye is made with gill nets and purse seines. In the ocean they may wander 2000 miles before returning to the mouth of the river in which they were hatched.

Coho, or silver, salmon *(Oncorhynchus kisutch)*, average 8 pounds in weight and have become very popular with anglers in recent years. This growth in popularity has resulted from widespread transplanting from its native west coast to the Great Lakes and rivers of the east. In 1966 the Conservation Department of Michigan introduced about 800,000 Pacific coast cohos into streams tributary to Lake Michigan and Lake Superior. The transplanting was very successful, but the cohos in the Great Lakes developed a high concentration of DDT in their tissues. Anglers find that coho readily take spoons, jigs, and streamer flies when conditions are favorable.

Pink salmon, *Oncorhynchus gorbuscha,* account for about a third of the canned salmon pack of the United States. Found in the waters of California, Puget Sound, and Alaska, they are also known as humpbacks, or humpies, because of the hump of cartilage that forms behind the head of breeding males.

Chum, or dog, salmon *(Oncorhynchus keta),* occur along Pacific coast waters from San Francisco to Kamchatka. Some chum salmon are known to travel 1500 miles up the swift Yukon River to spawn in Canada's Teslin Lake. They are sometimes called dog salmon because their pale pink flesh was at one time used as dog food.

Why have salmon continued to decline? Man is the greatest culprit. He has changed the environment of streams through pollution. Chemicals and sewerage cast into rivers lower the oxygen content vital to all fish life. Toxic mill wastes have made many streams uninhabitable for salmon and other fishes. DDT and other insecticides sprayed on forests and orchards adjacent to watersheds have killed millions of larval fishes. Dams have prevented salmon from successful spawning. Wanton harvesting of salmon without leaving a spawning stock has done away with the fish in some rivers.

Will Atlantic salmon ever reach their former abundance? Fishways may lead salmon around dams, and reared fishes may be released into streams, but it is unlikely that the Atlantic salmon population will regain the magnitude of former years. Agencies such as the Atlantic Sea-Run Salmon Commission of Maine, the U.S. Fish and Wildlife Service, and the Fishery Research Board of Canada are devoting their efforts to improvement of our Atlantic salmon resources.

White Perch—Neither White Nor Perch

The white perch, *Morone americana,* may be neither white nor perch, but it is one of the most universally popular panfish along the Atlantic seaboard. The white perch is a member of the bass family, Percichthyidae, and is closely related to the striped bass, *Morone saxatilis.* The white perch was first described by Gmelin in 1788 as *Perca americana* because Gmelin mistakenly placed the fish with the perch. Since the white perch occurs only in North American waters, it is understandable that it would have the species name *americana.*

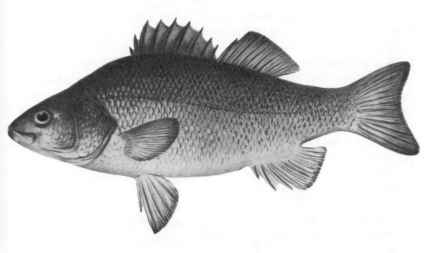

White perch are found from the Gulf of St. Lawrence and Nova Scotia to South Carolina, principally in bays, estuaries, salt ponds, and rivers. They thrive in salt and brackish waters, but can live in fresh water, too; when they have become landlocked in freshwater lakes and ponds, they seem to thrive there.

Coloration is variable, mostly silvery but often olive to bluish or gray above, with greenish sides and silvery belly. Large individuals often have a bluish head; young ones, less than 5 inches, are silvery gray. The fins are usually gray with the ventrals sometimes whitish. In the southern part of their range, white perch are sometimes called gray perch, black perch, or blue-nosed perch.

Usually this species' average size is 7 to 9 inches long, ½ to ¾ pound in weight. They reach maximum lengths of 15 inches, weights between 2 and 3 pounds.

White perch are seldom found in water deeper than 3 fathoms. During the winter months this species tends to congregate in the deeper estuaries and creeks and remains in a sluggish state until warmer weather arrives. Though the fish travel in small schools and tend to migrate nocturnally into shallow inshore areas during the daylight hours, they cannot be found in this locality.

The most common habitat of the white perch is fresh tidal rivers with clay or muddy bottoms. Those living in saltwater creeks tend to be darker than those found in fresh water. They ascend the tidal rivers soon after the melted ice has run off and spawn during the spring. Sometimes they are found in rivers in company with their close relatives, the striped bass, feeding in the same locations.

White perch feed greedily on the spawn of other fishes, particularly shad and alewives. Bigelow and Schroeder (1953) mention white perch following alewives around the edges of the ponds on Martha's Vineyard and eating the spawn as soon as it was released into the water. Also found in the diet of white perch are small fish such as smelts, minnows, young eels, squid, shrimp, crabs, and worms.

At Woods Hole, Massachusetts, white perch spawn in late May and June; around New York waters, in late April and early May; and in the Chesapeake Bay region, in early April. Ideal water temperature is a key factor in successful spawning of this species.

The average female releases about 40,000 eggs about ¾ millimeter in diameter. These stick together in masses or attach to any object they come in contact with. At a water temperature of 58 degrees F., the eggs hatch in about 3 days. Larvae feed and grow rapidly, reaching lengths of 4 to 5 inches by the end of their first year. Young white perch, 4 inches and less, feed mainly on insect larvae, annelids, amphipods, isopods, and copepods.

In their study of Rhode Island white perch, S. B. Saila and D. Horton (1957) found the average length of year-old fish was 3.9 inches; 2-year-olds, 6.5 inches; 3-year-olds, 8.2 inches; 4-year-olds, 9.3 inches; 5-year-olds, 9.7 inches; 6-year-olds, 10.6 inches; 7-year-olds, 11.1 inches; 8-year-olds, 11.4 inches. The age of a fish was determined by scale analysis, observing the annual growth rings.

During the early part of this century there was a considerable commercial fishery for white perch in the tidal rivers of Massachusetts and Rhode Island with many thousands of pounds being caught in seines, gill nets, pounds, and fyke nets. Today this commercial fishery has declined to a few hundred pounds taken annually. The 1958 U.S. Fish and Wildlife Service commercial landings list only 200 pounds from New England, and these were taken in Rhode Island.

Most of the white perch on the market today come from the Chesapeake Bay region where they are captured in seines and traps with the striped bass.

Occasionally the white perch suffer very serious mortalities. During the late spring of 1955 in a Newport, Rhode Island, pond, several thousand white perch were found dead or dying after spawning season had ended. The cause of death was found to be a bacterial infection known as Columnaris disease.

Similar kills of white perch have been reported in the same area in previous years. During July and August of 1959 large numbers of white perch died in Perch Pond, adjacent to the Pawcatuck River in Westerly, Rhode Island. Investigation showed the perch died from a lack of oxygen brought about by a large plankton bloom and considerable algae growth. G. W. Hunter (1942), in his study of the parasites of Connecticut fishes, found occasional parasitic worms present in white perch.

As a game fish for anglers, the white perch provides considerable sport. With a light rod and reel, the fisherman can expect a good fight. Early in the morning is the best time to fish for white perch. Shrimp are the most desirable bait, if available; next in preference are worms and live minnows.

White perch are delicious eating and can be fried, baked, or broiled.

16

The "Winged" Fish

Fins have been adapted for a spectacular variety of uses in fishes. Aside from many different swimming movements, fins are also utilized for gliding (flying fishes), flight (flying characins), progress on land (mudskippers), sailing (sailfish), digging (skates), and as fishing rods (anglerfish). The large, wide pectoral fins of angel sharks, skates, and rays provide a gliding stability analogous to the swept-back wings of jet aircraft.

Half-Human, Half-Monster—The Angel Shark

Did you ever see a fish shaped like a bass fiddle, with pectoral fins resembling an angel's wings, whose body is flat and depressed like that of a skate? Well, a fish answering this description was caught January 15, 1955, by Warren Vincent.

This strange sea creature was taken in 55 fathoms of water about 100 miles south of Block Island. Skipper Vincent landed his catch, and notified Charles J. Fish, director of the Narragansett Marine Laboratory of the University of Rhode Island. Dr. Fish identified the odd fish as an angel shark (not to be confused with the angler, or goosefish) and said that it was the second of its kind to be recorded in Rhode Island

waters during the eighteen years he had been director of the laboratory.

The weight of this angel shark, also known as a monkfish, was 22 pounds; it was 3 feet long. J. T. Nichols and C. M. Breder (1927) mention two monkfish taken in the traps of Menemsha Bight, Martha's Vineyard, one of 35 pounds and 4 feet long on September 1, 1873; another 3 feet 7 inches long on September 23, 1921. There is also a record of one from a Lynnhaven Roads, Virginia, pound net on July 15, 1916.

The common angel shark, *Squatina dumerili*, is found in the Atlantic from southern New England to Florida, the Gulf of Mexico, and Jamaica. The European monkfish, *Squatina squatina*, is known from

Fisherman holding up an angel shark caught off Port Judith, Rhode Island

Northern Europe to the Mediterranean. Other similar species of the same family are found off the shores of Peru, Chile, Mexico, California, Australia, and Japan. In Europe it is sometimes called fiddle fish, monkeyfish shark, and shark ray.

From its general appearance the angel shark closely resembles a ray or skate. This is brought out by its local names mongrel skate and shark ray. A close study of its internal anatomy shows it to be a true shark. This finding is confirmed by the location of the external gill clefts on the side of its head.

A further argument in favor of placing the monkfish with sharks rather than skates is provided by its method of swimming. It propels itself by means of a powerful sculling action of its oarlike tail and makes little or no use of its large pectoral fins for this purpose.

Angel sharks reach a maximum length of 8 feet but are usually considerably smaller. The base of the pectoral fins projects to form angular shoulders free from the head and body.

The color of the back of this fish is a brownish gray tending toward olive drab with the belly surface plain white. Its eyes are small and located on the top of its head. The mouth is near the end of the rounded head and equipped with several rows of sharp-pointed teeth set apart one from another. Its spiracles are large and crescent-shaped a short distance behind the eyes.

Fossil remains of *Squatina* date back to the Jurassic and Cretaceous periods. The well-preserved remains in the Lithographic Stone of Bavaria reveal angel sharks indistinguishable from their living descendants.

This species of shark has a historical reputation as a half-human monster of the deep. A. Hyatt Verrill, in his book *Strange Fish and Their Stories*, quotes French ichthyologist Rondelet describing a monkfish washed up on a Norwegian beach during a storm: "In our time in Norway, a sea monster has been taken after a great storm, to which all who saw it at once gave the name of monk. It had a man's face rude and ungracious, the head smooth and shorn. On the shoulders, like the cloak of a monk, were two long fins in place of arms, and the end of the body was finished by a long tail."

Otto Lugger, in a *Report* of the Commissioner of Fisheries of Maryland (1878), says of the angel shark: "The not very inviting looks of this fish are not the only reasons why fishermen dislike it. It has, to some extent, the unpleasant habits of the snapping turtle, since it can open its mouth very suddenly, to an alarming extent, and not to play, either. In consequence of this biting propensity, it is called by the fishermen the 'sand devil' and also the 'fair maid'; the first name not without any reason and the latter certainly not out of politeness."

The food of the monkfish is similar to that of the skate; its normal diet includes crabs, snails, small flatfish, and other animals found on the sea floor. One female examined was found to have in its stomach several dabs and plaice, portions of other fishes, scales of mullet, not less than 50 fish eyes, and a fair-size bundle of eel grass. On occasion the monkfish may be a voracious feeder; there is a record of one fish coming to the surface and seizing a live cormorant by the wing and holding it below the surface until it drowned. Another monkfish swallowed a lady's hat; a 2-pound can of mustard was found in the gut of another; and perhaps the oddest item, a piece of wood 18 inches long and 12 inches wide studded with nails.

The monkfish spends the winter offshore in rather deep water and approaches the coast in the spring for breeding purposes. The young are born alive, generally in June or July. Twenty-five baby monkfish have been recorded at a single birth.

The flesh of angel shark is rather coarse and was formerly despised as food. However, in England, an increasing amount of these fish are landed each year, the majority going to fried-fish shops. In olden times the rough skin of the angel shark, called shagreen, or chagrin, was much used as an abrasive to polish wood and ivory. The skin itself was dried and crushed as a remedy for itching and other skin complaints.

The angel shark has been found off Martha's Vineyard and Block Island. H. B. Bigelow and W. C. Schroeder have recorded it in *Fishes of the Western North Atlantic*, giving excellent figures, descriptions, habitat, and sizes.

Skates Have Mermaid's Purses

Familiar to fishermen on the Atlantic coast is a group of sand-colored, flattened fishes belonging to the family Rajidae and commonly known as skates, from the old Norse *skata*. Twenty-four species of the genus *Raja* are found in the waters of North and Middle America.

Skates are fishes that lack true bones. Instead they have cartilage

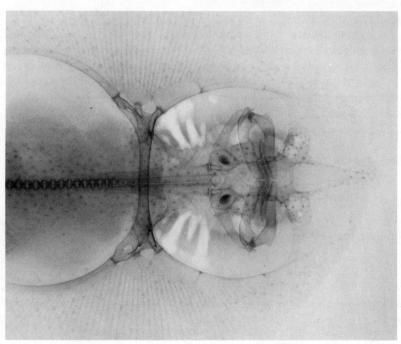

or gristle for skeletal support. This is true also of sharks.

Skates can be recognized easily by the lozenge-shaped body and rough-spined, narrow tail. They differ from flatfish, or flounder, in that the lower surface is the belly; in flounder it is the side. If a skate were divided down the middle line of the upper surface, the two portions would be identical. If the same division were made in a flounder, one-half section would be the back of the fish, containing the brain, while the other would be the belly, with the gills and intestines.

On the sides of skates are pectoral fins, the so-called wings. The tail does not provide the chief means of propulsion but is used chiefly for steering and defense. Skates are propelled by a series of wavelike movements of their wings. They can attain a good rate of speed.

The skate is primarily adapted to life on the sea floor. Even its breathing organs suit this habitat. While swimming or gliding through the water, it is able to breathe in the usual fish manner, taking water in through its mouth and expelling it through the gill openings on the underside of the head. However, when lying on the ocean bottom, the skate is in danger of taking in particles of sand with the stream of water, resulting in a clogging of the delicate gill filaments. Therefore, on the bottom, the skate switches to taking in water through spiracles on its back surface instead of its undersides. The spiracles are large openings regulated by valves just behind each eye. Oxygen is removed from the water as it passes through the gill filaments. The water is then expelled through the gill openings on the underside.

The eyes also are modified. The upper portion of the pupil is covered by a thick, dark lobe that can be enlarged or decreased so that light may be regulated. In dim, deep water the opening is made larger; in bright shallows, the aperture contracts.

For protection, skates rely chiefly on their mottled, sandy coloration, which camouflages them when they partially bury themselves in the sand. When tumbled from a net, skates roll themselves into a ball-like position. The head and tail are commonly studded with groups of small, rough spines, and many species are provided with electric organs on both sides at the end of the tail. These give additional protection.

In New England, the three leading species are the little skate *(Raja erinacea)*, known also as prickly skate, tobaccobox, or summer skate; the barndoor skate *(Raja laevis)*; winter skate, and the big skate *(Raja ocellata)*, known also as spotted skate or eyed skate. The barn-

door skate is the largest in New England waters, sometimes reaching lengths of 6 feet and weights of 35 pounds.

Usually in April and May the skates migrate into shoal water; they return to deeper water during the winter months. They glide along the bottom, feeding on crabs, mollusks, and small fishes. It has been stated that some skates uncover shellfish buried in the sand by a vigorous flapping of their wings.

All skates produce eggs, which hatch after they have been released by the mother. The egg case, usually released on muddy or sandy flats, is a dark capsule 3 to 7 inches long, with 4 stiff-pointed horns. (They are frequently called such names as mermaid's purses and mermaid's pinboxes.) Fertile eggs contain an embryo in a yolk sac. The incubation period ranges from 4½ months to nearly 15 months, depending upon the species and the temperature of the water. Eventually, the miniature skate leaves the egg case through a small slit at one end of the capsule.

Male skates are usually about one-third smaller than females. The males can be identified by the two fingerlike mating claspers found on their undersides.

In Europe, skates are considered a delicacy, appearing on the finest restaurant menus as "ray." French epicures relish skate as *Raie au beurre noire*, i.e., ray with browned butter. In the United States, skates occasionally are shipped to market as "rajafish."

Cownose Ray—Seven Feet Wide

When we first saw it swimming in the fish trap, its motion through the water resembled that of a soaring sea gull. With a gentle flapping of its winglike fins, it glided up, almost to the surface, and then down into the green, murky depths of the trap.

"Another ray," said Captain Clark. But we could see that this one was different from the usual skates and stingrays captured in the nets. Once the trap had been emptied and the ray examined closely, we could see the indented, lobed head that identified it as a cownose ray. Captain Clark remarked that each year they usually get one or two of this species in the trap. This specimen was about 4 feet across at the tips of its broad pectoral fins. It possessed a sharp spine at the base of its tail.

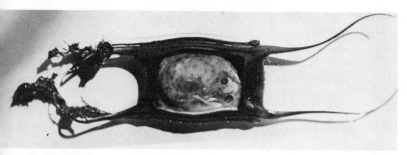

Skate egg case

Occasionally trawlers dragging in Block Island Sound capture the cownose ray in southern New England waters.

The most abundant species of cownose ray found off our Atlantic coast is *Rhinoptera bonasus*, which is found from southern New England to Brazil. Cownoses are warm-water fish but travel off the Middle Atlantic coast and into New England waters in late summer and fall. They have been recorded as late as October 16 in the general vicinity of Woods Hole and Nantucket.

There is fluctuation in the abundance of the cownose ray. During some seasons none are reported at Woods Hole, but on a single day in 1902, 145 members of this species were taken in the pound nets at Menemsha Bight near Woods Hole. On September 12, 1932, a single pound net in Sandy Hook Bay near New York captured 42 of these rays.

Cownose rays are about 14 inches wide at birth; they grow to a maximum breadth of about 7 feet and weigh over 100 pounds. Specimens examined in New Jersey have ranged from 25 to 70 pounds. They are yellowish brown above and white on the underside.

In southern waters, cownose rays are sometimes observed in shoal sandy water producing clouds of mud and sand while burrowing out the mollusks and crustaceans on which they feed, dislodging them from the bottom with their pectoral fins. Examination of stomach contents has shown clams, large snails, lobsters, crabs, and oysters. They have powerful dental plates with which to crush the hard shells. There is one record of a cownose ray caught off the New Jersey coast on a hook baited with a clam.

Cownose rays were much more abundant a century ago. Mitchell in 1815 wrote of this species in New York waters: "A shoal of cow-noses roots up the salt water flats as completely as a drove of hogs would do."

17

Man and Fishes

Fish have dwelt in the waters of our planet for 400 million years
Humans appeared much later, to capture and consume fish. Human
pollution and consumption have cast a shadow over future generation
of finned creatures.

Fish as Sea Monsters

Thriving in the dim depths of the sea are many varieties of large sea
creatures. Accounts of leviathans, giant sea serpents, and sea monster
have captivated the imagination of seafarers and landsmen for thou
sands of years. Fear and trepidation of large, unknown sea creature
were instilled in the minds of primitive people by myth, legend, and the
appearance of large fishes and aquatic mammals.

Ancient civilizations including the Babylonian, Philistine, Egyp
tian, Greek, and Roman worshiped sea deities and sea monsters.

Aristotle rejected as myth most of the tales of giant sea monsters
Yet Pliny in his *Natural History* records a profusion of sea monsters
For hundreds of centuries, since the beginnings of civilization, imagi
nary accounts of fanciful sea creatures have haunted the human mind

The largest fishes that ever dwelt in the waters of our plane

appear to have been the great sharks, *Carcharodon megalodon*. Fossil teeth and relics of this shark indicate a total length of 80 feet.

Giant eel-like sea monsters referred as sea serpents have been reported with some regularity by numbers of oceangoing ships during the past few centuries. Pontoppidon in his *Natural History of Norway* describes "The Kraken," an extraordinary sea monster of Norwegian waters. He states that its back looks like small islands, which rise as high as the masts of seagoing sailing ships.

In 1554 a serious volume on fishes, *De Picibus Marinus*, by Guillaume Rondelet, was published. It contained accounts, descriptions, and grotesque illustrations of marine monsters including a fish dressed as a monk and a bishopfish in full canonicals. Fabricated as a hoax, these "specimens" were contrived from the skins of large sharks and rays.

Rondelet also wrote in awe of the white shark, *Carcharodon carharias*. He stated that this fish was sometimes so large that when laid on a cart, it could scarcely be pulled by two horses. He also wrote about the huge stomach of this species. He said that local fishermen of Nice and Marseilles sometimes found whole men dressed in armor inside the huge fish. One great white shark Rondelet examined at Marseilles contained in its stomach two tuna and a fully clothed sailor.

The great white shark's huge stomach capacity has led some to speculate that the biblical sea creature that swallowed Jonah was not a whale but a great white shark.

In 1848 officers and crew of the British ship HMS *Daedalus* observed a large, snakelike sea monster in the South Atlantic off Africa. It was dark brown with yellowish white about the throat and something like the mane of a horse on its neck.

It is believed by some marine biologists that members of the ribbonfish family have given rise to some of the stories of sea monsters. One immature ribbonfish captured near Bermuda was more than 16 feet in length. It had a long row of flexible filaments on its back, which could represent the horse's mane seen by the crew of the *Daedalus*.

In 1893, the South African steamer *Umfuli* was off French West Africa, heading south for the Cape, when at about 5:30 P.M. Captain Cringle, several officers, some members of the crew, and passengers all clearly saw a large, serpentlike creature traveling north at a good speed, some 500 yards away. They estimated its length as about 80 feet. It was visible to the naked eye; through glasses it was seen to have the shape of an enormous conger eel, with huge jaws estimated at about 7 feet, armed with large teeth.

Captain Cringle turned his ship about and chased the creature, but it was moving so fast that the ship, which did 10 knots, was unable to overtake it and had to give up the chase as darkness fell. But they had the animal clearly in sight for a half hour.

The most valid evidence for a present-day sea monster involves the capture on January 31, 1930, of a 6-foot larval eel. This specimen, now in the Paris Museum, was captured in a tow net by the research vessel *Dana*.

Eels, as we have seen, undergo a change in form in their early development from a thin, almost transparent, ribbonlike form called leptocephalus (meaning narrow head) to that of a round tubular form like a garden hose. From the leptocephalus stage to the adult form there is a tremendous increase in length. Proportionally, the 6-foot larva taken in 1930 by the crew of the *Dana* would indicate a proportional adult length of 60 to 70 feet!

Reports of giant sea creatures washing ashore are stimulators of public curiosity. Crowds flocked to the shore in the fall of 1972 when radio, TV, and newspapers carried reports of a strange sea monster that had washed ashore in Scituate, Massachusetts. All roads leading into Scituate were jammed. People from all over North America and

Europe headed to Massachusetts to see the "sea monster." Close examination of the "beast" by the author showed that it was only the decayed cartilaginous skeleton of an ordinary plankton-feeding basking shark.

The largest living fish, the whale shark *(Rhincodon typus)*, was not known to scientists until April 1828, when it was accurately described and named. This giant has a maximum length of 65 feet.

One of the earliest accounts was a letter of November 25, 1834, which Lieutenant W. Foley of British Naval Intelligence published in the *Journal of the Asiatic Society of Bengal:*

> On my voyage to Madras (in May last), I saw a most extraordinary fish, which had never been seen by any seaman on board, although some of the officers and crew had been employed in the whale fishery. It was the size of a whale, but differing from that animal in shape, spotted like a leopard, in a very beautiful manner: it came close under the stern of the ship, during a calm, and we had a magnificent opportunity for viewing it. It had a very large dorsal fin which it moved about with great rapidity, when made angry, in consequence of the large stones we threw down on it rashly; for it possessed sufficient strength to have broken the rudder and stove in the stern of the ship. Several large fish [presumably dogfish], about a cubit in length and upwards, were gambolling about the monster, entering its mouth at pleasure and returning to the water again. The following will give you some idea of its shape. The mouth very large, dorsal fin black or dark brown, tail also; body covered with brown spots like a leopard, head lizard-shaped. May it not be the Plesiosaurus, or a species of that fish known to have existed formerly in the waters of the ocean?

One result of Lieutenant Foley's letter was that H. Piddington of Calcutta also wrote to the journal that he had observed a similar creature at the entrance to Manila Bay in the Philippines when he was in command of a Spanish brig. He said the fish was 70 or 80 feet long and 30 feet wide. Filipino sailors referred to the creature by the local name, *chacon.* Piddington found that local fishermen were afraid of the fish because it attacked and destroyed small fishing boats. It even swallowed a man who fell overboard in the panic to get a look at the monster.

Piddington also reported the account of an American boat in 1820 or 1821 rowing across Manila Bay. The crew suddenly saw a large, spotted creature rising from the depths. The terrified sailors dropped their oars, and the mate saw the large jaws coming down on him. Having nothing else available, the mate threw the tiller into its mouth. The fish closed its jaws with a tremendous crash and dived under the boat.

In 1828 a giant spotted sea creature of the same type was harpooned at Table Bay near the Cape of Good Hope. The carcass was examined by Andrew Smith, who described it as a new species called whale shark. The shark's skin was sent to the Paris Museum of Natural History where it was mounted and placed on display.

In 1919 a whale shark measuring 59 feet in length and weighing about 90,000 pounds was caught in a bamboo fish trap at Koh Chik in the Gulf of Siam. A giant Russian sturgeon 26 feet 3 inches long and weighing 3250½ pounds was caught in 1827 in the estuary of the Volga River.

The oceanic sunfish is probably the largest bony fish in the world. Forty miles off Sydney, Australia, on September 18, 1908, a huge mola was struck by the SS *Fiona*. This fish measured 14 feet between its anal and dorsal fins and weighed in at 4928 pounds.

Fish Farming—Ancient and Modern

In Japan, fish are invited to dinner by the ringing of harmonious gongs. In India, they are summoned out of the muddy depths of the waters at Dohlpore by the ringing of a handbell. Carp in Belgium respond promptly to the whistle of monks who feed them. In Tahiti, pet eels rise to the surface of ponds in response to the whistling of their masters. For many centuries humans have tried, with some success, to domesticate fish.

Known as aquaculture, mariculture, sea farming, pisciculture, fish culture, fish-stocking, marine agronomy, or hydroculture, fish farming advances human utilization of fishes from the primitive state of hunting to the more regulated state of agriculture. All the various types of land farming—ranching, truck farming, mechanized farming, and so on—have their aquatic equivalents.

Fish farming is one of the oldest forms of fishery science. A bas-relief found in the Egyptian tomb of Theban (2000 B.C.) shows the spiny-rayed fish *Tilapia* being harvested in an artificial pond. Fish ponds have been found by archeologists as adjuncts to Sumerian temples dating as far back as 2500 B.C.

Some historians assert that the ancient Chinese were the first to develop pisciculture. Wei-Ching W. Yen, in an address before the Fourth International Fishery Congress at Washington, D.C. (1908), described the fish-farming methods of T'ao Chu-kung, who lived in the fifth century B.C. His method was to dig a pond the size of an acre, leaving nine small islands scattered about it. In the pond he placed 20 female carp, 3 feet in length, and 4 males of a similar size. This was done in March. Exactly a year later, there were 5000 fishes 12 inches long, 10,000 fishes 2 feet long, and 15,000 fishes 3 feet long. According to Mr. Yen, "In the third year the number had multiplied ten or twenty times, and in the fourth it was impossible to keep count." T'ao put the nine islands in his pond to deceive the fishes, "who would believe they were in the big ocean, travelling round the nine continents." T'ao Chu-kung, who lived about 460 B.C., not only bred fish but also wrote about breeding methods under the name Fan Li in his book, *Yang Yu Ching (Treatise on Fish-Breeding)*. He mentions various ways of breeding carp and gives cooking suggestions, such as stuffing the carp with cabbage leaves.

In ancient and modern China, raising of fish in ponds resulted in the development of a lucrative commerce in fertilized fish eggs. The Chinese took pains to develop special traps and nets to collect fertilized fish eggs in lakes, rivers, and streams.

Classical Greeks cultivated fishes, and ancient Rome was noted for its fish ponds, which were called *piscinae* or *vivaria*. It was fashionable among proconsuls to try to outshine one another in the size and contents of their ornate fish ponds. Rich patricians were not satisfied with a single pond. They frequently had several, each for a different species of fish. In addition, wealthy Romans had fishkeepers, *nomenclators*, who would train fish decorated with jewels to answer to their names or wag their tails when called. Cicero stated: "Our leading people think that they attain unto Heaven if they own in their ponds bearded mullets who will come to them to be stroked."

Romans also gave their fish ponds a sinister role. Pliny and Seneca tell of the savage use to which Vedius Pollio put his fish ponds. At a banquet given for Caesar Augustus, one of Pollio's slaves broke a crystal decanter and was ordered thrown instantly into the *piscina*, there to be eaten alive by the nibbling voracious *Muraenae* (conger eels). The unfortunate slave, not wanting to become food for the fish, threw himself at the emperor's feet and begged the royal guest to intercede on his behalf. Caesar was moved by the slave's plea; he not only pardoned the slave but took further action. In order to show his dissatisfaction with his host's regular method of punishing slaves, he ordered that all the crystals, glasses, decanters, and vases that bedecked the banquet tables be smashed and the colorful fragments be thrown into the fish ponds.

Fish was a prized food for the Romans. It was the luxurious main course at most Roman banquets. The Romans not only carried on fish farming by stocking their ponds with fish brought in from other regions, but also carried on fish propagation. They placed in their fish ponds the spawn of lake, river, and sea fishes, which developed with some success into new fish stocks.

During the Middle Ages, fish ponds developed throughout Europe. They were frequently located near monasteries to provide fish during the Lenten period. Charlemagne took personal interest in the ponds and the species of fish for them.

A manuscript dated 1420 describes fertilizing of trout eggs. Dom Pinchon of the abbey of Reome near Montbara pressed out the eggs and milt from ripe trout and then placed the fertile eggs in a special wooden box. He gave the wooden box ballast by covering its bottom with fine sand. Both ends of the box and its top were covered with a willow grating, to allow water to flow through. The box with its contents of fertile eggs was then placed in a gentle stream where the larval trout would grow rapidly. This method was soon applied to carp, pike, perch, gray mullet, and other species. Large fish ponds developed in Prussia, Saxony, England, Scotland, and Scandinavia.

J. Ludwig Jacobi wrote of his experiments in artificially propagating trout and salmon in 1758 and 1763. Jacobi used a 12-foot-long wooden box that was 6 inches deep, 18 inches wide, and covered with a screen of wire mesh. Through this container ran spring water in a pebbly stream to aerate the fertile eggs.

The word pisciculture was probably first used by Baron de Rivière in 1840. Shortly thereafter, fish culture was extensively practiced throughout most of Europe and in India, Japan, and China.

American interest in fish culture seems to have started in 1804 when John Bachman of Charleston, South Carolina, hatched the eggs of fall fish and trout. Theodatus Garlick and H. A. Ackley of Cleveland, Ohio, were very successful in fertilizing the eggs of brook trout. They established the first American fish farm with a hatching house near Cleveland, using three ponds. Dr. Garlick published *A Treatise on the*

Artificial Propagation of Certain Kinds of Fish (1857). The first U.S. book on fish culture was published in 1854 by W. H. Fry, *A Complete Treatise on Artificial Fish-Breeding.*

At Simsbury, Connecticut, in 1855, E. C. Kellog and D. W. Chapman began successfully hatching brook trout. Kellog, with Colonel Samuel Colt of the revolver firm, set up an extensive hatchery.

One of the most notable fish culturists of this era was Seth Green, who purchased a mill site near Rochester, New York, with a water flow of 150,000 gallons per minute. Green constructed fish ponds by placing barriers in the millrace. A year later, Green sold 180,000 eggs; three years later, 800,000 eggs.

Green's original intention was to raise trout for fish markets. The demand for eggs and young fish for other culturists was so great that Green never raised his fish to market size. He received $8 to $10 per thousand for fertile trout eggs. Fingerling trout brought $30–$40 per thousand. At a time that the going wage was $1 per day, Green proved that fish farming could be profitable and in 1870 wrote a book on his fish-culture methods called *Trout Culture.*

Up to 1867, speckled trout and salmon were the only fish species that had been produced on any considerable scale in U.S. fish hatcheries, although experiments had been made with other species. At the invitation of the states bordering the Connecticut River, Seth Green surveyed the river and selected a locality for a successful shad hatchery.

Efforts to improve and restore salmon to New England rivers culminated in 1868 when Livingston Stone, under the patronage of Massachusetts and New Hampshire, established a salmon-breeding hatchery on the northwest branch of the Miramichi River, 8 miles above Newcastle, on the farm of Joseph Goodfellow. A hatching house, 100 feet by 27 feet, was built, and a spring breeding pond about an acre in size was used in successful salmon cultivation.

A little over a century after Stone started his salmon hatchery in New England, a tremendous growth in fish cultivation has occurred in the United States. Today there are about 334 state and federal fish hatcheries, which produce about 250 million trout and 300 million salmon for release into natural environments to contribute to commercial and sport fishery needs.

In addition to federal and state hatcheries, hundreds of private hatcheries produce fish for private stocking by fishing clubs and individuals for recreational fishing. There are also numerous commercial hatcheries that raise fish to maturity for direct marketing in stores and fish markets.

The largest commercial trout farm in the United States is the Snake River Trout Company in Buhl, Idaho. It usually maintains a stock of more than 10 million trout in various stages of development. This firm operates a complete cycle of fish farming from the egg to the packed frozen product. Trout are spawned in the hatchery, raised on special diets in raceways, then harvested at maturity and packaged as commercial food products. The firm's annual production is around 2 million pounds of trout. Intensive cultivation yields as much as 400,000 pounds per acre. A constant natural source of spring water of 58 degrees F. flows through the 10-acre facility at a rate of 60,000 gallons per minute.

Trout farming in fresh water is a well-established industry in many places, but in the past decade experiments have indicated that some trout will grow faster in fertile salt water. At Loch Ailort, Scotland, trout are raised in sea water and reach weights of 5½ pounds in 2 years. Not only do trout grown in salt water increase in weight faster, but the flesh of the trout develops light pink coloration resembling that of salmon.

Trout cultivation was greatly enhanced by the forty years of research carried on by Lauren Donaldson at the University of Washington. During his two score years as a member of the faculty at Seattle, Donaldson developed a strain of super rainbow trout with growth rate, survival, and egg production twenty times greater than the usual trout stock. In addition to his work with trout, Donaldson also developed better stocks of chinook, coho, and sockeye salmon through selective breeding for desirable characteristics. Donaldson was also instrumental in the successful introduction of salmon into the Great Lakes and Hokkaido Island, Japan.

The coho, a popular Pacific salmon, has been successfully transplanted into the Great Lakes. It also has been transplanted with moderate success in the North River of Massachusetts and other rivers of southern New England. In the mid-1970s, Marine Salmon Farms, Inc., of Wiscasset, Maine, has successfully raised crops of coho for market.

Cylindrical silos filled with circulated water and food pellets have proved successful in raising salmon and trout. These closed systems hold promise for raising high-value food fish.

Aquaculture in Japan provides 6 percent of the total fish production. Since the Japanese cultivate only those species that are sought after and easily marketable, fish farming provides 15 percent of the total value of their fishery.

One of Japan's major aquacultural species is salmon. The islands of Honshu and Hokkaido have many rivers. Three hundred of these rivers are inhabited by salmon. In 1970, along these rivers, some 150 incubating and hatching stations released 600 million salmon fry for the local fishery.

In Japan many of the coastal waters have become unsuitable for aquaculture due to pollution, filling in of marsh lands, and increased boat traffic. In addition, pens and fish cultivation in shallow coastal ponds, bays, and inlets are frequently buffeted by severe coastal storms with destructive waves and damaging turbulence.

A new approach to coastal sea farming has been developed to circumvent the perils of the shallow coastal zone—deep-water farming offshore. The Japanese have started undersea cultivation in the deeper waters off Japan at depths of from 30 to 130 feet.

Within the past decade, the Japanese have started systematic farming of salmon, trout, yellowtails, scallops, abalone, oysters, and other species on the ocean bottom. For swimming organisms such as fish, bottom-positioned pens made from resin-coated steel pipe frames are used to house the crop. The developing fish are fed through a "chimney net" rising to the sea surface. This deep-water farming method is proving successful in many locations.

A little-known fish in Western nations, the yellowtail *(Seriola quinqueradiata)*, called *buri* by the Japanese, is Japan's primary cultured-fish species. In the decade of development from 1960 to 1970 it has become a multimillion-dollar industry. In 1969, the Japanese raised 4.3 million yellowtail fingerlings to produce 36,725 metric tons of yellowtail worth the equivalent of $44.7 million.

The yellowtail is one of the fastest-growing fish in the world. In about 110 days, larval fish ¾ inch long will grow rapidly to over 1⅓ feet in length, gaining over 2 pounds in weight. The Japanese prefer to eat yellowtails 12 to 18 inches long. The larvae of yellowtails are normally caught by the Japanese in the early spring, drifting under seaweed off the Kyushu and Shikoku islands. They are then raised by the fish farmers in other embanked ponds, net-enclosed ponds, or floating net cages. The young fish fry are fed a mixture of artificial formula foods or frozen scrap fish. They seem to thrive on anchovy, sand louse, and jack mackerel.

Eel farming is also highly developed in Japan. About 13,000 tons of the Japanese eel, *Anguilla japonica*, are produced annually. The Japanese have been successful in getting eels to spawn, using hormonal applications from fish pituitary glands. This process to induce spawning is called "hypophysation" and is also used successfully on mullet.

One of the most widely cultivated fish species in the Asian world i the milkfish, *Chanos chanos*. Found notably in salt and brackish-wate ponds of Java, India, Hong Kong and the Philippines, milkfish ar herbivorous, feeding on aquatic plants. They are also a very hard species able to withstand a wide variation in salinity and temperature The annual milkfish harvest of the Philippines is about 21,000 tons wit a productivity in the ponds about 78 tons per square mile. In th Philippines the ponds are not usually fertilized to enhance production In Taiwan, where the Chinese fertilize milkfish ponds, productio reaches 520 tons per square mile of pond. In Indonesia, where sewage i diverted into the ponds instead of commercial fertilizers, the yiel reaches an astonishing 1300 tons per square mile.

The technical feasibility of raising flounder in dense cultures i small enclosures has been amply demonstrated by James E. Shelbourn and his colleagues in Great Britain since 1951. In the Lowestof Fisheries Laboratory, successful methods of raising flounder from egg spawned in captivity to mature fish has been developed. It was foun that the nauplii larvae of the brine shrimp, *Artemia salina*, wer suitable planktonic food for developing flounder larvae.

It is a well-known biological fact that marine organisms grow faste in warm water. Experiments to use the warm waste water of nuclea reactors to raise rapid growing flounder have been underway at th Scottish nuclear power plant at Hunterston since 1967. Water warme 15 to 20 degrees above normal by the nuclear reactor flows throug flounder-filled tanks. The fish thrive in the warm water and grow at much faster rate in it. Flatfish were found to reach market size in 2 months instead of the usual 48 months. In the United States experimen tal fish farms warmed by the thermal effluent of nuclear power plant are being developed in Maine, New York, Florida, and California.

Fish farming holds great potential for helping to alleviate th famine that threatens many nations around the world.

The Future of World Fisheries

The waters of our planet contain trillions of fishes of at least 30,00 different species. Yet less than 1 percent of the species of fishes make u over 90 percent of the world's fishery catch. Clupeoid fish, members c the herring family such as menhaden, sardines, and anchovies, comprise over 40 percent of the world's catch.

In the United States nearly three-quarters of the American fishery catch is made up of menhaden, tuna, salmon, hakes, flounder, alewives, and members of the cod family. Eighty percent of the dollar value of our commercial catch comes from just ten seafood items: shrimp, salmon, tuna, crabs, oysters, lobsters, clams, flounder, menhaden, and cod. And about 90 percent of the world's fishery catch is taken on the continental shelves. That is why the U.S. Congress has passed legislation extending exclusive American fishery rights from 12 to 200 miles out from shore, effective in 1977.

Countless proliferating organisms of the sea exist, ranging from plant microorganisms that are transformed from smallest to largest through the food chains into giant sharks and whales weighing many tons. In a fertile patch of seawater 15 million plankton microorganisms may be living in less than a gallon of water.

In a world where famine and starvation stalk over a third of the planet's growing population, it is significant that the oceans provide about 15 percent of the world's protein. For some time, people thought the fishery resources of the sea were virtually inexhaustible. Today we are aware that certain national fishing areas have already been seriously depleted by overfishing. Giant fishing trawlers with small meshed nets have endangered stocks of fish, such as haddock, cod, herring, and salmon. International fishery agreements have set catch quotas and limitations on formerly bountiful species such as herring, tuna, haddock, halibut, salmon, and yellowtail flounder. However, individual floating fish factories are "pirating" more than their share every day.

The late Dr. Wilbert M. Chapman said that, "it was reasonable to expect a demand for a global harvest of living aquatic resources of a little less than 100 million metric tons by 1975, nearly 175 million tons by 1985, and a little more than 400 million tons by the year 2000." He thought that 90 percent of this could be supplied from the sea.

The Food and Agriculture Organization (FAO) of the United Nations has estimated the upper limits of future catches of fish of the types now consumed to be in the vicinity of 120 million tons. This figure would be contingent on effective national and international management of fish stocks to maintain maximum sustainable yields.

At a recent session of the FAO Committee on Fisheries, the director-general of FAO said:

This is a critical moment for world ocean fisheries. The pattern so rapidly developed in the last two decades is already changing. Production of marine fish has increased, in the space of one decade, from 27 million tons in 1958 to 56 million tons in 1969. At the beginning of this period, virtually all fish stocks outside the North Atlantic and the North Pacific were underexploited or not exploited at all. Now there are few stocks of the types of fish readily caught and marketed which are not heavily exploited. This is a consequence of technological advances changing the very structure of fishing industries. There is a large number of long-range fishing vessels capable of fishing anywhere in the world which are deployed most effectively with the latest available managerial techniques and electronic aids.

The increase of such elaborate fishing vessels with advanced technological development reduced numbers of fish at an increasing rate. The increasing fishery effort and decreasing catches of desirable species has made more pressing the need for management and conservation of the traditional fish varieties and the development of new species for food.

Beneath the surface of the oceans lurk over 20 thousand species of protein-rich fish, weighing millions of tons, which are not yet utilized for human food. We are told by many fishermen that nearly 50 percent of their catch is discarded at sea because of a lack of market demand. We are also informed that there are enough fish in the sea to supply the total animal protein needs of between 5 billion and 30 billion people. Deep ocean waters hold hundreds of billions of sardinelike lanternfish, or myctophids, which have been unharvested and unknown as human food until recently because they dwell in the dark depths of the sea.

Near Cape Town, South Africa, in the major fishery for fishmeal and oil, small amounts of lanternfish began to be taken for reduction to meal. By 1973 this abundant deep-water fish accounted for more than 10 percent, 43,000 metric tons, of the total production of this important fishery.

Vast quantities of unharvested fish abound in the nutrient-rich waters of the Arctic and Antarctic seas. New varieties of fishes await exploitation as vital sources of food for future generations. It has been estimated that an additional 20 million tons of coastal and oceanic pelagic fish can be added to the world's fish catch. Few people realize that over 70 percent of the world's potential natural food resources lies beneath the surface of the sea.

Supplement: 250 Fishes From A to Z

AGNATHA. A class of jawless fishes that includes the hagfish and the lamprey. These primitive eel-shaped fish are dependent on other fish for food as parasites or saprophytes.

ALBACORE. *Thunnus alalunga* (derivation: *thunnus* from Greek for "tuna," *alalunga* meaning "long fin"). Small white-fleshed tuna of the Atlantic and Pacific with a long fin. Its light-colored flesh makes it a choice species for tuna canneries.

ALEVIN. A very young fish. Usually refers to early stage of newly hatched salmon.

ALEWIFE. *Alosa pseudoharengus* (derivation: *alosa*, "to nourish," *pseudoharengus*, "false herring"). A river herring of the Atlantic coast which migrates upstream in the spring to spawn. A bony fish that is sometimes smoked, salted, or used for fishmeal and fertilizer.

ALLIGATOR GAR. *Lepisosteus spatula* (derivation: *lepisosteus*, "bony scales," *spatula*, "spoon shaped"). The largest species of American gar, reaching a length of 10 feet and weighing 300 pounds. It is found in rivers flowing into the Gulf of Mexico.

AMBERJACK. *Seriola dumerili* (derivation: *seriola*, Italian name of "amberjack," *dumerili* in honor of André Dumeril, French physician and naturalist, 1774–1860). An oceanic fish of the jack family Carangidae. Inhabits the Atlantic and reaches a length of 6 feet and a weight of 120 pounds.

AMERICAN SMELT. *Osmerus mordax* (derivation: *osmerus*, "odorous," *mordax*, Latin for "biting"). Found along the east coast and enters streams from the Gulf of St. Lawrence to Chesapeake Bay. Landlocked in many New England lakes and all the Great Lakes where it was introduced in 1912. In the fall smelts move inshore and remain all winter. Smelts are predatory, eating all kinds of small fish. They grow to a length of 14 inches.

AMUR PIKE. Native to Russia, this species was first imported into the United States by the Fish and Wildlife Service in 1965. A second shipment of 60,000 amur pike eggs was received in 1969. Several thousand amur pike fingerlings were released into the Glendale Reservoir in southwestern Pennsylvania.

ANABAS or CLIMBING PERCH. *Anabas scandens* (derivation: *anabas*, from Greek meaning to "go up"). A group of perchlike freshwater fishes found in Southeast Asia and Africa. It is not a true perch but is known to climb tree trunks and move over moist land from one body of water to another.

ANCHOVY, ANCHOA, ANCHOVA. Any of a number of small herringlike species of fish of the family Engraulidae. Found in the Mediterranean Sea and in the Atlantic and Pacific oceans. They are at times very abundant and are pickled as a food fish, used as a bait fish, or processed into fishmeal. This name is from the Spanish *anchova*, meaning dried or pickled fish.

ANEMONEFISH. Any of a dozen species of damselfish that can live in close association with the toxic tentacles of the sea anemone. These fishes have a protective mucus secretion that prevents the stinging discharge of the anemone. The clownfish is a common example.

ANGELFISH. A name given to certain tropical fish of the families Chaetodontidae and Ephippidae.

ANGEL SHARKS. Raylike sharks of the family Squatinidae (from Latin *squatus*, "skate"). *Squatina californica* is a Pacific species while *Squatina dumerili* is found in the Atlantic.

ANGLERFISH. A species with a fleshy flap or projection to lure fish into its mouth. A common example is the angler, goosefish, or monkfish *(Lophius americanus)* common in Atlantic waters reaching a length of 5 feet. Smaller varieties occur in the deep-sea zones.

ARAPAIMA. *Arapaima gigas* (derivation: "giant arapaima"). A member of the South American freshwater fish group called Osteoglossidae (bony tongues), *Arapaima gigas* reaches a length of 10 feet and a weight of 440 pounds. It is the largest freshwater fish in South America.

ARAWANA. *Osteoglossum bicirrhosum* (derivation: "bony tongue with two projections"). A close relative of arapaima, living in northern South America, the arawana reaches a length of 2 feet and has 2 barbels projecting from its lower jaw. The female keeps fertile eggs in her mouth until the young fish emerge.

ARCHER FISH. *Toxotes jaculatrix* (derivation: *toxotes*, "bowlike," *jaculatrix*, "to shoot"). A fish of India, Southeast Asia, and the East Indies which shoots down insects by squirting water. The water is propelled by the fish pressing its tongue against a groove in the roof of its mouth. Insects 3 feet away can be knocked into the water.

ARCTIC CHAR. *Salvelinus alpinus* (derivation: *salvelinus*, an old name for char, *alpinus*, pertaining to lofty mountains). Found in streams tributary to the Arctic Ocean in Europe, Asia and North America, the Arctic char habitually enters the sea. The streams entering Hudson Bay produce fish up to 11 pounds.

ARGENTINE. Refers to the silvery scales of fish used in making artificial pearls. Also denotes small silvery fish closely related to smelts. In the Atlantic, *Argentina silus;* in the Pacific, *Argentina sialis.*

ASIAN WALKING CATFISH. Family Clariidae. This exotic Asian species was accidentally released in 1965 into the waters of southern Florida by aquarium dealers. It has spread overland into the waters of southern and central Florida. This species is considered by many fishery biologists to be out of control in Florida with no practical method of eradication.

ATLANTIC SALMON. *Salmo salar* (derivation: *salmo*, Latin for "salmon," *salar*, "to leap"). This salmon ranges the Atlantic from Portugal north to the Arctic and from West Greenland and northern Laborador south to Cape Cod. Fish from 80 to 100 pounds have been caught in Europe; in America 50 pounds is unusual. The average size varies from river to river but is usually between 10 and 20 pounds.

ATLANTIC STURGEON. *Acipenser oxyrhynchus* (derivation: *acipenser* is an old name for sturgeon, *oxyrhynchus* means "sharp snout"). Occurs from Quebec to Gulf of Mexico. It ascends rivers to spawn, the young returning to the sea to complete their growth. It feeds in both fresh and salt water on a great variety of bottom animals. This sturgeon reaches a length of 14 feet and weight of 811 pounds.

BACALAO. Spanish, Portuguese, and Italian name for cod.

BARRACUDA. Members of the elongated pikefish genera *Sphyraena*. With needlelike teeth the great barracuda reaches a length of 6 feet. The 1-foot northern barracuda strays into New England waters. Feared by swimmers and skin divers, it is a dangerous species due to its sharp teeth.

BARRELFISH. *Hyperoglyphe perciformis* (derivation: "overcarved perch form"). An Atlantic species found along American and European coasts; associated with floating seaweed and driftwood. It sometimes enters floating barrels and boxes. It feeds on barnacles.

BASKING SHARK. *Cetorhinus maximus* (derivation: name means "large whalelike shark"). One of the largest species of sharks; reaches a length of 40 feet. Harmless to man, has very small teeth and is a filter feeder. Has habit of lying in sea surface basking in sun. Found in the northern seas, it has been sought after for its liver which can yield several barrels of oil.

BASS. Mainly members of the family Serranidae. *See* Channel Bass, Largemouth Bass, Small-mouth Bass, Sea Bass, Striped Bass.

BATFISH. Members of family Ogcocephalidae. Close relatives of the frogfish and anglerfish, generally found in tropical Atlantic. Also sometimes used to describe species of *Platax* of family Platacidae which have large, winglike fins.

BEAUGREGORY. *Pomacentrus leucostictus* (derivation: *pomacentrus*, "central opercle," *leucostictus*, "white spots"). Small tropical marine species with brilliant blue and sulfur yellow coloration. Found among coral reefs in West Indies and Florida Keys.

BELLOWSFISH or LONGSPINE SNIPEFISH. *Macrorhamphosus scolopax* (derivation: *macrorhamphosus*, "long beak," *scolopax*, "snipe"). A small Atlantic species with tubular snout and deep compressed body, up to 6 inches in length. Found at edge of continental shelves.

BETTA or SIAMESE FIGHTING FISH. *Betta splendens* (derivation: "beetlike splendor"). Tropical fish of Southeast Asia, red, blue, beetlike in color. In Thailand male specimens are prized for their ferocity and are made to fight each other in captivity with bets being placed on participating fishes. Reaches a length of 2–3 inches.

BELUGA. *Acipenser huso* (derivation: *acipenser* is an ancient name for sturgeon, *huso* an old Germanic name). Largest sturgeon, native to Russia, called *bylukha*. Once abundant in Volga River, Ural–Caspian Sea area where specimens over 100 years old, 28 feet long, weighing 3300 pounds have been recorded. Produces best-quality caviar.

BICHIR. *Polypterus bichir* (derivation: "many feather wings"). A primitive elongated fish of the rivers of tropical Africa. Body has rhombic enameled scales and the dorsal fin is made of a series of finlets. Found in the Nile, Congo, and Niger rivers, it is a nocturnal predator.

BIGEYE. *Priacanthus arenatus* (derivation: *priacanthus*, "sawlike spine," *arenatus*, "sandy"). Small carnivorous tropical fish with big eyes and oblique mouth. This Atlantic species is found from Brazil to Rhode Island.

BIG SKATE. *Raja ocellata* (derivation: *raja*, Latin for "skate," *ocellata*, "with eye-like spots"). Found at depths of about 30 fathoms. Feeds on rock crabs and squid. Only importance, nuisance to fishermen. Average size: 32 inches long, 20 inches wide.

BILLFISH. Any of many types of fish with elongated bill or snout, such as swordfish, marlin, sailfish or gar.

BLACK BASS. *See* Black Sea Bass, Largemouth Bass, Smallmouth Bass.

BLACK BULLHEAD. *Ictalurus melas* (derivation: *ictalurus*, "catfish," *melas*, "black"). Not as large as other bullheads; maximum size is 17 inches, weight under 3 pounds. Lives well in farm ponds and small streams where there is a soft mud bottom.

BLACK CRAPPIE. *Pomoxis nigromaculatus* (derivation: *pomoxis*, "sharp opercle," *nigromaculatus*, "black spots"). Freshwater species mottled with dark green or black spots. Nests and lives in waters 3 to 8 feet deep but moves into shallows at night to feed.

BLACK RUFF. *Centrolophus niger* (derivation: "black central crest"). A European deep-water fish which sometimes strays into American waters. Elongated and purplish black, it reaches a length of 3 feet. It feeds on other fishes.

BLACK SEA BASS. *Centropristis striata* (derivation: "streaked sawlike spines"). Atlantic food and game fish reaching a weight of 8 pounds. It is found among rocks and shipwrecks from Maine to northern Florida.

BLACKFISH or TAUTOG. *Tautoga onitis* (derivation: *tautoga*, Narragansett Indian for "sheep's heads"). Edible coastal North Atlantic species sought after by anglers and spearfishermen. Adult form is black, sometimes with brown and greenish gray blotches.

BLENNY. One of the many species of small elongated fish of the family Blenniidae. Usually found in marine or brackish water among rocks and pebbles. Worldwide in distribution.

BLIND FISH. Fish with degenerated eyes usually found in total darkness of caves or abyssal depths of the sea.

BLOATER. A common sea herring which has been salted, smoked and half dried. Also sometimes refers to species of North American whitefish found in lakes, *Coregonus* genus.

BLOWFISH, SWELLFISH, or NORTHERN PUFFER. *Sphoeroides maculatus* (derivation: *sphoeroides*, "resembling a sphere," *maculatus*, "spotted"). A small fish with the ability to inflate its body to twice its normal size. Its elastic skin is rough with minute prickles. It is common from Cape Cod to South Carolina.

BLUE CATFISH. *Ictalurus furcatus* (derivation: *ictalurus*, "catfish," *furcatus*, "forked"). The blue catfish reaches a size of over 100 pounds. Individuals 25 to 30 pounds are caught but most are 5 to 15 pounds. Blue catfish move from larger rivers into bayous and backwaters in spring, even ranging into salt water in Louisiana. They bite on trotlines baited with small fish and crawfish.

BLUEFIN TUNA. *Thunnus thynnus* (derivation: Greek for "tuna"). The bluefin, sought after by sport and commercial fishermen, is the largest tuna species reaching 1800 pounds and 14 feet in length. A recent decline in numbers of this species has brought about international conservation measures.

BLUEFISH. *Pomatomus saltatrix* (derivation: *pomatomus*, Greek for "operculum cutting," *saltatrix*, "jumper"). A marine swift-swimming species. Among the most savage and bloodthirsty of all fish. Recorded to have attacked swimmers in Florida waters. A desirable food and game fish of worldwide distribution.

BLUEGILL. *Lepomis macrochirus* (derivation: "scaled opercle with long pectoral"). The bluegill is one of the most common and best known of the sunfish.

Omnivorous, they feed on plants, snails, insects, crustaceans and plankton. An excellent freshwater food and game fish, it reaches a length of 15 inches and a weight of 4½ pounds.

BLUE MARLIN. *Makaira nigricans.* Found chiefly off coasts of Florida and Cuba. An outstanding game fish, it reaches a length of 9 feet and a weight of 500 pounds.

*****BLUE PIKE.** *Stizostedion vitreum glaucum.* This valuable species was once a commercial fish of importance in Lake Erie and Lake Ontario. Swift decline in the 1950s due to pollution and environmental changes. In 1969 a pair of blue pike successfully spawned at a Pennsylvania fish station and 9000 fry successfully transferred to a national fish hatchery in South Dakota. Some fry later planted in an isolated Minnesota lake to renew this valuable species. Endangered.

BLUE SHARK. *Prionace glauca* (derivation: Greek *prion,* "saw," in reference to serrated teeth; *glauca,* "blue-gray"). Known also as bluedog and blue whaler, the blue shark is a swift voracious shark reaching 15 feet in length and 410 pounds. Known to attack whales during cutting in on whaleships. It feeds on fish but is considered dangerous to swimmers.

BOARFISH. Family Caproidae. A small oceanic deep-water fish with a projecting snout. There are several species worldwide which reach a length of 7 inches.

BONITO. *Sarda sarda* (derivation: *sarda* from Sardinia where species was found in abundance). Small tunalike oceanic fish reaching a length of 3 feet. A swift-swimming migratory species, it is sought after by deep-sea anglers.

BOSTON BLUEFISH. This is a local name in the New England region given to pollack.

BOSTON SCROD. A trade or restaurant menu name, given to 1½- to 2½-pound cod, haddock, or pollack.

BOWFIN. *Amia calva* (derivation: *amia* is ancient Greek fish name, *calva,* Latin for "bald"). Primitive soft-flesh freshwater fish of Great Lakes and sluggish waters from Vermont to Florida, Texas and Dakota. Reaches 2 feet in length; olive color with dark spots.

BOXFISH. *Ostracion diaphanum* (derivation: "translucent bony shell"). Boxfish or trunkfish are usually tropical with head and body enclosed in a solid box of bony plates. Most are brightly colored and slow swimmers. Having sharp spines and toxic effects, this species is not edible. Used as dried ornaments.

BRAMBLE SHARK. *Echinorhinus brucus* (derivation: "spiny shark," in reference to its thorny hide). Also called alligator dogfish. Reaches 10 feet in length in temperate and tropical waters. Its hide is covered with buttonlike curved spines. It feeds on fish and is sometimes taken by anglers.

BREAM. Name used to describe carplike European freshwater fish. Family Cyprinidae, grows to a weight of 12 pounds. Sea bream refers to marine members of family Sparidae found in Mediterranean, European, and Australian coastal waters.

BROOK TROUT. *Salvelinus fontinalis* (derivation: *salvelinus* is an old name for trout from German *Sälbling; fontinalis,* "living in fountains"). Found from Labrador to Saskatchewan and from Maine to Alabama, west to Minnesota. Brookies can remain landlocked in lakes, rivers and brooks where the summer temperatures are not much greater than 65 degrees. In northern regions some races go to sea, returning to small streams to spawn. Large individuals weigh as much as 9 pounds.

BROTULID. Among the most abundant fishes of the abyssal zone. One species, *Bassogigas*, taken from 27,236 feet, was the deepest fish ever collected.

BROWN TROUT. *Salmo trutta* (derivation: *salmo*, Latin for "salmon"; *trutta* is low Latin for "trout"). Introduced from Europe into North American waters, the brown trout are now very widespread. They can tolerate warmer water, up to 75 or 80 degrees, and this increases stocking value in marginal trout waters. The size attained varies widely: maximum average weight is between 6 and 12 pounds; largest is around 40 pounds.

BULLHEAD. *See* Catfish.

BURBOT. *Lota lota* (derivation: Latin for "bearded"). The only member of the cod family found in freshwater rivers and lakes. Feeds on frogs and small fish, reaching a maximum size of from 2 to 3 feet.

BUTTERFISH. *Peprilus triacanthus* (derivation: "oval and three spined"). Small, delicious oval panfish found along east coast of United States from Maine to North Carolina. Reaches maximum size of about 10 inches. Young butterfish sometimes take shelter under floating jellyfish.

BUTTERFLYFISH. Family Chaetodontidae. Bright-colored marine coral fish. Resembles butterfly with winglike fins. This name is also sometimes given to African freshwater flying fishes.

CALIFORNIA SHEEPHEAD. *Pimelometopon pulchrum* (derivation: *pimelometopon* from the Greek, "fat-forehead"; *pulchrum*, "beautiful"). Also known as California redfish and fathead, this food fish is found in Pacific kelp beds. Reaches a length of 3 feet and weight of 15 pounds.

CANDLEFISH or EULACHON. *Thaleichthys pacificus* (derivation: "Pacific sea fish"). A marine species of the Pacific of the smelt family. An edible oily fish. It is so oily that when dried it can be used as a candle by placing a wick through it lengthwise.

CARP. *Cyprinus carpio* (derivation: *cyprinus*, Greek for "carp," *carpio*, "carp"). A large, small-mouthed, freshwater fish of Asiatic and European origin introduced into North American waters. Long used in fish farming, this edible species lives to a great age and reaches 55 pounds or more in weight.

CARPET SHARKS. Family Orectolobidae. Twenty to thirty species of this type of shark occur in Indo-Pacific region. The carpet shark of Australia is also called the wobbegong. This type is flattened and lies on the bottom more than most sharks. Its skin has a pattern similar to a carpet, which provides camouflage.

CATFISH, BROWN BULLHEAD, or HORNED POUT. *Ictalurus nebulosus* (derivation: *ictalurus* from Greek meaning "catfish"; *nebulosus*, "clouded"). Scaleless freshwater fish with chin whiskers or barbels. Found in quiet, muddy and weedy waters of the United States. Feeds readily on a variety of baits, especially worms.

CHAIN PICKEREL. *Esox niger* (derivation: "black pike"). Occurs in sluggish waters of the eastern and southern states. The creation of reservoirs by impoundments favors their increase. They remain active all winter so ice fishing for them is a popular sport. They reach a length of 30 inches and weight of 9 pounds.

CHANNEL CATFISH. *Ictalurus punctatus* (derivation: "catfish with spots").

Channel cats are found in medium to large rocky rivers. They generally feed on plant and animal matter during twilight including fish, algae, insects, seeds, etc. They are considered excellent food and game fish by many anglers.

CHICKEN HALIBUT. A name sometimes applied to small or young halibut. They are sold at a slightly higher price than regular-size halibut.

CHIMAERAS. Chimaeras are cartilaginous fishes allied to sharks, skates and rays, but differ anatomically. They have one gill opening on either side, no scales and are tadpole shaped, usually 2 or 3 feet long. Found in deep water from 160 to more than 1200 fathoms.

CHINOOK SALMON. *Oncorhynchus tshawytscha* (derivation: *oncorhynchus*, "hooked snout"; *tshawytscha* is from the Alaskan local name, *Choweecha*, and the Russian local name, *tshawytscha*). This salmon is often called spring salmon in British Columbia. It is also called king and quinnat. Like the other Pacific salmon, except the sockeye, the Chinook occurs from Southern California to Alaska and from there to Japan. Lengths of 5 feet and weights up to 126½ pounds have been recorded.

CHUB. A name frequently given to small baitfish of the family Cyprinidae.

CHUM SALMON. *Oncorhynchus keta* (derivation: *oncorhynchus*, "hooked snout," *keta*, "whale"). The chum salmon or dog salmon ranges from the Sacramento River to Bering Strait. This is usually the latest salmon to appear in migrating groups in the fall. The usual weight at maturity is 8 to 18 pounds.

CICHLIDS. Members of the family Cichlidae, a group of perchlike freshwater and brackish water fishes of Africa, South America and Asia. Over 600 species are in this group, which is prized by aquarists.

CLIMBING PERCH. *Anabas testudineus* (derivation: "up from the bottom with protective covering"). Found in southern Asia, can travel overland. It pulls itself along by the edges of its gill covers. It has a double gill. One part breathes water, the other breathes air.

CLINGFISH. *Gobiesox strumosus* (derivation: "swollen Gobioid fish"). Small carnivorous fish of warm seas. Usually lives in tide pools and clings firmly to stones. Also known as skilletfish.

CLOWNFISH. *See* Anemonefish.

COBIA. *Rachycentron canadum* (derivation: "central spine," from lower Silurian period). Elongated food fish of South and Middle Atlantic coast. Generally 2 to 3 feet in length.

COD. *Gadus morhua* (derivation: ancient name for codfish). One of the most important food fishes of the United States. Found along coast of New England, Iceland, Greenland. Usually weighs from 3 to 75 pounds.

COELACANTH. *Latimeria chalumnae* (derivation: after Courtney Latimer, who found first living specimen in 1938 and Chalumna River, near site of capture of first specimen). Primitive lobe-finned fish that first appeared 400 million years ago. Believed extinct until specimen was captured off South Africa in 1938.

COHO SALMON. *Oncorhynchus kisutch* (derivation: *oncorhynchus*, "hooked snout"; *kisutch* is a local name for this species in Kamchatka). The coho or silver salmon is an important species for anglers. It enters all kinds of rivers and may spawn only a short distance from the sea. It is not abundant south of Oregon. It has successfully been transplanted to the Great Lakes and certain New England streams.

*COLORADO SQUAWFISH. *Ptychocheilus lucius.* Once widely distributed throughout the Colorado River and its tributaries; throve in warm swift waters. Dams and reservoirs now obstacles to successful reproduction. Endangered.

COLUMBIA RIVER SQUAWFISH. *Ptychocheilus oregonensis* (derivation: *ptychocheilus* is from the Greek, "fold" and "lip," the skin of the mouth behind the jaws being folded; *oregonensis*, from Oregon). This member of the minnow family lives only in the Columbia River and its tributary rivers and in the large lakes and coastal rivers of Washington and Oregon. Also known as northern squawfish.

CONGER EEL. *Conger oceanicus* (derivation: ancient Roman name for this fish). Large carnivorous sea eel which reaches a length of 9 feet and weight of 84 pounds.

CREEK CHUB. *Semotilus atromaculatus* (derivation: *semotilus*, "spotted"; *atromaculatus*, "with black spots"). A widespread species found in small brooks and streams from Maine to Wyoming, south to Georgia and New Mexico. Creek chubs are important as live bait and as food for trout.

CREVALLE. *Caranx hippos* (derivation: "horse crevalle"). A food fish of eastern Florida and Gulf coasts. Average weight about 2 pounds.

CROAKER. *Micropogon undulatus* (derivation: *micropogon*, "small beard," *undulatus*, "undulating"). When this fish is out of water it produces a low rasping croak, underwater it makes a low drumming sound. Found in southern Atlantic and Gulf of Mexico.

CRUCIFIX FISH. A name given to some marine catfishes of the genus *Arius* found in West Indian and South American waters. The underside of its dried skull possesses the figure of a crucifix.

*CUI-UI. *Chasmistes cujus.* Occurring only in Pyramid Lake, Washoe county, Nevada, the Cui-ui (pronounced *kwee-wee*) sought after by the Paiute Indians. This lake sucker species reaches a length of 2 feet and a weight of 6 pounds. Once widespread in the southwest, now in danger of extinction due to dam construction on the Truckee River in which they spawn. Decline also due to predation on its eggs by Tui chubs, *Gila bicolor*, and the growth of a fungus, genus *Saprolegnia*, on the eggs. Endangered.

CUNNER. *Tautogolabrus adspersus* (derivation: "with lips like a tautog"). Small food fish abundant along rocky coastlines of northeast Atlantic coast.

CUSK. *Brosme brosme* (derivation: *brosme* is Danish name for this fish). A deep-water edible fish found in Atlantic off the New England coast northward.

CUTLASSFISH. Elongated members of the family Trichiuridae found in all oceans in deep water. Ribbonlike oceanic fishes related to swordfish. Compressed body resembles a cutlass.

CUTTHROAT TROUT. *Salmo clarki* (derivation: *salmo*, "salmon"; *clarki* after Captain William Clark, 1770–1838, American explorer). Found from northern California to Alaska. It sometimes migrates to salt water where it reaches a weight of 24 pounds. The largest on record is 41 pounds. In mountain regions they may average 2 pounds. Cutthroats are known by their two red streaks just below the jaw.

DOLLY VARDEN TROUT. *Salvelinus malma* (derivation: *salvelinus* is an old name for charr; *malma* "soft and mellow"). The Dolly Varden is related to the Arctic char. It inhabits rivers from northern California to Alaska and in Kamchatka on the Asiatic side. It reaches a length of 3 feet and a weight of 20 pounds. The largest recorded is 32 pounds.

DOLPHIN. *Coryphaena hippurus* (derivation: *coryphaena*, "helmet to show," *hippurus*, "horse tail"). A fish species of tropical seas brightly colored, not to be confused with the mammalian cetacean also called dolphin. Reaches a length of 3¼ feet.

DUSKY SHARK. *Carcharhinus obscurus* (derivation: *carcharhinus*, "rough shark," *obscurus*, "obscure"). A bluish gray shark of the Atlantic reaching a length of 12 feet. It occurs from New England waters to Brazil and is a fierce predator.

EEL or AMERICAN EEL. *Anguilla rostrata* (derivation: *anguilla*, Latin name for "eel," *rostrata*, "snouted"). Lives in fresh water but spawns in Sargasso Sea. Reaches weight of 16 pounds. A tasty snakelike fish with minute scales.

ELECTRIC CATFISH. *Malapterurus electricus* (derivation: "electrical bad fin"). This African species is found in the Nile and Zambesi rivers and African lakes. These fish grow to 4 feet and can discharge up to 350 volts of electricity.

ELECTRIC EEL. *Electrophorus electricus* (derivation: "electrical producing"). An inhabitant of South American streams, the electric eel is not a true eel but a member of the carp family. It produces electricity in specialized cells in its body to protect itself and to capture small fish and frogs for food.

FALLFISH. *Semotilus corporalis* (derivation: *semotilus* means "spotted" according to Rafinesque, who first described the genus; *corporalis*, "fleshy"). Abundant in New England, New York, and Pennsylvania in small, clear rivers near rapids and falls, also in some lakes. The largest individuals reach 18 inches in length. The young are important as bait fish.

FIERASFER. A name used for pearlfishes and cucumberfishes. Members of this group sometimes live in the anus of the sea cucumber.

FILEFISH. *Monacanthus ciliatus* (derivation: "one spine threadlike"). Atlantic species found from Brazil to Cape Cod with large rough edged spine on back above its eye. About 4 to 8 inches long. Not of economic importance.

FLAT BULLHEAD. *Ictalurus platycephalus* (derivation: *ictalurus*, "catfish," *platycephalus*, "flat head"). Lives in coastal streams from North Carolina to Florida. It does not grow to as large a size as the other catfish but is more often caught by anglers. Its maximum size is 12 inches.

FROGFISH. *Histrio histrio.* A brown fleshy fish that lives in association with sargassum seaweed which it resembles. Common in Gulf of Mexico and as far north as Cape Hatteras.

FROSTFISH. A name used on the New England coast for whiting and tomcod.

*GILA TROUT. *Salmo gilae.* Once abundant in the upper tributaries of the San Francisco and Gila rivers. Today, this golden yellow trout is found only in a few creeks in the Gila National Forest. Loss of forests, pollution, and competition for food from introduced species have caused decline. Endangered.

GOLDEN SHINER. *Notemigonus crysoleucas* (derivation: *notemigonus*, "back angled," *chrysoleucas*, "golden white"). A good-tasting panfish, though small. Average size is around 5 inches. Golden shiners are found throughout the United States east of the Rockies in sluggish and weedy water.

GOLDEN TROUT. *Salmo aguabonita* (derivation: *salmo*, "salmon," *aguabonita*, "pretty water"). Once living only in tributaries of the South Fork of the Kern River in California at elevations of 10,000 feet or more, golden trout have been planted in many other high-altitude lakes and streams of the

Sierras and Rockies. They often grow to a size of 4 to 6 pounds, the largest reaching 11 pounds.

GOLDFISH. *Carassius auratus* (derivation: "golden yellow carp"). Goldfish were introduced into the United States from China. An aquarium fish, their use as bait has spread the goldfish accidentally in streams and lakes. They reach a length of 12 inches and their habits are similar to carp.

GRAY SNAPPER. *Lutjanus griseus* (derivation: *lutjanus* from the Japanese name for the fish, *lutjang; griseus*, Latin for "gray"). This reddish green snapper occurs from New Jersey to the West Indies. It is a food fish and one of the most common members of the snapper family.

GREAT LAKES MUSKELLUNGE. *Esox masquinongy masquinongy* (derivation: *esox*, an old name of the pike, *masquinongy*, an Indian name for this fish). A long, slim freshwater game fish. Many are caught on the Great Lakes each year by spearing or angling through holes in the ice. This musky also lives in many inland lakes. Reaches a length of 7 feet 4 inches and weight of 110 pounds.

GREATER REDHORSE. *Moxostoma valenciennesi* (derivation: *moxostoma*, "sucking mouth," *valenciennesi* after the French zoologist, Achille Valenciennes, 1794–1865). Only found in the St. Lawrence, Great Lakes Region, and Upper Mississippi. Since they are often killed by excess turbidity they are nearing extinction. This is the largest member of the genus, reported to reach 16 pounds.

GREEN SUNFISH. *Lepomis cyanellus* (derivation: *lepomis*, "scaled opercle," *cyanellus*, "dark blue"). A small fish, seldom more than 7 inches long; living in small brooks and creeks, but adaptable so they may be found in almost any habitat. Often mistaken for young bluegill. Found from Great Lakes to Mexico.

*GREENBACK CUTTHROAT TROUT. *Salmo clarki stomias.* Original cutthroat native to streams flowing into the South Platte River, Colorado. In 1968 only about ten pure specimens of this small strain were left. Diminished due to competition from larger stocked trout, hybridization, and stream pollution. Endangered.

HADDOCK. *Melanogrammus aeglefinus* (derivation: *melanogrammus*, Greek for "black line," *aeglefinus*, low Latin for "haddock"). A desirable marine fish found offshore in water 25 to 75 fathoms deep. An overfished species caught for fish market. Average size, 12–24 inches; weight, 1–5 pounds.

HAGFISH. *Myxine glutinosa* (derivation: *myxine*, Greek for "slime," *glutinosa*, "glutton"). Eel-like body, cartilaginous, jawless mouth. Lives in cool waters. Blind, it finds food by specialized smell organs. Nuisance fish, damaging haddock crop. Average size: 1½–2 feet.

HALIBUT. Largest member of the flatfish family sometimes weighing over 625 pounds.

HAMMERHEAD SHARK. *Sphyrna zygaena* (derivation: *sphyrna*, Greek for "hammer," *zygaena*, Greek for "crossbeam"). This peculiar hammerhead-shaped shark is found in the warm and tropical Atlantic, Pacific, and Indian oceans. They feed on fish, stingrays, and sharks, reaching 13 feet in length.

HATCHET FISH. Small-body, deep-water, bathypelagic fish. Photophores along lower edge of body.

HORSE MACKEREL. A local name for tuna.

*HUMPBACK CHUB. *Gila cypha.* Found in small numbers in the drainage of the Green and Colorado rivers of western United States; diminishing species due to pollution and predators. Little known; is small mouthed and small eyed. Fishery biologists are investigating. Endangered.

INCONNU or SHEEFISH. *Stenodus leucichthys* (derivation: *stenodus,* "narrow," *leucichthys,* "white fish"). The name *inconnu* means "unknown"; *sheefish* is the Alaskan Eskimo name. Found in rivers of the Arctic Basin from the White Sea of Europe to northwestern Canada. In springtime, when the ice breaks up, sheefish migrate up rivers to the headwater lakes. Reported to reach 80 pounds, the size is known to vary from river to river. The largest recorded from the Mackenzie Delta is 63 pounds; from the Yukon River, 14 pounds.

KNIFEFISH. These are electricity-producing South American freshwater fishes comprising three families. These include the gymnotid eels, Gymnotidae, which grow to 2 feet; the Rhamphichthyidae of the Amazon River which reach 4 feet; and the Sternachidae, which grow to a length of 18 inches.

*LAHONTAN CUTTHROAT TROUT. *Salmo clarki henshawi.* Found in the highly alkaline lakes of the Lahontan Basin in Nevada and California; large, 10 to 15 pounds; diminished greatly in the past few decades due to lumbering activities, forest fires, and overgrazing in its watershed areas. Near extinction in some lakes. U.S. government established Lahontan National Fish Hatchery to bring back to a strong natural population.

LAKE HERRING. *Coregonus artedii* (derivation: *coregonus* is an old name for European whitefish; *artedii* after Petrus Artedi, 1705–1735, sometimes called the father of ichthyology). Found in Upper Mississippi Valley, the Great Lakes and smaller lakes north to the Northwest Territories. Often run in schools where they are taken by anglers using minnows. Lake herring are called ciscoes in Lake Erie where they may reach a length of 25 inches and weight of 8 pounds. A length of 12 to 15 inches and weight of about 1 pound is the average size in most lakes.

LAKE STURGEON. *Acipenser fulvescens* (derivation: *acipenser* is an old name for sturgeon; *fulvescens,* "tawny"). Found from Alberta across Quebec and south in a broad triangle to Alabama, in lakes and rivers. In feeding, it avoids silty bottoms, selecting areas of clean sand or gravel where clams, snails and insect larvae are abundant. Reaches a length of over 7 feet and weight of 275 pounds.

LAKE TROUT. *Salvelinus namaycush* (derivation: *salvelinus* is an old name for charr; *namaycush* is an American Indian name for this fish). Living in deep lakes, these trout are found from Labrador to Alaska and south through New England and the Great Lakes. In the Great Lakes predation by invading sea lampreys has greatly reduced their numbers. Lake trout weighing more than 100 pounds have been reported.

LANCETFISH. A deep-water group of the Atlantic and Pacific oceans. A long, slender fish with soft bones and flabby flesh. It sometimes rises from great depths in the open ocean, reaches a length of 6 feet.

LANTERNFISH or MYCTOPHID. A member of the family Myctophidae, small oceanic fishes which normally live at depths between about 100 meters and 2000 fathoms. Very abundant at great depths, these fishes have small numerous light organs called photophores on the sides of their body. They undergo daily vertical feeding migrations.

LARGEMOUTH BASS. *Micropterus salmoides* (derivation: *micropterus,* "small fin," *salmoides,* "salmonlike"). A freshwater food and game fish introduced into streams and ponds all over the United States. The largemouth is very popular and sought by anglers.

LARGEMOUTH BUFFALOFISH. *Ictiobus cyprinellus* (derivation: *ictiobus* Greek for "buffalo fish," *cyprinellus* Latin for "small carp"). The largemouth lives in larger streams of the Mississippi River System and Lake Erie. At spawning time, they move over flooded lowlands. Maximum length is 35 to 40 inches, weight to 80 pounds.

LING. A local name given to members of the hake family.

LITTLE PICKEREL. *Esox americanus* (derivation: Latin for American pike). Occurs from Maine to Florida, usually found in small streams or sheltered weedy bays of lakes. Little pickerel seldom grow more than 12 inches long, though some giants reach 15 inches.

LITTLE SKATE. *Raja erinacea* (derivation: *raja,* a "ray," *erinacea,* "prickly" like a hedgehog). A flat bottom dwelling cartilaginous fish of the Atlantic from Virginia northward. Reaches a length of 1½ feet.

LOGPERCH. *Percina caprodes* (derivation: *percina* is a diminutive of perca; *caprodes,* "like the wild boar"). The largest of the darter group, this perch reaches a length of 5 to 7 inches. In the Great Lakes they can live in depths to 130 feet. Like other perches, they remain active all winter. Their food is small crustaceans and insect larvae. Caught by anglers sometimes by accident, while fishing for yellow perch.

LONGEAR SUNFISH. *Lepomis megalotis* (derivation: *lepomis,* "scaled opercle," *megalotis,* "large ear"). A brilliant blue and orange freshwater fish found in the Great Lakes and Mississippi Basin, Gulf States, South Carolina to Mexico. Of small size, seldom more than 5 inches.

LONGHORN SCULPIN. *Myoxocephalus octodecemspinosus* (derivation: *myoxocephalus,* Greek for "dormouse-head," *octodecemspinosus,* "eighteen-spined"). A bony head, spines and prickles exemplify this North Atlantic species found from Nova Scotia to Chesapeake Bay.

*LONGJAW CISCO. *Coregonus alpenae.* Known also as longjaw chub. Caught commercially in Lake Michigan and Lake Huron until decline in the 1950s. Average 12 to 14 inches. Declined because of intensive commercial fishing and predation by the sea lamprey. Endangered.

LONGNOSE GAR. *Lepisosteus osseus* (derivation: *lepisosteus,* "bony scales," *osseus,* "bony"). Long jaws with many needlelike teeth and a slender body are typical of this freshwater species. Feeding on other fish the adult longnose gar reaches a length of 3 feet.

LONGNOSE SUCKER. *Catostomus catostomus* (derivation: *catostomus* Greek for "lower mouth"). Found from the Great Lakes, New England and Labrador through Alaska and into Siberia; habitat usually in lakes. Maximum length is 24 inches, weight just over 4 pounds.

LUMPFISH. *Cyclopterus lumpus* (derivation: "circular fins, lumpy"). Northern marine species captured in numbers off Iceland. Its eggs, liver and meat when salted, smoked or canned are edible. In Norway lumpfish are used as bait for halibut.

LUNGFISH. Air-breathing freshwater bony fish found in lakes and swamps of South America, Africa, and Australia. The presence of a lung in all species is a significant evolutionary change. Their location in the three southern continents supports the concept of continental drift.

MACKEREL. *Scomber scombrus* (derivation: *scomber,* Greek for "mackerel"). A streamlined, migratory species which swims in schools. An excellent food and game fish.

MAKO. *Isurus oxyrinchus* (derivation: *isurus,* "equal tail," *oxyrinchus,* "sharp nose"). The most sought after shark as a game fish by anglers. When hooked it sometimes makes spectacular leaps. Reaches a length of 10 feet. It is an edible species.

MAN-EATER SHARK, GREAT WHITE. *Carcharodon carcharias* (derivation: *carcharodon* Greek for "jagged tooth," *carcharias* old Greek name for large sharks). Most voracious of all sharks. Found in Atlantic and Pacific, reaches a length of 38 feet and a weight of over a ton. Known to attack man.

MOLA or OCEANIC SUNFISH. *Mola mola* (derivation: *mola* Latin for "mill-stone"). Odd-shaped oceanic species found in Atlantic, Indian, and Pacific oceans. Often observed sunning itself on sea surface. It feeds on jellyfish, plankton, and seaweed. May reach lengths of over 8 feet and weights of 1000 pounds. The most prolific of all fishes, releasing 300 million eggs during spawning season.

MORMYRID or ELEPHANT SNOUT FISH. Found in tropical Africa, these electricity-producing fishes have trunklike snouts and large brains. Their electrical impulses are discharged at a variable frequency which can reach 80 to 100 impulses per minute.

MOSQUITOFISH. *Gambusia affinis* (derivation: *gambusia* from Cuban *gambusino,* "nothing." Poey, a Cuban fishery scientist, said one fishes for gambusinos when he catches nothing). Reaches a length of 3 to 4 inches. Feeds on mosquito larvae and has been transplanted to many parts of the world to control mosquitoes.

MUDSKIPPER. Gobylike fish of Asian brackish waters which move across sand and mudflats at low tide. They range from 5 to 12 inches in length. One species known to make jumps of 2 feet.

MUMMICHOG. A small baitfish of brackish water; also known as killifish and fundulus.

MUTTON SNAPPER or PARGO. *Lutjanus analis* (derivation: *lutjanus* from Japanese name for the fish, *lutjang; analis* refers to large anal fin). Found from the Gulf of Mexico to Brazil this large snapper reaches 2 feet in length and a weight of 25 pounds. A popular food fish.

NEEDLEFISH. *Scomberesox saurus* (derivation: *scomberesox,* "mackerel pike"; *saurus* is an old name for lizard fish). Elongated surface-dwelling fish. Preyed upon by bluefish, cod, and porpoises. Sometimes used as a baitfish by fishermen. Also known as the Atlantic saury.

NILE PERCH. *Lates niloticus.* Native to Africa and the Nile River valley, this species is being evaluated for introduction into freshwater bodies in Texas by the Texas State Parks and Wildlife Commission and the University of Texas.

NORTHERN KINGFISH. *Menticirrhus saxatilis* (derivation: *menticirrhus,* "chin thread," *saxatilis,* "of the rocks"). A food and game fish of the Middle Atlantic coast. Reaches a weight of 3⅓ pounds. Very tasty, it is caught with worms, squid, or clams for bait.

NORTHERN PIKE. *Esox lucius* (derivation: *esox* and *lucius* are ancient names for pike). One of the most widely distributed species of strictly freshwater fish ranging across the whole width of northern Eurasia and North America and south to about latitude 39 degrees. Young less than 11 inches have oblique bars on their sides like the little pickerel. The maximum length of the northern is about 4 feet.

NORTHERN PUFFER. *Sphoeroides maculatus* (derivation: *sphoeroides*, "resembling a sphere," *maculatus*, "spotted"). A saltwater puffer which can inflate itself with air or water as a defense mechanism. Reaches a weight of 2½ pounds.

OARFISH. A seldom seen, ribbonlike fish reaching a length of 20 feet. Sometimes falsely believed to be a sea serpent.

OCEAN WHITEFISH. *Caulolatilus princeps* (derivation: *caulolatilus* is from Greek meaning "stem" and "tiled"; *princeps*, "leader"). A Pacific saltwater food fish found from California to South America. Grows to a length of 3 to 4 feet.

*PAIUTE CUTTHROAT TROUT. *Salmo clarki seleniris.* This rare orange and red trout is native only to creeks near Yellowstone National Park in California. Overfishing and hybridization with rainbow trout have cut down local population. Some creeks believed to contain this species closed to fishing as protective measure. Endangered.

PALLID STURGEON. *Scaphirhynchus albus* (derivation: *scaphirhynchus*, "shovel snout," *albus*, "whitish"). Found in the Missouri River system and Lower Mississippi. The snout is more pointed and its barbels are attached nearer to the mouth than in the shovelnose. It is a bottom inhabitant of the channels of large rivers. Largest size known is 5 feet and weighs between 30 and 40 pounds.

PALOMETA. *Trachinotus goodei* (derivation: *trachinotus*, "rough back"; *goodei* after George B. Goode, American ichthyologist). This is one of the largest members of the pompano family, reaching a weight of 30 pounds. Common in the West Indies. A fine food fish.

PEACOCK FISH. *Cichla temensis.* Native to South America, this species of peacock fish was imported from Colombia and Brazil by the Texas Park and Wildlife Department as a sport-predator fish. In November 1974, a Texas biologist brought 300 month-old fish from Brazil to Texas. It is hoped that this species can be made to thrive in Texas reservoirs.

PEARLSIDE. *Maurolicus mulleri.* A deep-water bathypelagic fish of all the oceans with large light-producing photophores on its sides. Found in depths from 500 feet to 3000 feet. Sometimes found in the stomachs of cod, tuna, pollack, and other fish. Usual length about 3 inches.

PINK SALMON. *Oncorhynchus gorbuscha* (derivation: *oncorhynchus*, "hooked snout"; *gorbuscha* is from Russian *gorbuscha* meaning "hunchback"). Although the pink salmon or humpback is abundant from the Straits of Juan de Fuca to Alaska, few are taken by anglers. Practically the entire catch is canned. Weights up to 10 pounds have been recorded and lengths up to 30 inches. The bodies of breeding males become distorted between the head and the dorsal fin, earning them the name humpback.

PIRANHA. South American freshwater fish of the family Characidae with ferocious carnivorous appetites. Reach a length of 15 inches and will kill living animals wading into their stream or river.

PLAICE. A European member of the flounder family.

PORBEAGLE. *Lamna nasus* (derivation: Greek for "a kind of shark"). This member of the mackerel shark family is widespread throughout the Atlantic and Pacific oceans. It reaches a length of 10 feet feeding on most kinds of fish. Its meat is tasty and its liver oil has commercial value.

PORCUPINEFISH. (*Diodontidae,* two-toothed.) Tropical marine puffers with erectile spines. They sometimes stray into northern waters. As a defense mechanism it will sometimes gulp in water to swell into a protective sphere.

PUMPKINSEED. *Lepomis gibbosus* (derivation: *lepomis,* "scaled opercle," *gibbosus,* "humpbacked"). This is the common freshwater sunfish found in northern United States to Colorado to South Carolina. Has been planted in many western U.S. waters and abroad. It builds nests.

RAINBOW TROUT. *Salmo gairdneri* (derivation: *salmo,* "salmon"; *gairdneri* after Dr. Gairdner, a naturalist who was in the employ of the Hudson Bay Company). Probably the most important game fish in western North America, where it is native, and many other swift, cold waters where it has been introduced. Sea-run rainbows are known as steelheads. They are known to reach a weight of 40 pounds.

RAY. A general name for the cartilaginous skates, torpedos, and mantas.

RED DRUM or CHANNEL BASS. *Sciaenops ocellata* (derivation: *sciaena* is an ancient fish name; *ocellata,* "having eyelike spots"). Important food and game fish from Cape Cod to South Atlantic and Gulf coasts. It can produce loud sounds by means of its air bladder.

REDEAR SUNFISH. *Lepomis microlophus* (derivation: *lepomis,* "scaled opercle," *microlophus,* "small crest"). Found in fresh water from the lower Mississippi drainage and from Texas to Florida. Introduced farther north. Sometimes enters brackish water but does not spawn there.

RED HORSE. A name applied to several species of suckers of the American West and South. Also applied to redfish of Florida and the Gulf of Mexico.

REMORA. *Remora remora* (derivation: an ancient name meaning "one who holds back"). Occurs chiefly in tropical waters, occasionally up into northern waters. Known for hitchhiking habits on a host, usually a shark, using its sucking plate. Average size: 12–18 inches.

ROCK BASS. *Ambloplites rupestris* (derivation: *ambloplites,* "blunt armed," *rupestris,* "living among rocks"). An olive green to dark green freshwater fish most often found in clear waters over gravel or rocky bottom, but tolerates a wide variety of habitats. Congregates in deep holes in small streams.

RUBBERLIP SEAPERCH. *Rhacochilus toxotes* (derivation: *rhacochilus,* "rubber lips," *toxotes,* "bow like"). A food fish found on the California coast from Cape Mendocino to San Pedro. Also called alfone and sprat. Reaches a length of 18 inches and weight of 5 pounds.

SACRAMENTO SQUAWFISH. *Ptychocheilus grandis* (derivation: *ptychocheilus* from Greek, "folded lip"; *grandis,* "large"). A member of the minnow family found in tributaries of the Sacramento River and streams flowing into Monterey and San Francisco bays.

SAILFISH. *Istiophorus platypterus* (derivation: *istiophorus* Greek for "bearing a sail," *platypterus* Greek for "flat-finned"). One of the fastest species of fish known to travel at speeds up to 68 mph. Reaches a weight of over 200 pounds and is an excellent game fish.

SAND TIGER. *Carcharias taurus* (derivation: *carcharias* is an old name for sharks; *taurus,* "bull"). A sluggish migratory shark averaging 15 to 40 pounds but can reach a weight of 400 pounds. A ground shark usually found a few feet above the bottom.

SARGASSUMFISH. *Histrio histrio* (derivation: *histrio,* Latin for "stage player"). Resembling the sargassum weed in which it dwells, this camou-flaged anglerfish reaches a length of 6 to 8 inches.

SAUGER. *Stizostedion canadense* (derivation: *stizostedion*, "pungent throat," *canadense* refers to species being found in Canadian waters of St. Lawrence region). Saugers live in large lakes and large streams but move into tributary streams or backwater lakes to spawn. The eggs are scattered and sink to the bottom. Saugers can tolerate a muddier bottom and more turbid water than the walleye. They reach a length of 20 inches and weight of 3 pounds.

SAWFISH. *Pristis pectinata* (derivation: *pristis*, "one who saws," *pectinata*, "comb-toothed"). A sharklike fish with a snout resembling a double-edged saw. Found in the tropical Atlantic, it reaches a weight of 1000 pounds.

SCUP or PORGY. *Stenotomus chrysops* (derivation: *stenotomus*, "narrow cut-ting teeth," *chrysops* Greek for "gold eye"). A perchlike Atlantic coastal fish taken by commercial and sport fishermen. Reaches a weight of 5 pounds.

SEA HORSE. *Hippocampus erectus* (derivation: *hippocampus*, "bent horse," *erectus*, "upright"). Unusually shaped small fish. Found in tropical and some temperate seas among seaweed. Feeds on plankton and larvae, sucking them in. Average size: 3-6 inches.

SEA LAMPREY. *Petromyzon marinus* (derivation: *petromyzon* Greek for "stone sucker," *marinus*, "marine"). Eel-like body with soft cartilaginous skeleton. Known for preying on many types of fish, including trout, cod, and salmon. Once considered a delicacy, now very scarce. Average size, 2–2½ feet; weight, 2 pounds.

SHEEPSHEAD. *Archosargus probatocephalus* (derivation: *archosargus* means "chief sargus," an old name for a related fish, *probatocephalus* Greek for "sheep-head"). A spiny-finned perchlike fish, usually from 3 to 15 pounds. Usually found on Middle Atlantic and Gulf coasts.

SHORTHEAD REDHORSE. *Moxostoma macrolepidotum* (derivation: *moxostoma*, "sucking mouth," *macrolepidotum*, "large-scaled"). Found from central to eastern Canada and south to New York and the Ozarks. The shorthead is easily distinguished by the bright orange to blood-red tail fin and straight lower lip. Reaches a length of 2 feet.

SHORTNOSE GAR. *Lepistosteus platostomus* (derivation: *lepistosteus*, from "scale" and "bone," *platostomus*, "flat-mouth"). An elongated cigar-shaped freshwater fish found in sluggish, weed-choked southern waters of Mississippi River and southeastern United States. Reaches a length of 2 to 3 feet.

***SHORTNOSE STURGEON.** *Acipenser brevirostrum* (derivation: *acipenser* is an old name for sturgeon; *brevirostrum* is from the Latin meaning "short snout"). Once abundant from New Brunswick to Florida, it is now an endan-gered species, due to pollution and overfishing. Often is not recognized by fishermen to be different from the Atlantic sturgeon. Maximum length, about 3 feet long. Endangered.

SHOVELNOSE STURGEON. *Scaphirhynchus platorhynchus* (derivation: *scaphirhynchus*, "shovel snout," *platorhynchus*, "flat nose"). Found in the Mississippi River system and Upper Rio Grande in New Mexico. It is most abundant in channels and on bars where it feeds on snails and clams. Can be caught on line baited with worms.

SILVER REDHORSE. *Moxostoma anisurum* (derivation: *moxostoma*, "sucking mouth," *anisurum*, "unequal teeth"). Found in eastern tributaries of the Mississippi River and Iowa and Missouri. Seldom grows larger than 12 to 16 inches, and the maximum length is 20 inches.

SLEEPER SHARK. *Somniosus microcephalus* (derivation: "sleeper with small head"). Known also as Greenland shark, this species is sluggish and slow moving. It reaches a length of 24 feet.

SMALLMOUTH BASS. *Micropterus dolomieui* (derivation: *micropterus*, "small fin," *dolomieui* after M. Dolomieu, a French scientist). A freshwater game fish that has been introduced widely in this country and abroad. Prefers to nest on a firm gravel bottom.

SMALLMOUTH BUFFALO FISH. *Ictiobus bubalus* (derivation: *ictiobus* Greek for "buffalo fish," *bubalus* Latin for "buffalo"). Found through the Mississippi system, buffalofish rarely take a hook but are caught in nets by commercial fishermen and are an important food fish. Maximum size is around 40 pounds.

SMOOTH PUFFER or RABBITFISH. *Lagocephalus laevigatus* (derivation: "smooth rabbit head"). A smooth-skinned puffer found from Cape Cod to Brazil, which reaches a length of 2 feet or more.

SOAPFISH. Marine fish of the family Grammistidae that are covered with a layer of slippery mucus and are difficult to hold.

SOCKEYE SALMON. *Oncorhynchus nerka* (derivation: *oncorhynchus*, "hooked snout"; *nerka* from Russian *nyarka*, "red"). Although only occasionally taken in salt water, this is the most prized Pacific salmon for canning purposes because of the deep-red color of its flesh. Some sockeyes do not go to sea but remain landlocked. These are called kokanees. Sockeyes seldom grow larger than 33 inches and 5 to 7 pounds.

SONIC FISH. Fish that are able to produce sound by means of specialized organs, such as an air bladder or pharyngeal teeth.

SPANISH MACKEREL. *Scomberomorus maculatus* (derivation: *scomber* was the ancient name of mackerel; *maculatus*, "spotted"). Swift-swimming, spotted, silvery warm-water fish. Found from Florida to Mid-Atlantic states with strays to New England waters.

SPLAKE. A fish that is a cross between brook trout and lake trout.

SPINY DOGFISH. *Squalus acanthias* (derivation: *squalus* Latin for "shark," *acanthias* Greek for "having spines"). A small shark reaching a maximum length of 3 feet and weight of 20 pounds. It occurs on both sides of the Atlantic and the northern Pacific. A pest fish to many fishermen, it is a useful food fish in Europe.

SPOTTED BASS. *Micropterus punctulatus* (derivation: "spotted small fin"). A freshwater bass that is greenish above, silvery below. It reaches a length of 17 inches. Ranges from Upper Mississippi Valley south to the Gulf States. Survives adverse conditions better than either smallmouth or largemouth.

SPOTTED GAR. *Lepisosteus oculatus* (derivation: *lepisosteus*, "bony scales," *oculatus*, "eyed"). Has spots on head. Prefers habitat of clear water with an abundance of aquatic vegetation. Reaches length of 44 inches.

SPOTTED SEA TROUT. *Cynoscion nebulosus* (derivation: *cynoscion*, "dog weakfish," *nebulosus*, "clouded"). Atlantic salt and brackish water sea trout. Reaches 16½ pounds. Taken by anglers with live bait and lures.

SPOTTED SUNFISH. *Lepomis punctatus* (derivation: *lepomis*, "scaled opercle," *punctatus*, "spotted"). Found in fresh water in southeastern United States from North Carolina to central Texas. Develops brick-red color during the breeding season.

SPRAT. A local New England name for alewife. A European species is *Sprattus*

sprattus, which resembles herring. Some are canned by the Norwegians as sardines.

STARGAZER. Two families of bottom-dwelling marine fishes with eyes set on the top of their head. Some species use flaps of tissue resembling worms to lure food. Some have electric organs that can produce up to 50 volts. Stargazers possess poisonous spines that can prove fatal to human beings.

STICKLEBACK. Any of several species of coastal and brackish water dwelling small fish of the family Gasterosteidae. They generally build nests for their eggs and guard them carefully. Reach a length of 3 to 4 inches.

STONE CAT. *Noturus flavus* (derivation: *noturus*, "back tail," *flavus* Latin for "yellow"). The yellowish stone cat is a freshwater catfish that reaches a length of 12 inches. All catfishes have glands near the base of their spines, so a wound from the spines is quite painful. The secretions from the glands of stone cat and madtoms are particularly virulent.

STONEFISH. Members of the genus *Synanceja*. Fish of coral reefs of the Indo-Pacific and among the most poisonous of all fish due to venomous spines.

STRIPED BASS. *Morone saxatilis* (derivation: *morone* is a name chosen by Mitchell; *saxatilis* Latin for "living among rocks"). Found on the Atlantic Coast from New Brunswick to Florida and on the Gulf Coast from Texas to Alabama. It was introduced into San Francisco Bay in 1879, and now ranges from Southern California to Washington. Some grow to a very large size. A specimen 36 inches in length weighs about 18 pounds, but lengths of 4 to 5 feet and weights of 50 to 125 pounds are on record.

STURGEON. Members of family Acipenseridae. Marine and freshwater primitive fish with 5 rows of bony or ganoid plates along the back and sides. A bottom-dwelling food fish. Its eggs are made into caviar.

SUCKER or WHITE SUCKER. *Catostomus commersoni* (derivation: *catostomus* Greek for "below-mouth," *commersoni* in honor of Philibert Commerson, 1727–1773, a French naturalist). Common freshwater fish in North American waters reaching a length of about 12 inches. Its circular mouth is under projecting snout. It has thick, soft lips that can be protruded.

SUNAPEE TROUT. *Salvelinus aureolus* (derivation: *salvelinus* is an old name for charr; *aureolus* Latin for "gilded"). A golden-colored trout produced from eastern brook trout. Sunapee originally lived in Sunapee Lake, New Hampshire. The largest size recorded is 11½ pounds.

SWORDFISH. *Xiphias gladius* (derivation: *xiphias* from Greek "sword," *gladius* from Latin "sword"). Worldwide spearfish reaches a weight of 1000 pounds. Sought after by commercial and sport fishermen.

TARPON. *Megalops atlantica* (derivation: *megalops* Greek for "large eye," *atlanticus*, "Atlantic"). A large herringlike fish of the Gulf of Mexico and South Atlantic. Reaches a weight of 350 pounds and length of 7 feet. Taken by anglers, it is a fighting game fish.

TENCH. *Tinca tinca* (derivation: *tinca* is Latin name for tench). Native to Europe and introduced into many American streams but established in only a few places in Washington, Idaho, New Mexico and California. It reaches a length of 2 feet and weight of several pounds. It is not very highly regarded as a food or sports fish.

TETRA. A minnowlike silvery freshwater characid that reaches a length of 3 or 4 inches. It is found in pools of the main streams of the Pecos and Rio Grande rivers of North America.

THREADFIN. Perchlike fishes with elongated fins.

THRESHER SHARK. *Alopias vulpinus* (derivation: name means "fox" in Greek and Latin, as this species is sometimes known as the fox shark). This shark has an unusual tail fin which extends to a length as great as the rest of the body. It uses its tail to stun small fish and it reaches a length of 20 feet.

TIGER MUSKELLUNGE. *Esox masquinongy immaculatus* (derivation: musky that is immaculate with small round blackish spots). The tiger musky lives in lakes of northern Wisconsin, Minnesota and southwestern Ontario. This muskellunge is a prized game fish, owing to its reputation of putting up a good fight.

TIGER SHARK. *Galeocerdo cuvieri* (derivation: *galeocerdo* Greek for "fix shark," *cuvieri* in honor of George Cuvier, 1769–1832, a French naturalist). This voracious shark of all warm seas feeds on sea turtles, other sharks, horseshoe crabs, etc. It can reach a weight of about 1500 pounds and a length of 20 feet.

TILAPIA. African and Asian fish of the genus *Tilapia* feeding on plants in lakes and rivers. Widely utilized species in aquaculture.

TOADFISH. *Opsanus tau* (derivation: the back of the head has a bony structure shaped like a *T* or Greek tau). Atlantic species found from Cuba to Cape Cod. Reaches a length of 15 inches with large head and tapering body. Has fleshy flaps around lower jaw. Has no scales and snaps vigorously when caught.

TORPEDO or ELECTRIC RAY. *Torpedo nobiliana* (derivation: "noble torpedo"). A rounded or oval disc shape. Has two large electric organs which make up one-sixth of the total weight of the fish. Found on both sides of the Atlantic in temperate waters. This fish-eating ray reaches a length of 4 to 5 feet and 200 pounds. It can produce 170 to 220 volts.

TRIGGERFISH. *Balistes carolinensis* (derivation: *balistes*, "to shoot," *carolinensis*, "Carolina"). Oval tropical fish with erectile protective dorsal spine. Reaches a weight of 4 pounds.

TRUMPETFISH. An elongated tropical group of several species with long flat snouts.

TURBOT. A large European flatfish. Reaches a weight of 40 pounds.

VIPERFISH. A group of slender-bodied deep-water fish with needlelike teeth dwelling at about 6000 feet (1800 meters).

WALKING CATFISH or MAILED CATFISH. Members of the Clariidae and Loricariidae families. Air is taken in and passed down into the intestine. Walls of the intestine have blood vessels through which gas exchange can take place. It can move over land and has become an exotic pest in Florida.

WALLEYE or WALL-EYED PIKE. *Stizostedion vitreum* (derivation: according to Rafinesque, who first described this species, *stizostedion* means "pungent throat," *vitreum*, "glassy"). This freshwater species is sometimes called glass-eye and pike perch. An important game and food fish of the United States and Canada, widely introduced into areas they did not originally occupy. Walleye reach a length of over 3 feet and weight of just over 22 pounds.

WARMOUTH. *Chaenobryttus coronarius* (derivation: *chaenobryttus*, "large mouth," "to yawn"; *coronarius*, "crowned"). Most abundant in quiet waters over mud bottom where there is abundant aquatic vegetation. Feeds on snails, aquatic insects, and when larger, on small fishes.

WEEVERFISH. Poisonous bottom-dwelling marine fish related to stargazer.

WHALE SHARK. *Rhincodon typus* (derivation: *rhincodon*, "nose mouth"; has wide mouth at end of snout). Largest of all living fishes, reaching a length of 65 feet. It feeds on small plankton which it strains from seawater.

WHITE AMUR or GRASS CARP. *Ctenopharyngodon idellus.* Native to Asia the white amur was imported into the United States in 1963 by the Fish and Wildlife Service. It was hoped that this species would become established throughout the Mississippi River basin.

WHITE BASS. *Morone chrysops* (derivation: "golden-eyed fish"). Found in the Great Lakes (except Lake Superior), in the Mississippi Valley, and across Texas to northeastern Mexico. White bass are very prolific, grow rapidly, and mature early. They are good to eat, easy to catch with minnows, grubs, or worms. Sometimes they will rise to a fly. They reach a length of 17 inches and a weight of 3 pounds.

WHITE CATFISH. *Ictalurus catus* (derivation: *ictalurus*, "catfish," *catus* "catlike"). Ranges in coastwise streams from New Jersey to Texas. They reach a length of 2 feet and weight of around 4 pounds.

WHITE CRAPPIE. *Pomoxis annularis* (derivation: *pomoxis*, "sharp opercle," *annularis*, "ringed"). A freshwater species that is silvery olive. Lives in lake along with black crappie, one usually more abundant than the other, the white dominant in South, the black in North.

WHITEFISH. *Coregonus clupeaformis* (derivation: *coregonus* is an old name for European whitefish; *clupeaformis*, "herring-shaped"). Whitefish are found from Labrador to New England, the Great Lakes north to the Arctic coast. The young eat plankton; adults feed on the bottom on snails, insec larvae and small fishes. The largest whitefish may reach 30 inches and 10 to 1 pounds; average is 12 to 20 inches and weight of 2 to 4 pounds. They are important commercial products as smoked fish.

WHITE PERCH. *Morone americana* (derivation: American white perch) Found from Nova Scotia to Georgia in coastal waters, bays and estuaries They are often landlocked and introduced into lakes and reservoirs. Recently white perch have been found in Lake Erie from Lake Ontario. White perch live in shallow water. They commonly grow to a length of 10 inches and weight of 1 pound, but some reach 15 inches and 2 to 3 pounds in weight.

WHITE STURGEON. *Acipenser transmontanus* (derivation: *acipenser* is an old name for sturgeon; *transmontanus*, "across the mountains"). Occurs from Alaska to Monterey, California, ascending large rivers in the spring. High dams on western rivers have probably doomed this fish to extinction. This species vies with the Atlantic sturgeon for the title of largest anadromous fis. in North America, as the white reaches a length of 12½ feet and weight of 128 pounds.

WINTER FLOUNDER. *Pseudopleuronectes americanus* (derivation *pseudopleuronectes*, "false side swimmer"). Important marine flounde reaches a weight of 8 pounds, averages 1½ pounds. Enters bays and sal ponds to spawn from December through February. A favorite with saltwate anglers.

WRASSE. A family of perchlike fish related to parrotfish and tautog.

YELLOW BASS. *Morone interruptus* (derivation: "with interrupted blac stripes"). It is most abundant in rivers and some lakes of the Upper Missi sippi drainage area. The yellow bass does not grow as large as the white bas but still is an excellent game and food fish. They spawn in late spring over gravel bars or rocky areas and commonly reach a length of 8 to 11 inches

YELLOWBREAST SUNFISH. *Lepomis auritus* (derivation: *lepomis,* "scaled opercle," *auritus,* "long-eared"). With an olive belly and red fins, this freshwater species is found on the East coast from New Brunswick to Florida and Gulf states to Texas. Introduced into warm waters farther north. Prefers clear running water, takes artificial bait readily, affording real sport on light tackle.

YELLOW BULLHEAD. *Ictalurus natalis* (derivation: *ictalurus,* "catfish," *natalis,* "having large nates," i.e., adipose fin). Lives in shallow parts of lakes, ponds and streams where there is not much current and where the water is clear with abundant water plants. Reaches 18 to 20 inches in length and a weight of 4 to 4½ pounds.

YELLOW PERCH. *Perca flavescens* (derivation: from Latin meaning "dusky, growing yellow"). Small, spiny-finned, banded yellowish fish found in ponds and lakes of northeastern North America from Canada to North Carolina. A favorite with youthful anglers.

YELLOWTAIL. *Seriola dorsalis* (derivation: *seriola* is Italian name of the amberjack; *dorsalis* means "back," with reference to the long back fin). Swift-swimming, slender food and game fish of California and Mexican coasts, reaching a weight of 60 pounds.

YELLOWTAIL DAMSELFISH or JEWELFISH. *Microspathodon chrysurus* (derivation: "yellowish small tooth"). A small, bright reef fish of the Caribbean and Gulf of Mexico. One of the most common fishes of the West Indies, it reaches a length of 8 inches.

ZAMBEZI SHARK. A tropical and subtropical shark that swims into estuaries and rivers and sometimes becomes established permanently in fresh water.

ZEBRA FISH. A common name for small tropical fish with dark horizontal or vertical stripes.

ZEBRA SHARK. Another name for carpetshark.

ZEIDAE. The family includes the John Dory and other dories.

ZOARCIDAE. The eelpout family. Derivation: *zoarces* Greek for "viviparous."

These fishes are listed under the Endangered Species Act, *U.S. Federal Register,* September 26, 1975.

Appendix A

FISHES ENDANGERED OR THREATENED WITH EXTINCTION*

*From *U.S. FEDERAL REGISTER* 40, no. 188 (September 26, 1975).

Common Name	Scientific Name	Distribution
Ala Balik	*Salmo platycephalus*	Turkey
Ayumodoki	*Hymenophysa curta*	Japan
Blindcat, Mexican	*Prietella phreatophila*	Mexico
Bonytail, Pahranagat	*Gila robusta jordani*	U.S. (Nevada)
Catfish	*Pangasius sonitwongsei*	Thailand
Catfish, Giant	*Pangasianodon gigas*	Thailand
Chub, Humpback	*Gila cypha*	U.S. (Arizona, Utah, Wyoming)
Chub, Mohave	*Siphateles mohavensis*	U.S. (California)
Cicek	*Acanthorutilus handlirschi*	Turkey
Cisco, Longjaw	*Coregonus alpenae*	U.S. (Lakes Michigan, Huron, Erie)
Cui-ui	*Chasmistes cujus*	U.S. (Nevada)
Dace, Kendall Warm Springs	*Rhinichthys osculus thermalis*	U.S. (Wyoming)
Dace, Moapa	*Moapa coriacea*	U.S. (Nevada)
Darter, Fountain	*Etheostoma fonticola*	U.S. (Texas)
Darter, Maryland	*Etheostoma sellare*	U.S. (Maryland)
Darter, Okaloosa	*Etheostoma okaloosae*	U.S. (Florida)
Darter, Watercress	*Etheostoma nuchale*	U.S. (Alabama)
Gambusia, Big Bend	*Gambusia gaigei*	U.S. (Texas)
Gambusia, Clear Creek	*Gambusia heterochir*	U.S. (Texas)
Gambusia, Pecos	*Gambusia nobilis*	U.S. (Texas)
Killifish, Pahrump	*Empetrichthys latos*	U.S. (Nevada)
Madtom, Scioto	*Noturus trautmani*	U.S. (Ohio)
Nekogigi	*Coreobagrus ichikawai*	Japan
Pike, Blue	*Stizostedion vitreum glaucum*	U.S. (Lakes Erie, Ontario)
Pupfish, Comanche Springs	*Cyprinodon elegans*	U.S. (Texas)
Pupfish, Devil's Hole	*Cyprinodon diabolis*	U.S. (Nevada)
Pupfish, Owens River	*Cyprinodon radiosus*	U.S. (California)
Pupfish, Tecopa	*Cyprinodon nevadensis calidae*	U.S. (California)
Pupfish, Warm Springs	*Cyprinodon nevadensis pectoralis*	U.S. (Nevada)
Squawfish, Colorado River	*Ptychocheilus lucius*	U.S. (Colorado River System)
Stickleback, Unarmored Threespine	*Gasterosterus aculeatus williamsoni*	U.S. (California)
Sturgeon, Shortnose	*Acipenser brevirostrum*	Atlantic Coast of U.S. and Canada
Tanago, Miyako	*Tanakia tanago*	Japan
Topminnow, Gila	*Poeciliopsis occidentalis*	U.S. (Arizona), Mexico
Trout, Gila	*Salmo gilae*	U.S. (New Mexico)
Trout, Greenback Cutthroat	*Salmo clarki stomias*	U.S. (Colorado)
Woundfin	*Plagopterus argentissimus*	U.S. (Utah)

1976 MARINE FISH WORLD RECORDS
Caught by Anglers on Hook and Line
Recognized by the International Game Fish Society

Common Name	Scientific Name	Weight	Where	Date	Angler
Albacore	Thunnus alalunga	74 lb. 13 oz.	Canary Islands	Oct. 28, 1973	Olof Idegren
Amberjack, Greater	Seriola dumerili	149 lb.	Bermuda	June 21, 1964	Peter Simons
Barracuda, Great	Sphyraena barracuda	83 lb.	Lagos, Nigeria	Jan. 13, 1952	K. J. W. Hackett
Bass, Black Sea	Centropristis striata	8 lb.	Nantucket Sound, Massachusetts	May 13, 1951	H. R. Rider
Bass, Giant Sea	Stereolepis gigas	563 lb. 8 oz.	Anacapa Island, California	Aug. 20, 1968	James D. McAdam, Jr.
Bass, Striped	Morone saxatilis	72 lb.	Cuttyhunk, Massachusetts	Oct. 10, 1969	Edward J. Kirker
Bluefish	Pomatomus saltatrix	31 lb. 12 oz.	Hatteras Inlet, North Carolina	Jan. 30, 1972	James M. Hussey
Bonefish	Albula vulpes	19 lb.	Zululand, South Africa	May 26, 1962	Brian W. Batchelor
Cobia	Rachycentron canadum	110 lb. 5 oz.	Mombasa, Kenya	Sept. 8, 1964	Eric Tinworth
Cod	Gadus morhua	98 lb. 12 oz.	Isle of Shoals, Massachusetts	June 8, 1969	Alphonse J. Bielevich
Dolphin	Coryphaena hippurus	85 lb.	Bahamas	May 29, 1968	Richard Seymour
Drum, Black	Pogonias cromis	113 lb.	Lewes, Delaware	Sept. 15, 1975	M. Townsend
Drum, Red	Sciaenops ocellata	90 lb.	Rodanthe, North Carolina	Nov. 7, 1973	Elvin Hooper
Flounder	Paralichthys spp.	30 lb. 12 oz.	Chile	Nov. 1, 1971	Augusto Nunez Moreno
Jewfish	Epinephelus itajara	680 lb.	Fernandina Beach, Florida	May 20, 1961	Lynn Joyner
Mackerel, King	Scomberomorus cavalla	90 lb.	Key West, Florida	Feb. 16, 1976	Norton I. Thornton

Common Name	Scientific Name	Weight	Where	Date	Angler
Marlin, Atlantic Blue	*Makaira nigricans*	1142 lb.	Nags Head, North Carolina	July 26, 1974	Jack Herrington
Marlin, Black	*Makaira indica*	1560 lb.	Cabo Blanco, Peru	Aug. 4, 1953	Alfred C. Glassell, Jr.
Marlin, Pacific Blue	*Makaira nigricans*	1153 lb.	Ritidian Pt., Guam	Aug. 21, 1969	Greg D. Perez
Marlin, Striped	*Tetrapturus audax*	415 lb.	Cape Brett, New Zealand	Mar. 31, 1964	B. C. Bain
Marlin, White	*Tetrapturus albidus*	159 lb. 8 oz.	Pompano Beach, Florida	Apr. 25, 1953	W. E. Johnson
Permit	*Trachinotus falcatus*	50 lb. 8 oz.	Key West, Florida	May 15, 1971	Marshall E. Earnest
Pollack	*Pollachius virens*	46 lb. 7 oz.	Brielle, New Jersey	May 26, 1975	John T. Holton
Roosterfish	*Nematistius pectoralis*	114 lb.	La Paz, Mexico	June 1, 1960	Abe Sackheim
Runner, Rainbow	*Elagatis bipinnulata*	30 lb. 15 oz.	Kauai, Hawaii	Apr. 27, 1963	Holbrook Goodale
Sailfish, Atlantic	*Istiophorus platypterus*	128 lb. 1 oz.	Luanda, Angola	Mar. 27, 1974	Harm Steyn
Sailfish, Pacific	*Istiophorus platypterus*	221 lb.	Galapagos Island	Feb. 12, 1947	C. W. Stewart
Sea Bass, White	*Cynoscion nobilis*	83 lb. 12 oz.	San Felipe, Mexico	Mar. 31, 1953	L. C. Baumgardner
Sea Trout, Spotted	*Cynoscion nebulosus*	15 lb. 6 oz.	Jensen Beach, Fla.	May 4, 1969	M. J. Foremny
Shark, Blue	*Prionace glauca*	410 lb.	Rockport, Massachusetts	Sept. 1, 1960	Richard C. Webster
Shark, Hammerhead	*Sphyrna spp.*	703 lb.	Jacksonville Beach, Florida	July 5, 1975	H. B. Reasor
Shark, Porbeagle	*Lamna nasus*	430 lb.	Channel Island, England	June 29, 1969	Desmond Bougourd
Shark, Shortfin Mako	*Isurus oxyrinchus*	1061 lb.	Mayor Island, New Zealand	Feb. 17, 1970	James B. Penwarden
Shark, Thresher	*Alopias vulpinus*	739 lb.	Tutukaka, New Zealand	Feb. 17, 1975	Brian Galvin
Shark, Tiger	*Galeocerdo cuvieri*	1780 lb.	Cherry Grove, South Carolina	June 14, 1964	Walter Maxwell
Shark, White	*Carcharodon carcharias*	2664 lb.	Ceduna, Australia	Apr. 21, 1959	Alfred Dean
Snook	*Centropomus undecimalis*	52 lb. 6 oz.	La Paz, Mexico	Jan. 9, 1963	Jane Haywood

Common Name	Scientific Name	Weight	Where	Date	Angler
Swordfish	Xiphias gladius	1182 lb.	Iquique, Chile	May 7, 1953	L. Marron
Tanguigue	Scomberomorus commerson	81 lb.	Karachi, Pakistan	Aug. 27, 1960	George E. Rusinak
Tarpon	Megalops atlantica	283 lb.	Lake Maracaibo, Venezuela	Mar. 19, 1956	M. Salazar
Tautog	Tautoga onitis	21 lb. 6 oz.	Cape May, New Jersey	June 12, 1954	R. N. Sheafer
Tuna, Atlantic Bigeye	Thunnus obesus	335 lb. 1 oz.	Canary Islands	July 11, 1975	Wilheim Rapp
Tuna, Blackfin	Thunnus atlanticus	38 lb.	Bermuda	Jan. 26, 1970	Archie L. Dickins
Tuna, Bluefin	Thunnus thynnus	1120 lb.	Islamorada, Florida	May 22, 1973	Elizabeth Jean Wade
			Prince Edward Island, Canada	Oct. 19, 1973	Lee Coffin
Tuna, Dog-Tooth	Gymnosarda unicolor	153 lb. 8 oz.	Cooktown, Australia	Sept. 25, 1975	William E. Chapman
Tuna, Longtail	Thunnus tonggol	60 lb.	Bermagul, N.S.W., Australia	March 17, 1975	N. Noel Webster
Tuna, Pacific Bigeye	Thunnus obesus	435 lb.	Cabo Blanco, Peru	Apr. 17, 1957	Russel V. A. Lee
Tuna, Skipjack	Euthynnus pelamis	39 lb. 15 oz.	Walker Cay, Bahamas	Jan. 21, 1952	F. Drowley
Tuna, Southern Bluefin	Thunnus maccoyii	172 lb.	Cape Pillar, Australia	May 8, 1959	C. I. Cutler
Tuna, Yellowfin	Thunnus albacares	308 lb.	San Benedicto Island, Mexico	Jan. 18, 1973	Harold J. Tolson
Tunny, Little	Euthynnus alletteratus	21 lb. 12 oz.	Key Largo, Florida	June 29, 1975	Paul F. Leader
Wahoo	Acanthocybium solanderi	149 lb.	Cat Cay, Bahamas	June 15, 1962	John Pirovano
Weakfish	Cynoscion regalis	19 lb. 8 oz.	Trinidad, West Indies	Apr. 13, 1962	Dennis B. Hall
Yellowtail	Seriola dorsalis	111 lb.	Bay of Islands, New Zealand	June 11, 1961	A. F. Plim

Appendix C

As reported to World Record Fish Department, *Field and Stream*

Common Name	Scientific Name	Weight
Bass, Largemouth	*Micropterus salmoides*	22 lb. 4 oz.
Bass, Redeye	*Micropterus coosae*	7 lb. 8 oz.
Bass, Rock	*Ambloplites rupestis*	3 lb.
Bass, Smallmouth	*Micropterus dolomieui*	11 lb. 15 oz.
Bass, Spotted	*Micropterus punctulatus*	8 lb. 10½ oz.
Bass, White	*Morone chrysops*	5 lb. 5 oz.
Bass, Yellow	*Morone mississippiensis*	2 lb. 2 oz.
Bluegill	*Lepomis macrochirus*	4 lb. 12 oz.
Bowfin	*Amia calva*	19 lb. 12 oz.
Buffalo, Bigmouth	*Ictiobus cyprinellus*	47 lb. 2 oz.
Buffalo, Smallmouth	*Ictiobus bubalus*	22 lb. 11 oz.
Bullhead, Black	*Ictalurus melas*	8 lb.
Carp	*Cyprinus carpio*	55 lb. 5 oz.
Catfish, Blue	*Ictalurus furcatus*	97 lb.
Catfish, Channel	*Ictalurus punctatus*	58 lb.
Catfish, Flathead	*Pylodictis olivaris*	79 lb. 8 oz.
Char, Arctic	*Salvelinus alpinus*	29 lb. 11 oz.
Crappie, Black	*Pomoxis nigromaculatus*	5 lb.
Crappie, White	*Pomoxis annularis*	5 lb. 3 oz.
Dolly Varden	*Salvelinus malma*	32 lb.
Drum, Freshwater	*Aplodinotus grunniens*	54 lb. 8 oz.
Gar, Alligator	*Lepisosteus spatula*	279 lb.
Gar, Longnose	*Lepisosteus osseus*	50 lb. 5 oz.
Grayling, American	*Thymallus arcticus*	5 lb. 15 oz.
Kokanee	*Oncorhynchus nerka*	5 lb.
Muskellunge	*Esox masquinongy*	69 lb. 15 oz.
Perch, White	*Morone americana*	4 lb. 12 oz.
Perch, Yellow	*Perca flavescens*	4 lb. 3½ oz.
Pickerel, Chain	*Esox niger*	9 lb. 6 oz.
Pike, Northern	*Esox lucius*	46 lb. 2 oz.
Salmon, Atlantic	*Salmo salar*	79 lb. 2 oz.
Salmon, Chinook	*Oncorhynchus tshawytscha*	92 lb.
Salmon, Chum	*Oncorhynchus keta*	24 lb. 4 oz.
Salmon, Coho	*Oncorhynchus kisutch*	31 lb.
Salmon, Landlocked	*Salmo salar*	22 lb. 8 oz.
Sauger	*Stizostedion canadense*	8 lb. 12 oz.
Shad, American	*Alosa sapidissima*	9 lb. 2 oz.
Sturgeon, White	*Acipenser transmontanus*	360 lb.
Sunfish, Green	*Lepomis cyanellus*	2 lb. 2 oz.

Where	Date	Angler
Montgomery Lake, Ga.	June 2, 1932	George W. Perry
Lazer Creek, Ga.	April 9, 1975	Jimmy L. Rogers
York River, Ontario	Aug. 1, 1974	Peter Gulgin
Dale Hollow Lake, Ky.	July 9, 1955	David L. Hayes
Smith Lake, Alabama	Feb. 25, 1972	Billy Henderson
Ferguson Lake, Calif.	Mar. 8, 1972	Norman W. Mize
Lake Monona, Wis.	Jan. 18, 1972	James Thrun
Ketona Lake, Alabama	April 9, 1950	T. S. Hudson
Lake Marion, S.C.	Nov. 5, 1972	M. R. Webster
Tippecanoe Lake, Ind.	May 10, 1975	David F. Hulley
Lake Wylie, N.C.	Aug. 25, 1975	Douglas E. Brogden
Lake Waccabuc, N.Y.	Aug. 1, 1951	Kani Evans
Clearwater Lake, Minn.	July 10, 1952	Frank J. Ledwein
Missouri River, S.D.	Sept. 16, 1959	Edward B. Elliott
Santee-Cooper Res., S.C.	July 7, 1964	W. B. Whaley
White River, Indiana	Aug. 13, 1966	Glenn T. Simpson
Arctic R., N.W.T.	Aug. 21, 1968	Jeanne P. Branson
Santee-Cooper Res., S.C.	Mar. 15, 1957	Paul E. Foust
Enid Dam, Miss.	July 31, 1957	Fred L. Bright
L. Pend Oreille, Idaho	Oct. 27, 1949	N. L. Higgins
Nickajack Lake, Tenn.	Apr. 20, 1972	Benny E. Hull
Rio Grande, Tex.	Dec. 2, 1951	Bill Valverde
Trinity River, Texas	July 30, 1954	Townsend Miller
Katseyedie River, N.W.T.	Aug. 16, 1967	Jerry Verge
Priest Lake, Idaho	June 9, 1974	Melissa Stevens
St. Lawrence River, N.Y.	Sept. 22, 1957	Arthur Lawton
Messalonskee Lake, Me.	June 4, 1949	Mrs. Earl Small
Bordentown, N.J.	May, 1865	Dr. C. C. Abbot
Homerville, Georgia	Feb. 17, 1961	Baxley McQuaig, Jr.
Scandaga Reservoir, N.Y.	Sept. 15, 1940	Peter Dubuc
Tana River, Norway	1928	Henrik Henriksen
Skeena River, B.C.	July 19, 1959	Heinz Wichman
Margarita Bay, Alaska	Aug. 19, 1974	Richard Coleman
Cowichan Bay, B.C.	Oct. 11, 1947	Mrs. Lee Hallberg
Sebago Lake, Maine	Aug. 1, 1907	Edward Blakely
Lake Sakakawea, N.D.	Oct. 6, 1971	Mike Fischer
Enfield, Connecticut	April 28, 1973	Edward P. Nelson
Snake River, Idaho	April 24, 1956	Willard Cravens
Stockton Lake, Missouri	June 18, 1971	Paul M. Dilley

Common Name	Scientific Name	Weight
Sunfish, Redear	*Lepomis microlophus*	4 lb. 8 oz.
Trout, Brook	*Salvelinus fontinalis*	14 lb. 8 oz.
Trout, Brown	*Salmo trutta*	39 lb. 8 oz.
Trout, Cutthroat	*Salmo clarki*	41 lb.
Trout, Golden	*Salmo aguabonita*	11 lb.
Trout, Lake	*Salvelinus namaycush*	65 lb.
Trout, Rainbow, Stlhd. or Kamloops	*Salmo gairdneri*	42 lb. 2 oz.
Trout, Sunapee	*Salvelinus aureolus*	11 lb. 8 oz.
Trout, Tiger	*Brown X Brook*	10 lb.
Walleye	*Stizostedion vitreum*	25 lb.
Warmouth	*Lepomis gulosus*	2 lb.
Whitefish, Lake	*Coregonus clupeaformis*	13 lb.
Whitefish, Mountain	*Prosopium williamsoni*	5 lb.

Where	Date	Angler
Chase City, Virginia	June 19, 1970	Maurice E. Ball
Nipigon River, Ontario	July, 1916	Dr. W. J. Cook
Loch Awe, Scotland	1866	W. Muir
Pyramid Lake, Nevada	Dec., 1925	John Skimmerhorn
Cook's Lake, Wyoming	Aug. 5, 1948	Chas. S. Reed
Great Bear Lake, N.W.T.	Aug. 8, 1970	Larry Daunis
Bell Island, Alaska	June 22, 1970	David Robert White
Lake Sunapee, N.H.	Aug. 1, 1954	Ernest Theoharis
Deerskin River, Wis.	May 23, 1974	Charles J. Mattek
Old Hickory Lake, Tenn.	Aug. 1, 1960	Mabry Harper
Sylvania, Georgia	May 4, 1974	Carlton Robins
Great Bear Lake, N.W.T.	July 14, 1974	Robert L. Stintsman
Athabasca River, Alberta	June 3, 1963	Orville Welch

GLOSSARY

ABDOMINAL: In the region of the belly.

ABYSSAL: Refers to the great depths of the ocean and the inhabitants found there.

ADIPOSE FIN: A fleshy, finlike structure without rays or spines that occurs in tilefish, salmon, and catfish.

AIR BLADDER: A sac found just below the backbone in most fishes that contains gases to increase buoyancy.

ANADROMOUS: Marine fishes that leave the ocean and ascend streams to spawn, such as shad and salmon.

ANAL FIN: The fin on the midline of the undersurface of the body just behind the anus or vent.

BARBEL: A fleshy projection usually about the lower portion of the head.

BENTHIC: Refers to bottom dwellers.

BENTHOPELAGIC: Fishes that inhabit both the bottom and surface layers.

CATADROMOUS: Freshwater fishes that travel to the sea to spawn, such as eels.

CAUDAL FIN: The tail fin at the end of the body.

CAUDAL PEDUNCLE: The region between the dorsal fin and the caudal fin.

CLASPERS: The male copulative organs of sharks and skates.

CRUSTACEAN: Member of the class Crustacea having jointed bodies and legs that are usually hard shelled, such as lobsters, crabs, shrimp, and sand fleas.

DECIDUOUS SCALES: Scales that readily fall off the fish under slight pressure, as in herring.

DORSAL: Relating to the upper part of the body or back.

DORSAL FIN: The fin or fins on the midline of the back.

ECOLOGY: The interrelations between living organisms and their environment.

ENDOPARASITE: A parasite that lives inside the body of its host.

EUTROPHICATION: The condition in a body of water in which a rich nutrient supply and overabundant plankton cause depletion or absence of oxygen.

FIN: A membranous winglike projection that extends out from the body of the fish and aids in propelling and stabilizing the fish.

FINLETS: Small fins following the dorsal and anal fins, as found on the tunas.

FISH: Aquatic vetebrate animals possessing gills and fins.

GAFF: Metal hook attached to a handle used to lift fish.

GILLS: The breathing apparatus of fishes generally composed of soft red filaments.

GILL RAKERS: Small fingerlike projections along the inner edge of the gills that serve to strain out small food particles from the water.

GILL SLITS: Openings leading into the gill from the outside.

GRAVID: Pregnant.

HETEROCERCAL TAIL: Tail fin with longer upper margin, a characteristic of sharks.

HOMOCERCAL TAIL: Most common type of tail fin; appears to be symmetrical.

ICHTHYOLOGIST: A scientist who studies the characteristics and habits of fishes.

INCISORS: Front or cutting teeth of the jaws.

INVERTEBRATE: An animal not having any backbone.

KEEL: A ridge along the side of the tail or caudal peduncle in some fishes.

LATERAL LINE: A series of pores forming a dotted line along the side of the fish. It may be light or dark and serves to detect vibrations and currents in the water.

LITTORAL: Shallow area close to shore.

LUNATE: Refers to tails with a concave outer margin such as in tuna.

MANDIBLE: The lower jaw.

MAXILLA: The upper jaw.

MERISTIC COUNTS: Refers to identification of species by counting fin rays, scales, gill rakers, etc.

MOLLUSKS: Squid, octopods, and most shellfish.

NEKTON: Large forms of aquatic life that swim actively and do not just drift with currents.

OCEANIC: Pertaining to the oceans and also the fishes that live in the surface waters of the oceans far from land.

OPERCLE: The principal bone of the gill cover.

ORBIT: The eye socket.

OVIPAROUS: Creatures that produce eggs that hatch outside the parent's body.

OVOVIVIPAROUS: Creatures that produce eggs that hatch inside the parent's body.

PECTORAL FINS: The first or uppermost of the paired fins.

PELAGIC: Living at or near the surface of the ocean.

PELVIC FINS: The pair of fins below or behind the pectoral fins, also called ventral fins.

PHYTOPLANKTON: The plant members of the plankton such as diatoms.

PISCIVOROUS: Fish-eating.

PLANKTON: Microscopic and small organisms which float or drift in the water such as small invertebrates, bacteria, fish eggs, plants. They provide food for all marine life directly or indirectly.

POSTERIOR: Rear end.

RAY: The supporting rod of the fin. It may be spiny or soft.

SERRATE: With notches like a saw edge.

SNOUT: The part of the head in front of the eyes.

SPINE: Any sharp projecting point.

SPIRACLES: Small openings in the head or neck of primitive fishes.

TELEOST: Any one of the bony fishes.

VENT: The opening at the end of the digestive tract.

VENTRAL: The lower part of the body; opposite of dorsal.

VERTEBRATE: An animal with a backbone.

VIVIPAROUS: Giving birth to live young.

ZOOPLANKTON: The animal constituents of plankton.

Bibliography

Ackerman, Edward A.
  1941. New England fishing industry. Univ. of Chicago Press, Chicago, 303
  pp.
Atkins, Charles G.
  1872–3, Rep. U.S. Comm. of Fish and Fisheries. U.S.G.P.P., Washington,
  D.C., pp. 226–337.
Bailey, R. M., et al.
  1970. A List of Common and Scientific Names of Fishes from the United
  States and Canada. 3rd ed. Spec. Publ. Amer. Fish. Soc. 6. 149 pp.
Bardach, J. E., Ryther, J. H., and McLarney, W. O.
  1972. Aquaculture. The farming and husbandry of freshwater and marine
  organisms. Wiley-Interscience, New York, 868 pp.
Bean, Tarleton H.
  1901. Catalogue of the fishes of Long Island with notes upon their distribu-
  tion, common names, habits, and rates of growth. 6th Ann. Rept. Forest
  Fish & Game Comm. of N.Y. State, pp. 373–478.
Beebe, William, and Tee-Van, John.
  1928. The fishes of Port-Au-Prince Bay, Haiti, with a summary of the known
  species of marine fish of the island of Haiti and Santo Domingo. Zoologica,
  Vol. 10, No. 1, 279 pp., illus.
  1933. Field book of the shore fishes of Bermuda. G. P. Putnam's Sons, New
  York, 337 pp., 343 illus.
Berg, Leo S.
  1947. Classification of fishes, both recent and fossil. Edwards Bros., Inc.,
  Ann Arbor, Mich., 517 pp., illus.
Bigelow, Henry B., et al.
  1948. Lancelets, by Bigelow, H. B., and Farfante, I. P., 28 pp., 3 figs.;
  Cyclostomes and sharks, by Bigelow, H. B. and Schroeder, W. C., pp.
  29–257, figs. 4–106; Fishes of the western North Atlantic. Sears Foundation Marine Research Mem., no. 1, pt. 1.
Bigelow, H. B., ed.
  1963. Fishes of the western North Atlantic (soft-rayed bony fishes); Sears
  Foundation Marine Research Mem., no. 1, pt. 3, 630 pp.
  1964. Fishes of the western North Atlantic (Isospondyli): Sears Foundation
  Marine Research Mem., no. 1, pt. 4, 599 pp.
Bigelow, Henry B., and Schroeder, William C.
  1953a. Sawfishes, guitarfishes, skates and rays; Chimaeroids, xv 588 pp., 127
  figs.; Fishes of the western North Atlantic. Part II. Sears Foundation
  Marine Research Mem., no. 1.
  1953b. Fishes of the Gulf of Maine. U.S. Fish and Wildlife Service, Fishery
  Bull. 74, vol. 53, pp. i–vii, 1–577, 288 figs.
Blair, Frank W.; Blair, Albert P.; Brodkorb, Pierce; Cagle, Fred R.; and
  Moore, George A.
  1957. Vertebrates of the United States. McGraw-Hill Book Co., New York.
Breder, C. M., Jr.
  1929. Field book of marine fishes of the Atlantic Coast from Labrador to
  Texas. G. P. Putnam's Sons, New York, 332 pp. 403 illus., 8 colored pls.

Briggs, John C.
1974. Marine zoogeography, McGraw-Hill Book Co., New York, 475 pp.
Casey, J. B.
1964. Angler's guide to sharks of the northeastern United States, Maine to Chesapeake Bay. U.S. Bur. Sports, Fishing, and Wildlife Circ. 179, 32 pp.
Chute, W. H., et al.
1948. Common and scientific names of the better known fishes of the United States and Canada. Am. Fish. Soc., Spec. Publ. 1, pp. 1–45.
Clark, John.
1975. Shark Frenzy. Grosset & Dunlap, New York.
Dean, B.
1917. A Bibliography of Fishes. Russell & Russell, Inc., New York. 3 vols.
Edwards, Robert L.
1958. Species composition of the 1957 industrial trawl fish landings in New England. Interim Report No. 2. N. Atlantic Fishery Investigations Woods Hole, 23 pp.
Evermann, Barton W., and Marsh, Millard C.
1902. The fishes of Puerto Rico. Bull. U.S. Fish. Comm. for 1900, vol. 20, pt. 1, pp. 49–350, 112 figs., 49 colored pls.
Field, David D.
1819. A Statistical Account of the County of Middlesex in Connecticut. Middletown, Ct., 154 pp.
Fowler, Henry W.
1906. The fishes of New Jersey. Ann. Rep. New Jersey State Mus., 1905, pt. 2, pp. 35–477, 103 pls., 81 figs.
1917. Notes on New England fishes. Proc. Boston Soc. Nat. Hist., Vol. 35, No. 4, pp. 109–138, 8 figs.
Ginsburg, Isaac.
1952. Flounders of the Genus *Paralichthys* and related genera in American waters. U.S. Fish and Wildlife Service Bull. 71, vol. 52, pp. 267–351, 15 pls.
Goode, George Brown.
1884. Natural history of useful aquatic animals. Pt. 3. The food fishes of the U.S. Fish. Ind. of U.S. Sec. 1, pp. 169–549, 610–612, 629–681.
Goode, G. B., and Bean, T. H.
1895. Oceanic ichthyology. U.S. Nat. Mus. Special Bull. 2, text, 553 pp., Atlas, 417 figs.
Gordon, Bernard L.
1954a. My bout with a lumpfish. Natural History, Vol. 63, No. 2, pp. 68–71.
1954b. The hungry anglerfish. Nature Magazine, Vol. 47, No. 9, pp. 469–471.
1954c. Lumpfish are good eating. Maine Coast Fisherman, Vol. 8, No. 8, p. 28.
1954d. Goosefish a hearty eater. Maine Coast Fisherman, Vol. 8, No. 9, pg. 32.
1955a. Tilefish taste like chops. Maine Coast Fisherman, Vol. 9, No. 6.
1955b. Hake live in scallop shells. Maine Coast Fisherman, Vol. 9, No. 7, pg. 8.
1955c. Good for itch (angel shark). Maine Coast Fisherman, Vol. 9, No. 8, pg. 8.
1955d. Butterfish eat sandfleas. Maine Coast Fisherman, Vol. 9, No. 9, pg. 8.

1955e. Lamprey eel not an eel. Maine Coast Fisherman, Vol. 9, No. 10, pg.8.
1955f. Scup eggs hatch in 40 hours. Maine Coast Fisherman, Vol. 9, No. 11, pg. 28.
1955g. Blowfish epicure's delight. Maine Coast Fisherman, Vol. 9, No. 12, pg. 32.
1955h. Old "Rough Tooth" (maneater shark). Maine Coast Fisherman, Vol. 10, No. 1, pg. 28.
1955i. Stingaree well armed. Maine Coast Fisherman, Vol. 10, No. 2, pg. 28.
1955j. Remora a hitchhiker. Maine Coast Fisherman, Vol. 10, No. 3, pg.9.
1955k. Anglers and eaters prize bonito. Maine Coast Fisherman, Vol. 10, No. 4.
1955l. Kingfish favor warm water. Maine Coast Fisherman, Vol. 10, No. 5, pg. 28.
1955m. When the tilefish died. Natural History, Vol. 64, No. 5, pp. 273–275.
1955n. The vicious sea lamprey. The Fisherman, Vol. 6, No. 10, pp. 32–37.
1956a. Dad pipefish minds kids. Maine Coast Fisherman, Vol. 10, No. 6.
1956b. Marlin powerful swimmer. Maine Coast Fisherman, Vol. 10, No. 7, pg.9.
1956c. Sea bass are good eating. Maine Coast Fisherman, Vol. 10, No. 8.
1956d. Glutton of the sea (bluefish). Maine Coast Fisherman, Vol. 10, No. 9, pg.9.
1956e. Shad the travelling fish. Maine Coast Fisherman, Vol. 10, No. 10, pg.9.
1956f. Dogfish ruin fish nets. Maine Coast Fisherman, Vol. 10, No. 11, pg. 9.
1956g. Blackfish a bottom dweller. Maine Coast Fisherman, Vol. 10, No. 12, pg. 9.
1956h. That sea serpent may be a basking shark. Maine Coast Fisherman, Vol. 11, No. 1.
1956i. . . . it's still weakfish. Maine Coast Fisherman, Vol. 11, No. 2.
1956j. Tuna, torpedo of the deep. Maine Coast Fisherman, Vol. 11, No. 3.
1956k. Lashing tail brings food to thresher shark. Maine Coast Fisherman, Vol. 11, No. 4.
1956l. The remora, a fish story old but ever new. Frontiers. Acad. Nat. Sci. Phila., Vol. 20, No. 3, pp. 76–78, 95.
1956m. The paternal pipefish. Nature Magazine, Vol. 49, No. 5, pp. 243–244, 276.
1956n. The amazing angel shark. Bull. of International Oceanographic Foundation. Vol. 2, No. 2, pp. 109–111.
1956o. Sea-going hitchhiker. The Fisherman, Vol. 7, No. 11, pp. 66–69.
1957a. The migrant mackerel. Maine Coast Fisherman, Vol. 11, No. 6, pg.10.
1957b. The menhaden. Maine Coast Fisherman, Vol. 11, No. 7, pg. 10.
1957c. The cod, Cape Cod turkey. Maine Coast Fisherman, Vol. 11, No. 8, pg. 10.
1957d. The nimble pollock. Maine Coast Fisherman, Vol. 11, No. 9, pg. 10.
1957e. The spiny boxfish. Maine Coast Fisherman, Vol. 11, No. 10, pg. 10.
1957f. The skate. Maine Coast Fisherman, Vol. 11, No. 11, pg. 10.
1957g. The striper a favorite fish. Maine Coast Fisherman, Vol. 12, No. 4, pg. 10.

1957h. The common cunner. Maine Coast Fisherman, Vol. 12, No. 5, pg. 10.
1957i. The eel. Maine Coast Fisherman, Vol. 12, No. 6, pg. 10.
1957j. Titan of the seas. Natural History, Vol. 66, No. 5, pp. 272–274.
1957k. The migratory shad. The Fisherman, Vol. 8, No. 2, pp. 14–16, 80.
1957l. A tale of thunnus. The Fisherman, Vol. 8, No. 9, pp. 25–26, 95.
1957m. The spiny boxfish. Frontiers, Vol. 22, No. 1, pp. 21, 22.
1957n. The skate, primitive fish. Frontiers, Vol. 22, No. 2, pp. 38–39, 64.
1958a. The flavorful smelt. Maine Coast Fisherman, Vol. 12, No. 6, pg. 10.
1958b. The sturgeon. Maine Coast Fisherman, Vol. 12, No. 7, pg. 10.
1958c. The rabbitfish. Maine Coast Fisherman, Vol. 12, No. 8, pg. 10.
1958d. The ocean pout. Maine Coast Fisherman, Vol. 12, No. 9, pg. 10.
1958e. The omnivorous codfish. Nature Magazine, Vol. 51, No. 4, pp. 205–207.
1958f. The John Dory. Maine Coast Fisherman, Vol. 12, No. 10.
1970. Man and the sea; classic accounts of marine explorations. Edited by Bernard L. Gordon. Foreword by Paul M. Fye. Published for the American Museum of Natural History by the Natural History Press, Garden City, N.Y., xxiv, 498 pp.
1974. The marine fishes of Rhode Island. Book and Tackle Shop, Watch Hill, R.I., 2nd ed., 136 pp.
1974. Marine Resources Perspectives. Book and Tackle Shop, Watch Hill, R.I., 370 pp.
Guenther, Klaus, and Deckart, Kurt.
1956. Creatures of the deep sea. Charles Scribner's Sons, New York, 222 pp., 140 figs., colored pls.
Halsted, B. W.
1959. Dangerous Marine Animals. Cornell Maritime Press, Cambridge, Md.
Herald, E. S.
1961. Living Fishes of the World. Doubleday, Garden City, N.Y., 303 pp.
Hildebrand, Samuel F., and Schroeder, William C.
1928. Fishes of Chesapeake Bay. Bull. U.S. Bur. Fish. for 1927, Vol. 43, pt. 1, 388 pp., 211 figs.
Johnson, Frank M.
1902. Forest, lake and river, the fishes of New England and Eastern Canada. Privately printed (ltd. to 350 copies) Boston, 681 pp., 2 vols.
Jordan, David S.
1905. A guide to the study of fishes. Henry Holt & Co., New York, 427 illus., 2 vols.
1925. Fishes. D. Appleton and Co., New York, 773 pp., 673 figs., 18 pls.
Jordan, David S., and Evermann, B. W.
1896–1900. The fishes of North and Middle America, a descriptive catalogue of the species of fishlike vertebrates found in the waters of North America, north of the isthmus of Panama. U.S. Nat. Mus. Bull. 47, in 4 vols., 3,313 pp., 392 pls.
1902. American food and game fishes. Doubleday, Page & Co., N.Y., 573 pp., 221 figs., 66 pls., 9 color pls.
Jordan, David S.; Evermann, B. W.; and Clark, H. W.
1930. Checklist of the fishes and fishlike vertebrates of North and Middle

America north of the northern boundary of Venezuela and Colombia. Rep. U.S. Comm. Fish. 1928 with Appendices, pt. 2, Doc. No. 1055, pp. 1–670. (Reprinted in 1956.)

Kendall, William C.
1914–1935. The fishes of New England. Mem. Boston Soc. Nat. Hist., vol. 8, pt. 1, 1914, 103 pp., 7 col. pls.; vol. 9, pt. 2, 1935, 166 pp., 11 col. pls.

LaGorce, J. O.
1952. The Book of Fishes. National Geographic Society, Washington, D.C.

LaMonte, Francesca.
1946. North American game fishes. Doubleday & Co., Garden City, N.Y., 202 pp., 71 pls.

Liem, A. H., and Scott, W. B.
1966. Fishes of the Atlantic coast of Canada. Canada Fisheries Research Bd. Bull. 155, 485 pp.

Linsley, J. H.
1844. Catalogue of the fishes of Connecticut. Amer. Jour. Sci. and Arts., vol. 47, 71 pp.

McCormich, Harold W., Allen, Tom, and Young, W. E.
1963. Shadows in the Sea. The Sharks, Skates and Rays. Chilton Books, New York, 415 pp. illus.

McFarland, Raymond.
1911. A history of New England fisheries. Univ. of Pennsylvania, 457 pp.

Merriman, Daniel M.
1941. Studies on the striped bass. Fish Bull. 35 U.S.F.W.S., U.S. G.P.O., Washington, D.C., 77 pp.

Merriman, Daniel M. and Sclar, Ruth.
1952. The pelagic fish eggs and larvae of Block Island Sound. Bull. Bingham Ocean. Coll., vol. XIII, art. 3, pp. 165–220.

Moore, Emmeline.
1947. The sand flounder *Lophopsetta aquosa* (Mitchill); a general study of the species with special emphasis on age determination by means of scales and otoliths. Bull. Bingham Ocean. Coll., vol. XI, art. 3, pp. 1–79.

Morrow, James E., Jr.
1951. The biology of the longhorn sculpin *Myoxocephalus octodecimspinosus* (Mitchill); with a discussion of the southern New England "trash" fishery. Bull. Bingham Ocean. Coll., vol. XIII, art. 2, pp. 1–89.
1956. The jolthead porgy, *Calamus bajonado*, Bloch and Schneider, a first record for New England waters. Copeia, No. 3, pp. 194–195.

Nichols, J. T. and Breder, C. M., Jr.
1927. The marine fishes of New York and Southern New England. Zoologica, New York Zool. Soc., New York, vol. 9, No. 1, 192 pp.

Norman, J. R.
1931. A history of fishes. E. Benn, Ltd., London, 464 pp. illus.

Norman, J. R. and Fraser, F. C.
1949. Field book of giant fishes. G. P. Putnam, New York, 376 pp.

Olsen, Y. H. and Merriman, Daniel.
1946. The biology and economic importance of the ocean pout *Macrozoarces americanus* (Bloch and Schneider) Bull. Bingham Ocean. Coll., vol. 9, art. 4, pp. 1–184.

Raney, E. C.; Tresselt, E. F.; Hollis, E. H.; Vladykov, V. D.; and Wallace, D. H.

1952. The striped bass. Bull. Bingham Ocean. Coll., vol. 14, art. 1, 177 pp.
Rounsefell, G. A.
1975. Ecology, utilization, and management of marine fisheries. C. V. Mosby Co., St. Louis, 516 pp. illus.
Rounsefell, G. A. and Everhart, W. H.
1953. Fishery science, its methods and applications. Wiley, New York, 444 pp.
Rounsefell, G. A. and Stringer, L. D.
1945. The New England alewife fisheries. Trans. Am. Fish. Soc. 73: pp. 394–424.
Sanders, Howard L.
1952. The herring *(Clupea harengus)* of Block Island Sound. Bull. Bingham Ocean. Coll., vol. 13, art. 3, pp. 220–237.
Schultz, Leonard P. (with Stern, Edith M.)
1948. The ways of fishes. D. Van Nostrand Co., New York, 264 pp., illus.
Shapiro, Sidney, ed.
1971. Our changing fisheries. Washington, D.C. N.O.A.A., U.S.G.P.O., 534 pp. illus.
Sharp, B. and Fowler, H. W.
1905. The fishes of Nantucket. Proc. Acad. Nat. Sci. Vol. 56. Phil., pp. 504–512.
Smith, J. B. L.
1949. The Sea Fishes of Southern Africa. Central News Agency, Capetown, xvi, 550 pp., 1,245 figs.
Sterba, G.
1963. Freshwater fishes of the World. Viking Press, New York, 878 pp.
Storer, David H.
1839. A report on the fishes of Massachusetts. Bost. Jour. Nat. Hist., Vol. 2, pp. 289–558.
1867. A history of the fishes of Massachusetts, Cambridge and Boston, 287 pp.
Taylor, Clyde C.; Bigelow, H. B. and Graham, H. B.
1957. Climatic trends and the distribution of marine animals in New England. U.S. Fish and Wildlife Service, Fishery Bull. 115, vol. 57, pp. 293–345.
Taylor, Harden F.; Marshall, N.; Ellison, W. A.; Roelofs, E. W.; and La-Monte, F.
1951. Survey of marine fisheries of North Carolina, with a comprehensive view of the economics of national and world fisheries, Univ. North Carolina Press, 555 pp.
Tressler, Donald K. and Lemon, James McW.
1951. Marine products of commerce; their acquisition, handling, biological aspects and the science and technology of their preparation and preservation. Reinhold, 782 pp., illus., 2d ed. rev. and enl.
Walford, Lionel A.
1975. Marine Game Fishes of the Pacific Coast from Alaska to Ecuador. Smithsonian Institution Press, Washington, D.C., 205 pp., 69 pls.
Warfel, H. E. and Merriman, D.
1944. An analysis of the fish population of the shore zone. Bull. Bingham Ocean. Coll. Vol. IX, art. 2, pp. 1–19.

INDEX

Boldface numbers refer to main entry.